ANSELM
AND
NICHOLAS OF CUSA

KARL JASPERS

ANSELM

AND

NICHOLAS OF CUSA

From *The Great Philosophers: The Original Thinkers*

Edited by Hannah Arendt

Translated by Ralph Manheim

A Harvest Book

A HELEN AND KURT WOLFF BOOK

HARCOURT BRACE JOVANOVICH

New York and London

"Nicholas of Cusa" was originally published in
Germany as *Nikolaus Cusanus.*

Library of Congress Cataloging in Publication Data

Jaspers, Karl, 1883-1969.
Anselm and Nicholas of Cusa.

(A Harvest book, HB 289)
"A Helen and Kurt Wolff book."
Previously published as part of v. 2 of the author's
The great philosophers, which is a translation of
Die grossen Philosophen.
Bibliography: p.
1. Anselm, Saint, Abp. of Canterbury, 1033–1109.
2. Nicolaus Cusanus, Cardinal, 1401–1464. I. Title.
B765.N54J2913   189′.4   74-4484
ISBN 0-15-607600-4

First Harvest edition 1974

A B C D E F G H I J

CONTENTS

ANSELM
AND
NICHOLAS OF CUSA

ANSELM

I. LIFE AND WORKS

Life: Anselm was born in 1033 in Aosta, an Alpine town in the border zone between Burgundy and Lombardy. His father Gundulph and his mother Ermenberga were descended from the old nobility. He quarreled with his father, left home, and wandered about for years in France until 1060, when he became a monk in the Benedictine monastery of Bec in Normandy and studied under the Abbot Lanfranc. In 1063 he became prior, in 1078 abbot of the monastery, and in 1093 Archbishop of Canterbury. Twice driven into exile in the course of his struggle in behalf of Church rights with Kings William II and Henry I, he lived in Rome, Lyon, and other cities. In 1106, when the dispute was ended, he returned to Canterbury, where he died in 1109 at the age of seventy-five. He showed equal greatness as a monk by his piety, as archbishop by his courageous defense of Church rights, and as a thinker by his originality, depth, and clarity.

Works: The greater part of his work was written in the monastery of Bec. His writings deal with God (*Monologium de divinatis essentia, Proslogium*), with God and man (*De veritate, De libero arbitrio, De casu Diaboli*). As archbishop he thought through the great dogmatic questions (in his controversy with Roscellinus: *De fide trinitatis,* 1093; on the occasion of the Synod of Bari with the Greeks: *De processione Spiritus Sancti;* in exile: *Cur deus homo* and *De conceptu virginali et originali peccato;* finally, in the last years of his life, on the conjunction between predestination and free will). He also wrote numerous sermons and letters.

The historical situation: The vast majority of the European population lived in villages, cut off from the world by lack of communications and education. Through the monastic orders, the Roman Catholic Church represented a force for order and civilization. Though not a large social group, the clergy numbered many men of distinction and possessed an imposing unity of language (Latin), knowledge, and faith. While the common people never left their home districts and were without vision of the outside world, the monks led a rich, active life, unrestricted by national frontiers. Born in Italy,

3

Anselm became a monk in France and in England Archbishop of Canterbury.

Carriers of the French language and mode of life, the Normans conquered
England in 1066 and founded a state, embracing Normandy and England,
which, under William the Conqueror, was more powerful, more unified,
and more solidly organized than any other political structure of the time.
The Normans were a barbaric people, energetic and cruel. The nobles
could neither read nor write, the entire population was devoted to the
Church. Sole possessors of education and tradition, the clergy provided
the men who organized and guided society. The conquerors appropriated
all the land and distributed it among Norman nobles. This nobility
spoke French, the clergy wrote Latin, the people spoke the despised
language of the oppressed, which later developed into English.

II. ANSELM'S FUNDAMENTAL PHILOSOPHICAL IDEA

A. *Exposition*. The fool hath said in his heart: there is no God. The faithful
believe Him to be. Can pure thought—unclouded by folly and uninfluenced
by the obedience of faith—acquire certainty of God's being? Yes, says Anselm.
His demonstration is as follows:

Think: God is "a being than which nothing greater can be conceived
(*Quo maius cogitari non potest*)."

The fool replies: There is no God, because the idea of the greatest is
only a thought in the mind; merely by being thought, its content does not
become real.

To this we answer: It is one thing to exist only in the mind and another
to exist also in reality. A painter can have a picture in his mind without
having painted it. But with the idea of God it is a different matter. The
fool must admit "that something exists in the understanding at least, than
which nothing greater can be conceived." This admission suffices. For a
thing, than which nothing greater can be thought, cannot exist only in the
understanding. Why not? Because then the greatest thing that really is
would be greater than the greatest that is only thought and does not exist
in reality. If the greatest were only in the understanding, the greatest which
in addition really existed would be greater than that which is present only
in thought.

To conceive of a greatest that is present only in the understanding and not
in reality, so that something greater can be thought, which exists also in
reality, gives rise to a contradiction. For then we have conceived of a greatest that is not the greatest. It is said to be the greatest thing conceivable,
but is not, because something greater, namely, that which is also real,
is conceivable. Thus pure thought gives us the certainty that that beyond

which no greater can be conceived exists both in the mind and in reality.

This certainty is free from doubt. It is perfect certainty, because we cannot, without contradiction, think that the greatest, beyond which no greater is thinkable, does not exist.

The same idea can be expressed in a number of variants:

If the greatest beyond which no greater can be conceived, is not conceived as existing, it is not the greatest.

It is so true that that beyond which no greater can be conceived really exists, that its nonexistence is not even conceivable.

If in my thought I really have that beyond which a greater cannot be conceived, this idea, though it seems at first to be present only in my thought, encompasses its Being.

It is possible to conceive of a being whose Nonbeing is inconceivable. But something whose Nonbeing is inconceivable cannot in reality not be. It is.

If I think of the being beyond which no greater is thinkable as non-existent, by that same token I have not thought of the greatest thinkable being.

As soon as I conceive of the greatest that can be thought as existing only in my idea, it also vanishes in my idea; it is no longer the greatest.

Either I must abandon the idea, or I must conceive of its content as real.

B. *Interpretation.* Anselm's fundamental thought is not mere mathematical juggling with the category of quantity. Considered out of context, it can be mistaken for a logical operation by which the existence of an object, e.g., the never visible far side of the moon, is "proved"; such a proof is immediately refuted, because it cannot be confirmed by experience. Seen in this light, Anselm's idea may appear to be a logical trick demanding to be exposed. This would be a misunderstanding, which we can avoid by examining the circumstances of Anselm's thinking.

1. *Inward quietness, not mysticism:* Anselm introduces his exposition of his idea with an invitation to silent inwardness: "Flee thy occupations, cast aside thy burdensome cares and put away thy toilsome business. Hide thyself from thy disturbing thoughts. Yield room to God and rest for a little time in him. Enter the inner chamber of thy mind; shut out all thoughts save that of God; close thy door and seek him."

This is more than an insistence on mere attentiveness, more than a summons to quiet thinking. With these words Anselm points to the realm of concentration, seclusion, withdrawal from the world and its cares, the realm which is not nothingness but where, on the contrary, through questioning, we can gain certainty of God's existence.

If we compare this with the prescriptions of the mystics, the crucial difference is that Anselm does not devise a technique of meditation and its stages, and does not strive for visions and ecstasies. His concern is pure thought. He aims not at psychic experience, not at emotional intoxication, but at sober, compelling clarity, in regard to the all-important.

2. *Insight and empty thought:* Anselm drew a clear distinction between authentic thinking and empty, purely rational thought. "For in one sense an object is conceived when the word signifying it is conceived; and in another, when the very entity, which the object is, is understood."

The nonexistence of God can be conceived in the first kind of thought, which contents itself with the literal meaning of words, but never in the second, authentic mode of thought. If I think authentically, with insight, that God is, I cannot think that God is not. The man who says the words "God is not" cannot think what he says.

This applies to the idea that something, nothing greater than which is conceivable, must be. If I understand the idea, I cannot at the same time believe that what is thus thought does not exist. I can speak of nonbeing only if I do not understand what I am saying.

Consequently the purely formal proposition that the nonexistence of the highest, beyond which nothing higher can be thought, is unthinkable, is not enough. As a logical proposition it is empty. But taken in relation to its ground and fulfillment, it engenders understanding.

Anselm's idea can be meaningful only if there is a thinking which is based neither on experience nor on previously defined concepts, but which, transcending all concepts, touches the heart of reality. Then the formal operation is filled with meaning by an "insight," which is at once impulsion and goal. In its application to the reality of thinking, Anselm's idea is an existential vicious circle expressed in a logical vicious circle.

3. *A unique idea, meaningful only in relation to God:* The idea in which the certainty that God exists springs solely from the fact that His non-existence cannot be thought is a unique idea applicable only to God. There is no other being besides God whose existence can be derived from its essence. The nonexistence of every other object is thinkable. The existence of every other object must be demonstrated by its existence in the world. But Anselm's idea is derived neither from universal premises nor from experience.

The ontological proof had already been conceived as a mere universal, that is, in rational abstraction, by Anselm's contemporary and adversary, Gaunilon. In disagreement with Gaunilon, Anselm denied that the idea of God as that being "than which nothing greater can be conceived," could apply to Gaunilon's "island which is more excellent than all islands." According to Anselm, the existence of such an island does not follow from its excellence. Invoking God, Anselm declares: "Everything that is, excepting thee alone, can be conceived as not being. Thou alone of all things hast Being in the truest sense, and hence most of all."

Thus the idea cannot be dissociated from its content and stated as a syllogism with the major premise: Every thing that is conceived as the most perfect of its kind also has existence. This relation between being-thought and being applies only to God. One who thinks of God can think of Him only as being. Consequently all other existents, which can be conceived also to be nonexistent, are other and poorer in being than God.

God's being or existence, or whatever we may choose to call it, is not the mode of reality of something, of any thing in the world, of an island (Gaunilon) or of a hundred thalers (Kant). It alone is the being by virtue of which it is impossible that it is not and that nothing is—and which as such is a certainty in our thinking.

This impossibility of nothingness takes the form of the unthinkable only in connection with God. It is manifested to thought, which is itself being, though only created being. As an image of God's creative thinking, it perceives the necessary being of God through itself.

4. *No object:* The "being than which nothing greater can be conceived" (*quo maius cogitari nequit*) must be conceived in its authentic essence. It is not, as Gaunilon said, "greater than all beings" (*maius omnibus*). For then it would merely be a thing. If God is conceived as the highest of beings, His nonbeing is not as unthinkable as Anselm supposes. As highest in the series, it is not the highest than which nothing higher can be conceived. For what is called the highest being in the series need not be highest in an absolute sense.

Anselm's God does not, in being thought, become an object. Thus, according to Anselm, God is "not only the being than which a greater cannot be conceived, but . . . a *being greater than everything that can be conceived.*" This is crucial: with the idea that the greatest must exist Anselm combines the more profound thought that this greatest is also unthinkable. In so doing he counteracts the intellectual pride for which thought and Being, thinkability and reality, coincide.

A painter paints the picture he had in his imagination. By thinking God, however, a thinker does not produce God, but only assures himself of God's reality. God gives Himself in man's thinking—again a corrective to the intellectual pride which supposes that man has power over God, that God is dependent on man's thinking.

5. *Anselm's "theory of contradiction":* Anselm operates with the assumption that contradiction is unthinkable. He does not use the word "contradiction"; no more than Parmenides does he formulate the logical proposition. He says only that it is impossible to think nonexistence. Contradiction is

employed as a function of an idea which goes far beyond the notions of contradiction or freedom from contradiction.

In an operation of transcending, formal logic cannot supply such proofs as are possible in connection with finite objects. Thus, measured by the logical rigor of object thinking, Anselm's proof discloses the same formal flaw as all transcending thought, that is, thought which tries by finite means to attain the infinite. The alternative: God is or is not, is lacking. Such an alternative would put God into the category of objects to which the "is" and the "is not" apply. If the concept of contradiction is to be used in a transcending proof, it must lose its usual meaning, which belongs to the realm of our finite thinking. It becomes a symbol by which to elucidate the impossibility of God's nonexistence. In his philosophy, Cusanus made the opposite use of the contradiction: God is and is not; here the *coincidentia oppositorum* becomes a means of attaining the godhead.

Such methodological reflections on the logical forms of transcending are far removed from the rich spontaneity of Anselm's thinking. Thus we can only assimilate his central idea by noting that it is developed with wonderful clarity in accordance with a method that was not explicitly formulated until much later. We can understand Anselm. With him we can work out the function of contradiction in his idea and so experience the perpetual mystery of man's ability to think, as a medium of transcending.

6. *Anselm's thought as an invocation of God:* Anselm does not set forth his thought as though expounding an objective, scientific truth, but as an invocation of God, a prayer: "Teach my heart where and how it may seek thee." "I was created to see, and not yet have I done that for which I was made."

He cannot succeed in his meditation by his own strength. "I strove toward God, and I stumbled on myself." "Enlighten us, reveal thyself to us." "Teach me to seek thee, and unveil thyself to me, when I seek thee, for I cannot seek thee, except thou teach me, nor find thee, except thou reveal thyself. I will seek thee in yearning, and yearn for thee in my seeking." Prayer and invocation are not only at the beginning and end; they permeate the whole thought process. It is not a mere logical operation applying to something seen from outside.

The treatise in which the idea is put forward is significantly entitled: *Proslogium, The Invocation of God;* Anselm had originally meant to call it *"Fides quaerens intellectum,"* "Faith Seeking Understanding," but this title was dropped. The work presupposes faith, not any dogmatic article of faith (nor a logical premise from which the idea would be derived), but a fundamental human state or attitude, or the being or essence of man. With this as his basis, Anselm strives "to lift his mind to the contemplation of God, and seeks to understand what he believes."

In an earlier work (*Monologium*) Anselm had given an example of reflection on the rational content of faith (*ratio fidei*). But now he is clearly striving for something more. He is looking for "a single argument which would require no other for its proof than itself alone; and alone would suffice to demonstrate that God truly exists." The change of title is essential. The foundation of the new treatise is not a definite Christian dogma but a believing invocation of God.

Consciously, to be sure, Anselm takes the Christian faith as his starting point. But in the idea of his "proof of the existence of God" a larger area is discernible (and there is no mention of Christ): all that remains is a faith without object, a fulfillment in the Encompassing; the actuality of being, as a source in which the believer finds himself.

Thus the whole treatise is marked by a seeming contradiction. Anselm begins: "For I do not seek to understand that I may believe, but I believe in order to understand. For this also I believe—that unless I believe, I should not understand." But at the end of the "proof" he writes: "What I formerly believed by thy bounty (*te donante*), I now so understand by thine illumination (*te illuminante*), *that if I were unwilling to believe that thou dost exist, I should not be able to understand this to be true.*"

Anselm's operation requires the first sentence at the beginning and makes possible the second at the end. But the second sentence tells us that in his idea, once attained, Anselm sees more than a mere interpretation of the *ratio fidei*.

In relation to God's being, the principle of contradiction takes on the force of revelation. The most formal thinking expresses the deepest meaning. What seems to be the simplest operation of the mere understanding becomes the medium of a knowledge that overwhelms the thinker, a knowledge that is more than knowledge, namely faith. This was possible only because in Anselm thinking did not break away from the source to become a purely intellectual process. Through the presence of the being than which no greater can be conceived, faith took on the certainty of necessary insight.

Such insight must also be termed faith. The authoritarian Christian faith which Anselm took as his starting point is not the only faith. The difference between an abstract idea, which is thought only in a formal sense, and actual thought, which fills such an idea with a fundamentally human consciousness of Being, is the difference between a mere intellectual operation (in which form the idea is without validity) and the insight of faith (which is accessible to all thinking men insofar as they are favored with God's illumination—*te illuminante*). This insight of faith is reason, which is freely given to itself in the Encompassing and knows God without recourse to authority. Just as Anselm's faith-knowledge of God's existence is not an interpretation of any dogma or of any revealed text, so philosophical prayer is not essentially Christian, but an expression of human life as such in relation to transcendence. It is thinking that becomes one with the thinker's existence.

Have we then two kinds of faith, Christian and rational? In Anselm's opinion, no, but in the reality of his thinking, yes. In Anselm the autonomy of philosophizing, of philosophical faith, implies no consciousness of self-sufficiency, no breach with, let alone opposition to, the unquestionable certainty of Christian faith. That was possible in the northern and central Europe of Anselm's age, when Christianity was the only true faith, because other faiths were unknown. It was only later that contact with Islam through the crusades had its extraordinary effect on men's thinking. In Anselm's day the one Christian Church was still the sole repository of all higher thinking, of all education and tradition, a position of pre-eminence to which a number of outstanding figures bear witness. There was nothing else. There was no ground for questioning it. Even heretics doubted only particular dogmas, not the foundation of the edifice.

7. *The significance of his "proof" in Anselm's life:* That Anselm's fundamental idea was not a rational finding but the climax and foundation of his existence as a thinker is stated by Anselm himself in the words: "Although I often and earnestly directed my thought to this, and at some times that which I sought seemed to be just within my reach, while again it wholly evaded my mental vision, at last in despair I was about to cease, as if from the search for a thing which could not be found. But when I wished to exclude this thought altogether . . . then more and more, though I was unwilling and shunned it, it began to force itself upon me, with a kind of importunity. So, one day, when I was exceedingly wearied with resisting its importunity, in the very conflict of my thoughts, the proof of which I had despaired offered itself, so that I eagerly embraced the thoughts which I was strenuously repelling." Anselm's biographer, Eadmer, writes: "This thought allowed him neither to sleep, eat, nor drink and, what troubled him still more, it interfered with his devotions at matins and at other times. He believed that such thoughts might be temptations of the Devil and endeavored to banish them from his mind entirely. But the more violently he sought to do so, the more they besieged him. And one night, as he lay awake, it happened: God's grace illumined his heart, the object of his quest lay bared to his understanding, and his whole innermost being was filled with boundless rejoicing."

This is far from being the only instance of a fundamental philosophical idea coming to a thinker as a gift, after a long period of inner struggle—somewhat in the same way as prophetic revelation or conversion. Parmenides built a temple in thanks to the god; Cusanus relates that his fundamental idea descended upon him as an "illumination from above," on his return journey from Constantinople; while Descartes tells us that his central idea came to him in winter quarters at Neuburg and that he gave thanks for it by going on a pilgrimage. The mere fact that great philosophers have attached so much biographical importance to certain thoughts forbids us to take them lightly.

8. *Gaunilon against Anselm:* Anselm maintained that his fundamental idea was true only in authentic thinking (*intelligere*), not in empty discourse, and secondly, that it derived its certainty from the impossibility of the contradictory (*in cogitare*).

The monk Gaunilon agreed with both these assertions but took them as premises with which to develop his objections to Anselm. To his mind, a thinking conscious of the reality of its object is not *cogitare* (understanding) but *intelligere* (higher insight). If Anselm took thinking in this specific sense as *intelligere,* he would not distinguish between the mere possession of an object in thought and knowledge of its reality. For in intellection the two coincide.

In answer to this Anselm said: It is the failure of thinking (in the sense of *cogitare*) that first leads to authentic intellection. For in relation to all finite things, the immediate knowledge (*intelligere*) of a reality does not preclude the possibility of conceiving its nonexistence. Only in one case, the knowledge (*intelligere*) of the highest being, is our knowledge (*intelligere*) of the reality grounded in our inability to think (*cogitare*) His nonexistence. Anselm, says Gaunilon, should have shown that the idea of the Supreme Being is of a kind that includes certainty of His existence. Anselm says that this knowledge of the reality of God is not immediate, but derives its certainty through cogitation, through thinking the impossibility of God's nonexistence.

In his way of operating with the principle of contradiction, it might be asked, did Anselm not employ the emptiest and most formal aspect of finite thinking in order to gain insight into the infinite? This would be so only if the infinite, the godhead, were considered as an object, a thing among others, and drawn into the sphere of finite knowledge. But for Anselm contradiction is only a lever whereby thought is raised above finite thinking to become insight into the reality of God, which is radically different from knowledge of the real things of the world.

Gaunilon did not doubt the reality of God, but denied that he could gain insight into this reality through thought and demonstration. It is impossible, he says, to gain an adequate idea of the Supreme Being. From this it follows that I must conceive of this being as real, not that it really exists. Actual reality does not follow from imagined reality or reality in representation. First the reality itself must be demonstrated; from this it follows that this reality is the highest reality.

Gaunilon says finally that it is not possible to contest God's existence. But, Anselm replies, it is always being contested by the fools who deny it.

True, they cannot really know what they are saying; but thinking (*cogitare*) can impel them to perceive the vanity of their discourse and put them on the path to authentic insight.

Gaunilon's arguments all have one thing in common. Based as they are on pious faith, they seem more reliable than Anselm's philosophical arguments. But they move in the realm of the understanding, into which they also draw the distinction between *cogitare* and *intelligere;* for actually Gaunilon's *intelligere* refers only to the reality of finite things. This prevents Gaunilon from getting to the heart of Anselm's thought. For Anselm arrives at his *intelligere* by way of *cogitare.*

With Gaunilon philosophical thinking breaks down into two parts: on the one hand the empty formalism of correct or incorrect statements (from which Anselm's meanings are excluded), and on the other hand, the immediate, indubitable, unthinking certainty of God. But neither the rationality of compelling but empty statements nor immediate unthinking faith is capable of gaining certainty in thought or of philosophical transcending. Such rationality degenerates into an indifferent correctness, while unthinking faith culminates in blind obedience to an unknown authority. The cleavage between the two stifles true, free philosophizing. It appeals to common sense, the common sense of godlessness as well as authoritarian faith. Where either of these becomes the supreme authority, philosophy dies.

c. *The history of Anselm's fundamental idea.* In Anselm Western philosophy is reborn. Like Parmenides, he stands at the beginning. But the historical difference between the two is this: Untrammeled by the historical presuppositions of faith, Parmenides took the great step to philosophy without hesitation. Bound to ecclesiastical faith, Anselm did not fathom the consequences of his own act of thought. There is in Anselm an authentic philosophical impulse, but it did not, for the present, gain wider influence. It was submerged in the mounting stream of specifically Christian dogmatism.

No one has ever achieved certainty of God's reality in the same way as Anselm, but his proof was to be taken up by other original thinkers. Anselm's proof carries force of conviction only for a reader of his text who thinks along with him, not when set forth in a bare rational form, separately from the whole. Thus separated from its context, Anselm's thought was transformed into a simple rational proof, in which God became an object in the realm of finite knowledge. In such form (though vestiges of Anselm's substance are still present as overtones) it was affirmed by Bonaventura, Duns Scotus, Descartes, Leibniz, and Hegel, rejected by Thomas Aquinas and Kant.

Thomas Aquinas discusses and refutes Anselm's proof: once God has been known in intellection, it is impossible to understand how anyone might think He does not exist. This Thomas denies. In his view someone can perfectly well think that God is not. He might think, for example, that there is no being than which a greater cannot be conceived. Thus Anselm's proposition actually starts from the premise that there is something than which no greater can be conceived. Since Anselm assumes this, he does not prove it. And elsewhere: according to Anselm, the knowledge that God's name signifies God signifies also that God is. The name signifies the being than which no greater can be conceived. What exists in reality and in the mind is greater than that which exists only in the mind. Hence from our insight into the meaning of God's name there follows the insight that He is in reality. Thus God's existence is self-evident. In answer to this, Thomas says: Granted that God is essentially His Being; but to us who do not know what God is, it is not self-evident that He is. We cannot assert that He really is unless we assume that there really is something than which no greater can be conceived.

What is the meaning of Thomas' position? Anselm and Thomas are one in the certainty that God is that being than which no greater can be conceived. But whence this certainty? It may derive from something out-side, from the reality of the world, which leads us to infer the existence of God as Creator—Anselm does not deny this possibility. For Thomas it is the only way open to the natural intelligence. Or else it may have its source in an assurance from within, in thinking as thinking, in the existence of thought; this is Anselm's view, which Thomas denies. Or finally—and here again both thinkers are agreed—the certainty of God's reality can come to us from outside, guaranteed by authority.

Two modes of thought confront one another in the crucial point wherein they differ. On the one hand, a thinking that I enact with my own existence, which consequently is not empty, but oriented, through its own inherent lucidity, toward the reality of God. Through the reality of my thinking, God becomes real to my insight. This is a thinking which withdraws from all distractions and dispersions to immerse itself in the One, a thinking into which the thinker gathers himself and all being. Anselm does not start from any facts, but from thoughts; he strives to demonstrate God's being in pure thinking, deriving it from thought as such.

Thomas, on the other hand, takes a radically different point of view: our thinking is dependent on the senses. We gain our concepts by abstraction from sensibility. We rise up to God by way of concepts. But the foundation remains the sensible world. From the world we can infer God, from the visible the invisible through which the visible is. In pure thought we find no reality. The understanding requires sense perception in order to arrive at reality.

Thus Thomas employs the traditional ancient proofs of God's existence. He arranges them in a clear order, which still has currency in textbooks. He regards them as compelling for the mere natural understanding, even without faith. Since our thinking must always start from our experience, all inferences must be based on sense perception in the world. These inferences are classified according to their grounds: from the fact of motion, we infer the existence of a first unmoved mover; from the series of causes, because of the impossibility of an endless *regressus,* we infer a first cause; from the contingency and mere potentiality of all things in the world, we infer a necessary being as ground of all reality (*via causalitatis*). Another group of inferences is based on the degrees of perfection in the world. From degrees of perfection the supreme perfection is inferred as the ground of all perfection. By rising in the scale of perfections, our thinking arrives at God (*via eminentiae*). Most particularly, the ground of purposiveness is derived from the purposiveness observed in the world. Natural phenomena endowed neither with consciousness nor knowledge nevertheless operate purposively; this is possible only if they are guided by a being endowed with knowledge: thus God is the cause which lays down purpose. But all these proofs are restricted by the old ideas of negative theology. Where the proofs impute determinations to God, these determinations must be annulled. God cannot be apprehended through determinations (*via negationis*).

Anselm knew all the proofs of the existence of God; he himself repeated them and thought them correct. But they did not suffice him. Enraptured by thought as thought, he found the fundamental idea to which he clung all his life. But for Thomas this idea was a fallacy of which he disposed in passing, so simply that one is amazed at Anselm as well as Thomas. What does this mean?

Thomas thought with the natural understanding, which for him was empirical and rationalistic. Or in receiving revelation, he thought mystery. Anselm knew no such cleavage. Because he understood revelation with reason, he was able, in his fundamental thought, to exercise pure reason even without revelation.

Thomas' proofs of the existence of God demand no other thinking than that of the natural understanding. What Thomas apprehends in this way is available to every man without the ground of existence, it is convincing reality to the common sense (though, to be sure, as we have known since Kant, this common-sense reasoning is deceptive). This mediocre, essentially anchorless common sense knows neither the play of thought in speculation nor the objectless apperception of reality through thinking existence. Thomas supposes himself to be in possession of tangible knowledge; he has the certainty of reality. In this reality, rising by degrees, he believes he can disclose the reality of God by demonstration. Over the poverty of this method and its contents arches the radiant mystery of revelation and its contents as formulated by theological thinking.

Anselm's fundamental idea belongs neither to the realm of the natural understanding, delimited by Thomas, nor to that of revelation. It lies in between, and in Thomas there is no place for it. For it is original philosophy, thinking filled with the philosopher's own existence. Anselm trusts profoundly in the unity of thought and faith in the source of reason, that is, of philosophy. In the age of Thomas, the danger of thought for authority had become far more evident than in Anselm's day. Thomas tried to conjure this danger, on the one hand by accepting common-sense thinking but defining its limits, and on the other hand by complementing it with the mystery of revelation. He accepted common-sense thinking at the cost of subordinating all thinking to mystery. There was no longer room for Anselm's great philosophizing. It slipped away between the two tangible corporeal realities. It might seem as though Thomas had sensed the enormous danger for Church authority inherent in Anselm's philosophizing. Of this, however, there is no indication in the writings of Thomas, but only the admirable theologian's utter incomprehension of everything that did not fit into his world, so vast, so well ordered, so brilliant, and yet so dogmatically limited. In Thomas fulfilled thinking, thinking as an existential act, has vanished. At this one point in Anselm's thinking the soul stands in direct contact with God without the mediation of realities or revelation.

Was Anselm extravagant? The advocates both of Thomism and of common sense, of naïve realism and of the highly developed rationalism of authoritarian religion, are agreed that he was, though the opinion is stated with varying sharpness. We still find it in Gilson's mild formulation: "To our feeling, St. Anselm deviated from the sound way . . . passing over experience to the mere necessity of the concept."

I shall not discuss the affirmations of Anselm's idea by Bonaventura, Duns Scotus, and Hegel, which in many variants disclose a trace of Anselm's spirit. I shall also pass over Spinoza, who simply made Anselm's fundamental idea into the first of his definitions, from which he constructs his figures of thought: "By cause of itself I mean that whose essence comprises existence or that whose nature can only be conceived as existing." Instead, I shall consider Descartes and Leibniz, who both affirm Anselm's idea, but degrade it into a proof of objectively compelling character, treating its object as a fact and trying to improve man's understanding of this fact.

Descartes: Descartes held Anselm's proof to be correct. Only of the highest being, of God alone, can it be said that His essence includes existence. Only in connection with God is the proof compelling: existence can no more be separated from the essence of God than from the essence of a triangle the fact that the sum of its angles is equal to two right angles or the notion valley from the notion mountain. My thinking does not impose this necessity on things. On the contrary, the reality itself, namely God's existence, imposes this necessity on my thinking. I am free to conceive of God without existence as I am free to think of a horse with or without wings.

But Descartes wishes to improve on Anselm's idea. Anselm's inference draws its cogency from the idea of the highest being, of perfection. Its indispensable premise is that I have this idea. Descartes takes it as a fact that I have it, and this fact becomes the ultimate ground of Anselm's proof. The idea of the most perfect being, even the idea of a being more perfect than I, cannot stem from myself and cannot come from nothing. It must have an adequate cause. I who have this idea could not exist if there were not such a being. "The whole compelling force of this proof lies in my recognition that I myself with my nature—insofar as I have the idea of God in me—could not possibly exist if God did not really exist." Existence as such, knowing itself to be finite and imperfect existence, presupposes the existence of God as standard of the infinite and perfect.

The idea of the infinite perfect God is in Descartes innate and unchanging; it has attained its object. In Anselm the idea is in motion: its content is not the *summum esse,* but the *quo maius cogitari non potest,* not an object but a task. The fixity of the object in Descartes suggests a transference of thinking to the infinite, which I now possess; while Anselm is perpetually in motion toward the infinite. In Descartes we have a transcendent godhead, in Anselm God is present without becoming an object.

Although Descartes transfers the proof to the level of objectively compelling knowledge, he knows how difficult the operation is. "There is surely nothing that I would know more easily and readily than God if my mind were not clouded by prejudices and if the images of corporeal things did not fully occupy my consciousness." Are these words spoken as one might speak of any difficult idea, in mathematics for example, or do they reveal an awareness of the source that was at work in Anselm?

Leibniz: Like Descartes, Leibniz does not regard the ontological proof as valid in itself and tries to improve on it by adding a new premise that will make it absolutely secure. This new premise lies in the very thought that God, or perfect Being, is possible. If this thought is possible, its object must be real. And it is possible. For nothing can impede the possibility of what knows no limitations, no negation, and consequently no contradiction. This idea in itself suffices to give me *a priori* knowledge of God's existence.

Descartes and Leibniz introduce Anselm's proof into the context of other proofs. They transform it into a fact among other facts, and remove it from existence, that is, from the thinking which experiences reality and not mere logical necessity, or rather which in logical necessity experiences something more. Both try characteristically to improve on the proof, injecting a new presupposition that is supposed to give it full validity. Nevertheless, something of Anselm's substance remains; God's uniqueness and relation to my own existence are still present. Without these, the proof, transformed into an objective logical operation, becomes empty and meaningless. This was understood by Kant, who did not know Anselm's proof in the original, but only as paraphrased by the rationalists. Finding Anselm's idea in this denatured form, Kant termed it the ontological proof of the existence of God, and refuted it.

Kant: Like Anselm, Kant perceived the unique value of the idea over against the many proofs of the existence of God. "If the absolute necessity of a thing is to be known in theoretical consciousness, this might be done solely on the basis of concepts *a priori,* never on the basis of a cause in relation to a being that is given in experience."

Since Kant it has been clear that all proofs of the existence of God based on facts in the world are false, because they move on the plane of reality, which is the experience of objects in the world. When Thomas with the ancients infers the unchanging from the changing, the mover from the moved, the most perfect being from the degrees of perfection, the absolute from the relative, his starting point is a set of facts. Interpreted in conceptual terms, these facts call for completion by something which is not a fact, but derived as a concept, and which can never occur as a fact.

Kant noted that all these proofs do essentially the same thing as the denatured ontological proof: they infer the reality of an object from its concept. This ontological proof is indeed at the heart of all proofs of God's existence.

Rejecting what he termed the ontological proof, Kant argues that no reality can ever be inferred from concepts. "When, therefore, I think a being as the supreme reality, without any defect, the question still remains whether it exists or not." How can I ascertain its real existence? If it were an object of sense perception, I should be dependent on the context of my experience; through it, my thinking would gain another possible perception. But if we wish to think of existence through pure category alone, "we cannot specify a single mark distinguishing it from mere possibility."

In other words: Our consciousness of existence pertains in every case to the unity of experience. Only in "relation to my whole state of thinking," namely to the fact that knowledge of an object is possible through the experience of perception, can its existence be demonstrated. In speaking of an object of sense perception, we would not confuse the existence of a thing with the concept of that thing. But in dealing with an object of pure thought, even if we impute every perfection to it, even if it is free from all contradiction, we still have no means of proving it to be real. For reality is not one of the predicates of a concept, but pertains to the relation of a thing to our existence and experience. "A hundred real thalers do not contain the least coin more than a hundred possible thalers. . . . My financial position is, however, affected very differently by a hundred real thalers than it is by the mere concept of them (that is, of their possibility)."

Here Kant radically rejects the possibility of attaining certainty of Being by thinking pure and simple. For thought is as such objectless (mere possibility) and, in order to gain objective significance, requires completion. From an idea we cannot "pick out" the existence of a corresponding object. The ontological proof must either take existence into the concept (the "most real being"): then the thought itself would have to be a thing, which is impossible; or else the being we wish to demonstrate must be presupposed: then we should have a "wretched tautology."

Kant's whole critique of the ontological proof remains within the category of being as an empirical reality. He considered Anselm's "idea of God" on the same plane as it occupies in Descartes and Leibniz, but in addition he dispelled the last vestige of Anselm's spirit, which is perhaps still discernible in Descartes and Leibniz. In his whole discussion of the matter, Kant moves exclusively in the realm of concepts which are indeed inappropriate to the idea of God. He speaks of empirical, not transcendent, reality. Kant sharply rejected the old philosophical habit of making transcendence a bodily reality, existing in some place and time.

If Kant rejects all proofs of the existence of God, including the so-called ontological proof, we must go beyond his particular arguments and ask: Why?

Kant's philosophical motive is the reality of the transcendent itself. I cannot know the transcendent as I know things in the world. I cannot gain possession of it by knowledge and have it as I can have an object. It is equally fallacious to objectify God, to consider Him as we consider the reality of the sensible world, and to demonstrate His existence by mathematical or logical reasoning.

For Kant the question is very much the same as for Anselm: How shall I gain certainty of God's reality? Anselm indicates the meditative path of transcending thought, Kant the practical path of ethical action. Anselm knows the philosophical experience of inner action, leading to the certainty of God's existence. Kant knows reflection on the ethical action of man, who understands the meaning of his action only through the practical postulates of freedom and the existence of God. Kant's intuition of God, which is essentially grounded in the reality of ethical action, appears at the limit of every realm of reason: as *Ding an sich,* as the created ground of the phenomenal world; as the supersensory substrate of humanity in the contemplation of the beautiful; as the unity of all our faculties of reason in the intelligible; as the source of ideas. Kant also develops from his thinking the "transcendental ideal," the "material of all possibility," but these, as he states expressly, are only representations of the "flawless ideal"; they do not imply a knowledge of the real God. "Necessity, infinity, unity, existence outside of the world (not as world-soul), eternity (without temporal conditions), omnipresence (without spatial conditions), omnipotence, etc."— all these are for Kant predicates of transcendence that can be thought *a priori.* To "work out the purified concept (of transcendence) that is so much needed by theology" is for Kant a philosophical task. But thought can give all these no reality. For the ultimate ground of existential insight, which first lends weight to all these limiting concepts, is not theory but ethical practice.

Between Anselm and Kant there is a kinship that skips over all the intervening historical links. An indication of this is that for both of them there is only *one* essential proof. This one proof is not a mere content of thought, but God's presence. Our thinking moves in several directions, actuality is one. In his famous saying about the two things—the starry heavens above me and the moral law within me—that fill the heart with ever-renewed wonder and awe, he adds: "I see them before me and link them directly with the consciousness of my existence."

In the consciousness of their own Existenz, elucidated in thinking, both gain certainty of God's existence. Kant, who rejects the ontological proof, does not call his "ethical" demonstration of the existence of God a proof, but a postulate. Because the certainty of God's existence is not grounded in an objective proof of the understanding, Kant, after setting forth the thought that leads to God, does not say "He is a certainty," but "I am certain."

Anselm and Kant apprehend the one source of a certainty that can be expressed in rational terms but not demonstrated by reason. Their thinking is not a thinking "about" something, but a thinking Existenz, in which what they think becomes real for them. All the others, Thomas, Descartes, or Leibniz, whether for or against Anselm's proof, think in a very different way from Anselm and Kant.

These two in turn differ in their fundamental experience. Both attain to being in thought, but Anselm does so in pure thought, which is not *cogitare* but *intelligere,* Kant in practical thinking governed by an absolute law. For Kant my thinking awareness of the law I ought to follow contains something more than law, namely God. For Anselm, my thinking of the being than which no greater can be conceived, contains more than thought. In both cases, God becomes a certainty through their existence.

For neither thinker is God an acquisition of disinterested knowledge; He is present only to believing reason. Certainty is sought in the never-ending movement of our existence in time. For Anselm it requires purity of heart, without which his "idea" cannot be realized. In Anselm reflection is meditative and leads back to Christian faith. For Kant it is reflexive, leading back to the rational existence of ethical action.

Such ideas may appear to be mere technical devices by which to gain certainty of God's existence, but for those who first enact them, they are events: these thinkers have found something never to be forgotten, that sustains their lives for ever after. Later, such ideas are disseminated in a rational simplification and become ineffectual, mere doctrine. Nevertheless, they preserve an inexhaustible power, for hidden within them is an impulse, a spark, which can take fire at any moment, whenever it falls on a soul prepared for the flame of certainty in God.

Kant moved in the same area of philosophical depth as Anselm, and it was for that very reason that he rejected the simplified logical form in which he encountered the idea. But the question remains: Is there room in the area of Kantian critical thinking for Anselm's idea as Anselm intended it: the power of logical thought to transcend thought with thought in an attitude of prayer?

III. CHARACTERIZATION OF ANSELM'S THINKING

A. *Anselm's original philosophy as Christian thinking:* There is a radiant power in Anselm's philosophy. It is not a preparatory stage; it is a fulfillment, but one belonging to an early period, unaffected by the cleavages resulting from the reflection and the realities of a later day.

His thinking treats of truth, free will, evil, and the doctrines of the God-man (*cur deus homo*) and the Trinity. He believed that faith could be made accessible to reason. When Kant writes of religion within the limits of mere reason and Anselm seeks reason in the contents of faith (according to the Augustinian principle: *credo ut intelligam*), the difference between them is that one did his thinking before the cleavage into faith and reason, theology and philosophy, the other afterward. In both the will to autonomous reason and a lofty concept of reason were at work; both knew that the reality of reason does not have its ground in itself.

Anselm was the great original thinker of the Middle Ages. To be sure, the continuity of Christian thinking paved the way for his philosophy. But this was only the source of the power which enabled him, like Augustine, to philosophize independently. Like Augustine, he saw faith as the source of thinking, so that he knew both formulations: believe in order to understand the content of faith; understand in order to gain the certainty of faith. The seeming contradiction between the primacy of faith and the independent power of thinking is a confluence of the motives of this original philosophizing.

His extensive, crystal-clear discussions of fundamental human knowledge and the great dogmas form a background against which we discern his central philosophical preoccupations: purity of thought as an effective force; the power of simplicity; the simple, spontaneous, ahistorical, which lends infinite depth to everything else; the nullity of ideas if they are treated as finite facts by the mere understanding. He was moved by the Existenz of the idea, and even in the most abstract thought he looked for the Existenz that fills it with meaning.

Philosophically Anselm stands at a beginning, which can neither be outdone nor be repeated. In reading him, we breathe a pure air that reminds us of Parmenides and Heraclitus. This is one of the rare moments in which Biblical faith is elucidated in philosophical thinking without self-deception or magic.

B. *What is thinking in Anselm?* In the Middle Ages thinking about the
nature of thought and cognition was situated in an area defined by the
antithetical views of realism (the universals, *universalia,* are real, *realia*)
and nominalism (the universals are mere names, *nomina*). The controversy
developed in connection with statements of Porphyry and Boethius. Considering that Plato speaks of an independent existence of ideas, separate
from things, and that Aristotle grants their existence only in things,
Boethius declared that he did not wish to decide whether they exist only
in our understanding (as mere words or names) or whether they exist
objectively (are real), whether, in other words, Plato or Aristotle was
right, and further whether they are corporeal or incorporeal.

Through the centuries the question was answered in radical antitheses
or in compromises. The one-sided standpoints are: (1) Only the universals
are truly real; particular things are only representations of the universal
that is identical in them all. (2) Only individuals are truly real. The
universals are words, which have reality only as audible, visible things
that signify something.

In both one-sided solutions a new fundamental problem makes its
appearance in opposite forms: (1) If the universal is the real, then the
question arises: Where do the individuals come from (the question of the
principium individuationis)? (2) If the individuals are the real, the opposite question arises: What is the source of the universal (the existence of
the universal as names, signs, meanings derived by abstraction)?

The insoluble difficulties inherent in both these one-sided answers gave
rise to a compromise solution. First it drew a distinction between the
divine and the human mind. The divine mind sees the universals in their
simplicity as models (*exemplaria*). The human mind starts from the objects
of sense perception and arrives at the universal. Hence in relation to the
human mind the universals have three modes of existence: *ante rem* (in
themselves, in the divine spirit), *in re* (in things, connected with individuals), *post rem* (in the human mind, as abstraction).

This simplified schema embodies an enduring problem that is formulated
in the questions: What is? What is the relation between my cognition and
real objects? What is the meaning of objective knowledge?

If the universal is real, then my cognition strikes the reality itself. If
it is not real, it is only an instrument of my knowledge, through which
I never attain reality itself, but can only play with unreal meanings; the
inferences drawn from this game enable me, it is true, to intervene in the
course of events and to subjugate nature, but I remain blind to the essence and the whole, since in this activity I am without knowledge of
reality.

The methodological awareness of the modern sciences developed
on the foundation of so-called nominalism. What the sciences actually know

and do not know is to this day a question of the first importance; an ultimate answer has never been given, but the question has come to be understood more and more clearly.

In the Middle Ages these sciences existed only in germ. But from time immemorial man's natural drive for knowledge has rebelled against the notion that science has no connection with reality itself. As early a thinker as Gerbert of Aurillac (c. 1000) wrote that the classification of the things of nature into genera and species was not the result of human designs but of the Creator of all arts, who produced it as part of the nature of things, where men of discernment discovered it.

Here we shall not enter into the question of the relation between knowledge and reality, or of the kind of reality that is revealed to scientific knowledge. Anselm and the great medieval thinkers—who recognized no difference between philosophy and science, who in their philosophy looked to the essential which even today is not accessible to any science—saw this question in a very different light; for them it was of the utmost gravity for faith and salvation.

To Anselm nominalist thinking was no true thinking at all. For it is no thinking that declares its concepts to be empty, mere words (*flatus vocis,* emissions of voice). Anselm attacks this manner of thinking, which he regarded as unbelief or dangerous to belief. These men, he says, are so ensnared by sensory images (*imaginationibus corporalibus*) that they cannot tear themselves free from them. They cannot see what reason must contemplate in its own light. In Anselm's dogmatic attacks on Roscellinus (a contemporary, often called the "founder" of nominalism, whose only extant work is a letter to his pupil Abelard) the rejection of nominalist thinking plays an essential role. If a thinker declares God to be a universal, an *abstractum,* but the three persons, God the Father, Christ, and the Holy Ghost, to be individuals, he is thinking like a nominalist and has three Gods. But if the universal, God, is Himself reality, then God is one, and the three persons are forms of the one: this idea is "realist," because it upholds the reality of the universals. Church dogma seems to demand "realist" thinking. Anyone, says Anselm, who fails to understand that several people are, as to species, *one* man, will surely not be able to understand that in the most mysterious of beings the three persons, though each is God, are nevertheless only *one* God.

Anselm speaks of the "modern dialecticians," who accept nothing as real unless they can form representations of it (*imaginationibus comprehendere*), and of people who are so beset by the multitude of images within them that they cannot rise to the simplicity of the idea (*intellectus*).

To Anselm the most natural kind of thinking is that which does not lose itself amid the emptiness of mere discourse or let itself be confined by representations, but rises to the essential. He knows the peace deriving from the identity of thought and object and attains to it by a kind of thinking which is not a technical instrument, not reflection, not a playful revolving around things, but which in its action is with reality itself, which is indeed itself this reality.

Such thinking attains to the place where truth is reality and there finds fulfillment, in God. In the created world the truth is split: into things and the knowledge of these things, into the reality of things and what they ought to be. Hence all created things are still in quest of their being, they are not yet that being; in our transient lives, we find it and lose it again. But this is made possible only by the reality of the truth; everything that is real without being perceptible to the senses relates to that reality, which, however is not a subjective fiction, produced *by* thinking, but objective reality *for* thinking.

This philosophical thinking is so different from finite object thinking that from the standpoint of the latter it can only seem empty and absurd. It presupposes that true being is itself the being of thinking, a thinking-being, and that our thought is not a mere abstraction, but also something very concrete, which penetrates to the thinking-being in the ground of all things. Only under this assumption can man's thinking lay claim to a higher reality than that of empirical events in time. If this presupposition is taken away, authentic thinking ceases, and I fall back into an existence which is real only to an outsider who thinks it, but which does not know itself and, because it lacks true self-knowledge, is not master of itself.

Being is actualized in thought, not to be sure in empty logical operations, not in mere discourse and opinion, but in the substantial thinking which is itself reality.

I seem to be threatened either by lifeless thought (a random splashing about with words and abstractions) or by unthinking life ("experience"). Authentic thought rises above both of these. It is the self-transformation of existence through an inner thinking action. Such thinking soars to touch upon Being itself. It is a life that moves closer to the infinite Being, which in its thinking it already is. My empirical actuality becomes human life only when my thinking finds and unfolds the Being within it.

To understand Anselm we must bear in mind that to him thought was real. The self-certainty of this thinking that takes its substance from God is attested by its action in existence. In the dichotomies of finite thinking the logical forms will always be man's instrument and medium of communication; in authentic thinking they point the way to something beyond themselves.

It is in this same light that we must judge the function of contradiction in Anselm. Contradiction in Anselm becomes a lever by which thought lifts itself from *cogitare* to *intelligere* and a means of securing the *intelligere* through the *cogitare*. As such it is a necessary element, but once this aim is attained, there is no further need for it. To Anselm contradiction was intolerable. It is not masked by factors of other origin, which hide

by clustering around a manifest contradiction. Nor is it represented as
something to which we must submit—believing in the absurd—because
it comes from God. Rather, it is valid as a method. It destroys that wherein
it manifests itself, but in so doing points the way to the place where there
is neither contradiction nor freedom from contradiction, where finite thinking becomes authentic, infinite thinking and achieves certainty in the
truth that is reality.

c. *Authority:* Man can live only under authority, and this has been true
at all times. If he is unwilling to accept authority, he will merely succumb
to a more external violence. The illusion of being free from all authority
causes men to fling themselves into the most absurd and destructive
obedience. The claim that each individual is entitled to absolute freedom
of opinion dulls men's minds and leads to some form of total subjugation.
Man has only the choice of which authority to accept, that is, on what set
of beliefs to ground his life. There is no outside vantage point from which
to survey all authority. To stand outside means to stand in nothingness
and to be blind. But my choice of authority is not deliberate; I can only
gain a purified awareness of the authority in which I am already living,
that is, I can awaken the latent authority within me by recollecting the
ground of my being. I cannot look deep enough for this ground, because
it is there that I shall find what has absolute validity for me.

In Anselm we see the bond of authority and the freedom of reason in
its acceptance. He knows that empty reasoning achieves nothing. But he
also knows that faith is not enough: "It strikes me as negligence if, once
we are secure in faith, we do not try to understand what we believe."

Anselm's faith is still sheltered in the authority of the Church. He finds
authority for his thinking in the Catholic Church Fathers. He desires above
all that what he himself thinks "should accord with what was written by
St. Augustine."

Anselm could not be aware of the special historical character of his
time. To him it could not seem extraordinary that in a still barbarous world
the Church, thanks to the self-sacrificing lives of the monastic orders,
should be the sole source of all intellectual greatness, of all philosophy and
education, and indeed of all reading and writing, and that not only the
most learned but also the noblest men of the day were members of the
clergy. The Church still signified an identity of spirit and power; this
most "catholic" of Western organizations still signified the power of the
spirit against raw violence. And it meant absolute certainty. To question
the Church and its monastic orders in those days would have been to
question everything that men live by.

Hence the magnificent self-certainty that Anselm possessed as a monk,
as an abbot, and as an archbishop, creating in order to transmit the one
and only truth and impress it on the minds of men, terrified at the abyss

of arbitrary thinking. Thus when a conflict arose, he called for submission to Church authority. He insisted that there should be no debate with Roscellinus; he should first be made to retract. Once this was done, Anselm tried to persuade him by his treatise on the Trinity. But faced with the alternatives of martyrdom and hypocrisy, Roscellinus—for fear of death, as he said later—chose hypocrisy.

Anselm's thinking is the free thinking of a man of the Church, whom the reality of God's rule through the Church made humble, but at the same time courageous and mighty in the struggle against the King and the world. Anselm's attitude might be called grandiose naïveté, were it not a sublimated awareness, lacking in only one thing, which in that age was unthinkable: doubt in the legitimacy of the kingdom of God claimed by the Church, in the ethical rank of the Church as a real political power. Like Plato's political venture in Syracuse, Anselm's struggle in behalf of the Church was a phenomenon of transition, possible only once with true integrity, without superstition and magic, without the help of demagogically aroused mass instincts. That such action was taken once, with such human power, purity, and greatness, is inspiring forever, even if the concrete solution has proved questionable and a source of violence whenever it has been attempted since.

This was the period of meditative Romanesque piety, discernible in its architecture, a time when it seemed that Plato's idea of philosopher-kings might become a reality. Even then, to be sure, there was a divergence between aspiration and reality, but it was still possible to believe, sincerely and without restriction, that the two would someday be one. That the peak—the eleventh century—was at the same time a period of crisis is historically self-evident. For in temporal existence every maturation is at the same time a dying. All history is transition. The sublime cannot endure. It makes its appearance in some form at all times, and at all times it passes away. But seldom does the sublime reside in the reality of institutions, so that the kingdom of God and the secular kingdom, spiritual rank and physical power, coincide. In Anselm's lifetime the tendency was downward. At the moment of its supreme action, the Church became an evil power. But what was overpoweringly great in the idea, what for a moment achieved reality in approximations, what fired men's enthusiasm while preserving a discipline of moderation, does not lose its substance through failure. It endures for memory in the eternal realm of the spirit. In a new world, where men seek transcendence under new conditions, this thing that once happened can still serve as an orientation.

NICHOLAS OF CUSA

INTRODUCTION

Nikolaus Krebs (or Chryffs) was born in Kues on the Moselle, the son of a prosperous winegrower and boatman. He has come to be known as Cusanus after Cusa, the Latinized form of Kues, his birthplace. He is the only one of the great philosophers to have led a busy life in the world from an early age to the day of his death. He served the Church as a member of the Council of Basel, as cardinal, bishop, and vicar general in Rome.

The great Christian thinkers had all been members of religious orders; monastic life left its imprint upon them. Cusanus was a secular priest. Deeply religious, he enjoyed the friendship of monks. In his old age, a monk's cell was always kept in readiness for him in Tegernsee in case he should wish to retire into a life of meditation. Though his stormy political activities and arduous travels might have sufficed to consume his energies, he produced a body of philosophical writings whose great importance is generally recognized today.

This work was not a hobby or avocation pursued in his free time: it grew out of his practical activities and was intended to give them meaning. But while his quest for a union between theory and practice endows both with a character of grandeur, his attempts to achieve that union proved more and more disappointing as he grew older. He wished his actions to be an integral part of the intellectual order embracing God and the world, man and the Church. He must have been inspired by a fundamental impulse that transcended both his thought and his action. Having failed in his primary intention, he fell back on philosophical speculation, but his philosophy was not of a kind that could provide him with a constant serenity and equanimity in dealing with things of the world.

His modesty, his renunciation of the ostentatious splendors attaching to his position as a prince of the Church, his simplicity free from the rigors of asceticism, gave him dignity. We cannot doubt his sense of responsibility or the genuineness of his commitment. But the realities confronting him were not what he believed them to be, and he was essentially unaware of this fact and its consequences. What is "reality"? The question becomes especially urgent when we consider this man whose worldly activities were oriented toward God and eternity, yet in the end it remains unanswered.

Cusanus was a German who became a European at an early date; yet though his life was centered in Rome, he did not forget his origins. In his native Cusa he left a memorial to himself, upon which he lavished most of the income he gained from his position: he founded a home for the aged with extensive living quarters and farm buildings, a church, and considerable land holdings. It survived many wars and revolutions and today, five centuries later, is still standing. The old building, Cusanus' library, his manuscripts, and his instruments remain intact. The institution still owns the vineyards he inherited from his father and is still governed by the statutes he drew up for it. (The charter is reprinted in Scharpff, 1843, pp. 387 ff.) It is a living symbol of historical continuity—as we shall see, the will to endure is inherent in his thought.

In his testamentary dispositions the Cardinal directed that he be buried in S. Pietro in Vincoli, the church in Rome attached to his cardinalcy, where his tomb with an impressive portrait engraved in stone can be seen today. His heart was transferred in a casket to the church of his foundation in Cusa.

LIFE

Cusanus (1401-64) left home at the age of twelve. According to tradition, he was estranged from his father, who mistreated him. At all events, he became independent at an early date. Still according to tradition, a certain Count von Manderscheid sent him in 1413 to the Brothers of the Common Life at Deventer to be educated. Here he must have obtained his elementary schooling and lived in an atmosphere of mystical piety, of the type known to us from Thomas a Kempis' *Imitation of Christ*. In 1416 he was a student at Heidelberg (this is the earliest fact of which we have documentary evidence); in 1417 he went to Padua, where he studied for six years. In Padua he was initiated into the intellectual world of his period. At least two of his teachers became his friends—Toscanelli, the physician, geographer, and physicist, who was with Cusanus when he died, and Giuliano Cesarini, later Cardinal and President of the Council of Basel, who sponsored his ecclesiastical career at its beginnings in Basel. Cusanus studied with the zeal of a young man determined to master all knowledge. He familiarized himself with mathematics and astronomy, physics and medicine, ancient literature and the new humanism. His principal study was law; in 1423 he became a doctor of Canon Law at Padua.

Only then did he take up the study of theology, at the University of Cologne, where he was registered as *doctor in jure canonico* (1425). He wrote legal opinions. In 1427 he was appointed Dean at the St. Florin Foundation in Coblenz, and in 1430 he became secretary to Ulrich von Manderscheid, who had been elected Archbishop of Trier by the local chapter. In 1432 his patron sent him to the Council of Basel to defend his claim to his ecclesiastical post against an archbishop appointed by the Pope. In this mission Cusanus was unsuccessful. In 1435 he declined a chair at the University of Louvain.

Cusanus' youth must have been marked by the spirit of the times. In 1417, with the election of Pope Martin V, the Council of Constance had finally put an end to the papal schism. Nevertheless, it was clear that the world had undergone a major change. By what reforms might the disorder in Church and Empire be surmounted? The problem confronting the Council of Basel began with great expectations on all sides. The accident of his mission led Cusanus into the main stream of world events. At first he became a passionate champion of the conciliar principle against the views of Pope Eugenius, and defended this position in his first, most voluminous work, *De concordantia catholica*. Later, deeply disappointed by the threat of a new schism, he went over to the papal party and became its most successful propagandist in Germany. In recognition of his extraordinary contributions to Church unity and the power of the papacy, he was in 1448 appointed cardinal and assigned the Church of S. Pietro in Vincoli as his titular parish. This was an unusual distincton for a German.

In 1450 Nicholas V appointed him Bishop of Brixen (in southern Tyrol). This spelled his political doom. His unremitting efforts in behalf of internal reform and his defense of the rights of the Church against secular rulers (such as Duke Sigismund of Austria) fired conflicts which did not cease until shortly after Cusanus' death, when the Church agreed to a compromise.

In 1451 and 1452 Cusanus traveled through Germany as papal nuncio, charged with the mission of reforming the churches and monasteries, and of promulgating the Jubilee indulgence of 1450. On the whole his mission was a resounding failure.

Right down to his death he continued to work for the papacy, the last six years in the post of vicar general in Rome, the highest ecclesiastical office next to the papacy itself. During these last years he acted as the most trusted adviser of Pius II (Enea Silvio de' Piccolomini), who had been his friend for decades.

Cusanus died in the midst of his last mission, on August 11, 1464, at Todi in Umbria. Three days later Pius II died in Ancona and the fantastically unrealistic crusade against the Turks, which the Pope had championed against Cusanus' advice, came to an inglorious end.

Some writers have described Cusanus in his last years as tired and resigned. I cannot agree. His last writings show the keenest intellectual energy and concentration. They bear witness to an undiminished preoccupation with fundamentals. For all his great disappointments in the field of active politics, he never carried out his earlier plan of withdrawing to a monastery in his old age. His turning away from the political activity which had provided an outlet for the stormy exuberance of his youth had nothing in common with weariness.

WORKS

Nicholas of Cusa was familiar with the scholastics and mystics, with the philosophers of antiquity and the Church Fathers. He was interested in all the sciences of his time. As a jurist and statesman and priest, he was a powerful and effective speaker. Nearly all his thinking revolved around a single idea: God is revealed in everything that is, in everything that is known and done.

The literary form of his writings is very different from that of the *summae* characteristic of the Middle Ages. Cusanus gives us no vast, all-inclusive conceptual system. Nor do his works display anything like the precision of Anselm's treatises, which, though written in sections composed over the decades, fall into place like parts of a planned totality. Cusanus' writings are a loose sequence of treatises, dialogues, letters, sermons. Only one, the first (*De concordantia catholica,* 1435), is relatively voluminous. Only one (*De docta ignorantia,* 1440), taken in conjunction with *De coniecturis* (1440), can be said to provide a complete outline of his philosophy. Philosophical writings in the narrower sense make up barely one-third of the whole.

His actual writing was done in days or hours of leisure over a period of years, but his mind can never have been inactive. He wrote rapidly and seems to have revised very little if at all. But his thought had long been ripening in his mind. He was particularly productive between July and September 1450: from this period date two mathematical works and the books *Idiota de sapientia, Idiota de mente, De staticis experimentis.* From 1463 date some especially fine and mature works in which he once again takes cognizance of the whole: *De venatione sapientiae, De ludo globi, Compendium theologiae, De apice theoriae,* and the letter to Albergati. Outstanding among the other philosophical writings are *De deo abscondito* (1445), *De visione dei* (1453), and his letters to the monks at Tegernsee: *De beryllo* (1458), *De possest* (1460), *De non aliud* (1462).

At times, when he was most caught up in practical affairs, he did not, if writing is equated with production, produce at all (e.g., 1437-39, 1451-52, 1454-57).

The language and literary form of Cusanus' works are not classical. Self-sufficient little masterpieces such as *De deo abscondito* are rare, though there are admirable passages in nearly all his writings. There is a great deal of incidental matter. Magnificent, unforgettable formulations turn up in otherwise complicated, difficult texts. His Latin is never simple, clear, or exact. But an inimitable philosophical tone is sustained over long passages. His awareness of God is richly expressed in flashing insights as well as grave meditations, and many of the dialogues abound in vivid, dramatic images. But he can also lapse into traditional, schematic thinking or become painfully long-winded.

It has been maintained, especially with reference to a statement about himself at the beginning of *De apice theoriae,* that Cusanus' philosophy develops progressively. I cannot accept this view. His writings as a whole represent, rather, the continual transformation and enrichment of a single insight. In each of them, one or another aspect is stressed, e.g., experience or, on the contrary, the need to transcend the limits of our conceptual thinking. But this does not imply a progressive development in which earlier theses are rejected as false, and new and purer truth attained.

A different question is whether the kind of thinking first disclosed in *De docta ignorantia* now clearly and methodically, now soaring in full flight, betokens a sudden advance in the development of Cusanus' thought. In his letter to Cardinal Giuliano Cesarini, which concludes *De docta ignorantia,* he says: "Now receive what I have long sought by different paths, but found only while I was on shipboard, returning from Greece; I think it was by a gift from on high, from the Father of Light whence comes all that is best, that I was led to conceive the incomprehensible in an incomprehensible way in the knowledge of nonknowledge, by going beyond [*per transcensum*] the indestructible truths as they are known in the human way." Is this merely a literary effusion, or does it refer to some reality such as we encounter in the autobiographical references of other great philosophers (Anselm, Descartes, Kant, Nietzsche)? I am convinced that the latter is the case. The illuminating power of the new idea, whose development was now to supply the content of his intellectual life, had left an indelible impression. This was not just one more idea, it was a new kind of thinking. It marked Cusanus' "initiation" into philosophy. His extraordinary intelligence and his underlying faith remained unchanged; but all this was now absorbed in a new intellectual perspective, carried into a new dimension of depth. An insight into this new dimension is indispensable for an understanding of Cusanus.

Part One: Philosophical Speculation

I. THE FUNDAMENTAL IDEA

Cusanus tells us that the concepts of *docta ignorantia* ("learned ignorance") and *coincidentia oppositorum* ("the coincidence of opposites") were bestowed upon him by a higher power: this implies a claim to have been the first to introduce them. The claim would appear unjustified. The *coinciden-*

tia oppositorum, or at least the idea that all opposites are transcended, is very old: it is to be found in Neoplatonic writings. As for the term *docta ignorantia,* it occurs once in St. Augustine. As it is not unusual to make such discoveries in philosophical texts from Plato on, we are tempted to ask the disabused old question: What, then, is really new? If we look long and hard enough, we find that everything has already been said. And this is true enough for the mere verbal formulations. But it is not true in respect of the thought itself. The originality of an idea lies in the thinker's sudden insight, perhaps touched off by something he is studying or perhaps by something he once read and has since forgotten. The objective novelty of an idea is recognizable by the fact that, when related to the other ideas in a work, it discloses a unique, irreplaceable quality, a fundamental tone, so to speak, which governs the development of the work as a whole. I shall try to outline what is fundamental in Nicholas of Cusa's philosophical speculations.

A. *Discursive thinking and the finite.* When I think, I think something distinct and apart from other things. At the same time the things I think of in this way are related to one another. I compare one with another (*comparatio*). I apply some standard of measurement to whatever is, so as to define it (*mensuratio*). To think is to judge. In propositions that express judgments, a subject is related to a predicate. But what is thought or judged confronts the thinking subject as the object of his thought.

Thus we always think in dichotomies: a dichotomy between the thinking I and the object of thought, a dichotomy we bring about in the object by drawing distinctions, by discerning oppositions or contradictions.

Every object is particular, distinct. When I perceive, represent, or think something, I remain in the world of the determined, i.e., the world of limited, finite things.

Between the standard of measurement and the thing measured there is always a difference. There are always further differences, and as we progress we discover endless degrees of difference. This is the domain of the more and the less, the larger and the smaller, the domain of the relative, not of the absolute.

In the more or less of finite things I never reach either the largest or the smallest. Every limit reached has a beyond. Beyond every smallest there is a smaller, beyond every largest a larger.

Whenever we transcend a limit, we have limited that which we transcend, and we immediately discover a new limit. This goes on endlessly.

B. *Beyond the domain of the finite.* Such is the world as it appears to our discursive reason. But to stay within it leaves us dissatisfied. We should like to go beyond this world in which there is always a larger and a smaller, into a world of the absolutely largest and the absolutely smallest, that is, we should like to pass from the domain of limits to the unlimited, from the domain of the finite to infinity.

c. *Between the finite and the infinite there is no common term.* This impulse encounters strong resistance. We can have knowledge only of finite things, not of the infinite. Nowhere do we reach the infinite, no matter how far and how unendingly we progress in the finite: our work of comparing and measuring never ceases. No matter how great or how small the finite as we discern it may be, it remains finite.

The fundamental situation of our cognition is this: there is no common term between the finite and the infinite (*finiti ad infinitum nulla est proportio, De doc. ignor.,* I, 3). All relations remain within the finite. Hence there is a gap, a discontinuity between the finite and the infinite. If the term "world" denotes the finite and the cosmos of the finite and "God" the infinite, then this gap, this discontinuity, this unbridgeable gulf lies between the world and God. Plato called it *tmēma* (cut, incision).

"Thus, in the concrete, there is no ascent to the absolutely greatest and no descent to the absolutely smallest. Therefore, just as the divine, absolutely greatest being cannot be diminished to such an extent that it becomes limited and finite, so the concrete cannot relinquish its concreteness to the extent of becoming absolute" (*De doc. ignor.,* III, 1).

d. Docta ignorantia *and the* coincidentia oppositorum. Even though the infinite eludes all relating to the finite, it is nevertheless present to our awareness: it is that in the face of which our reason breaks down when we try to understand and define it. It discloses itself in the awareness of the thinker who, when his reason breaks down, discovers in himself a power bursting the bonds of discursive reason, whose logic is valid only within its own sphere. This power is the intellect, or speculative reason (*intellectus*), which makes use of discursive reason (*ratio*) but is able to obtain insights into what is not accessible to discursive reason.

The infinity of the godhead is not accessible to discursive knowledge, but the intellect can touch upon it as long as discursive reason is in a state of ignorance. Now this ignorance is not the empty ignorance of someone unaware of not knowing, or indifferent to what he is incapable of knowing. It is, rather, a "learned ignorance" (*docta ignorantia*), which is developed in thinking and can be filled with content.

Learned ignorance requires a new kind of logic. When discursive thinking breaks down, a different kind of thinking comes into being, which has no object. The oppositions and contradictions—which in the world of the finite are either tied to distinctions or destroy them by reducing them to absurdity—coincide in this latter kind of thinking (*coincidentia oppositorum*).

Thus, "learned ignorance" is not resignation, not the expression of an agnosticism indifferent to the unknowable. Rather, it is achieved through speculation, which provides it with content by methods that can be discerned through truly metaphysical thinking. This is the sense of Cusanus' lifelong intellectual effort, the fruit of the meditations expressed in his writings—a series of variations on this theme: "No man, even the most learned in his discipline [*doctrina*], can progress farther along the road to perfection than the point where he is found most knowing in the very ignorance that characterizes him; and he will be the more learned [*doctior*], the more he comes to know himself for ignorant [*ignorantem*]" (*De doc. ignor.*, I, 1).

The *coincidentia oppositorum* is one form this ignorance takes. It defies discursive reason, which can only condemn it as absurd. It presupposes a resolve—stemming from an experience essentially different from sensory and rational experience—to elucidate this new experience in a logical-alogical, internally disciplined, methodical manner, and thereby to unfold it, producing it by thought, in ever greater richness.

E. *The "Wall."* Cusanus had his own way of describing the boundary line between the finite objects of discursive reason and the domain of the infinite to which the intellect aspires. There is a wall around the domain of the godhead, too high for us to climb over. Yet what lies behind the wall is active, present, all-underlying. We fail when we try to break through the wall, but in the process of coming up against it, we recognize it as the sign of godhead.

Cusanus addresses God: "I give Thee thanks, my God, because . . . Thou hast shown me that Thou canst not be seen elsewhere than where impossibility meets and faces me. Thou hast inspired me . . . to do violence to myself, because impossibility coincides with necessity, and I have learnt . . . the place where Thou art found unveiled" (*De vis. dei,* pp. 43-44).[1]

This place "is girt round with the coincidence of contradictories," and this is "the wall of Paradise" wherein God abides. The spirit of discursive reason guards the door, "and unless he be vanquished, the way in will not lie open. Thus it is beyond the coincidence of contradictories that Thou mayest be seen" (*ibid.,* p. 44). "That which seems impossible is necessity itself. . . . This is why for him who approaches Thee, they meet in the wall surrounding the place where Thou abidest in coincidence" (*ibid.,* p. 50).

Cusanus calls the godhead *complicatio* (enfolding), and the world *explicatio* (unfolding)—these metaphorical terms will be discussed below. The wall is the point where *complicatio* and *explicatio* meet. These terms provide Cusanus with a way in and a way out. "When I find Thee as

[1] *The Vision of God.* Translated by Emma Gurney Salter. Frederick Ungar Publishing Co., New York. Republished 1960 by arrangement with E. P. Dutton & Co., New York. First published 1928. The translation is here slightly modified.

the power that unfolds I go out. When I find Thee as the power that alike enfolds and unfolds, I go in and out alike. . . . When I behold Thee, My God, in Paradise, girt by this wall of the coincidence of opposites, I see that Thou dost neither enfold nor unfold. . . . For disjunction and conjunction alike are that wall of coincidence beyond which Thou existest, set free from all that can be spoken or thought" (*ibid.,* p. 53).

F. *Examples illustrating the* coincidentia oppositorum

1. *Polygon and circle:* The square and the circle are specific finite figures. They are opposites and can never be geometrically congruent. I can replace the square (quadrangle) by a regular pentagon, hexagon . . . and so on, that is, by a polygon with ever more sides, but the polygon will never coincide with the circle. Yet if the number of sides is infinite, the situation is altered: a polygon with an infinite number of sides is identical with a circle.

"The infinite polygon"—in which the opposites polygon and circle coincide—is an inherently contradictory term. It is not an objective reality. We conceive of it as the result of an endless progression, not of a finite operation—we cannot actually run through an infinite series.

The infinite is conceived as that in which polygon and circle coincide. The mathematical ideal of infinity leads to the idea that all opposites are synthesized in the infinity which is called God.

2. *God and Christ:* I think the very greatest that is, than which there can be no greater (the absolute fullness, *De doc. ignor.,* I, 2). This can be only one, not many, for if it were more than one, any member of the multiplicity would fall short of absolute fullness, because it could be still greater. Which signifies: the One, the Greatest, is Unity, whence follows its uniqueness.

This Unique One cannot be a compound. It is one and not many. It is free from all relation to the Other. The infinite can have nothing outside it. It is all and all is within it. Nor can it be opposed to any Other, to the finite. Rather, it has transcended all oppositions within itself.

Because all opposites coincide in it, the greatest and the smallest also coincide in it. In it the absolutely greatest and the absolutely smallest are identical.

Cusanus makes use of this in his interpretation of Christ, the God-Man: When God becomes man, visible in the world, the extreme opposites must coincide in this mystery. "Then the smallest coincides with the greatest: the greatest humiliation with the greatest elevation, the most ignominious death of the pious with life everlasting, and the same is true of the rest, as we are shown by Christ's life, passion, and death on the Cross" (*De doc. ignor.,* III, 6).

3. *Time and Providence:* The eternity of God is timeless, the things of the world are temporal. But God's infinity comprehends finitude;

finitude is not opposed to infinity, but contained in it. In it the opposites of time and timelessness coincide. "For in eternity in which Thou conceivest, all succession in time coincides in the same Now of eternity" (*De vis. dei, loc. cit.,* p. 49).

This insight elucidates the meaning of "Providence." Providence does not signify a decision by God anticipating things to come in time, such as would make them inevitable. Rather, it signifies that time is abolished in eternity. "I may read or not read tomorrow, yet whatever I do, I cannot escape that Providence which comprehends all opposites, and hence whatever I do will be in conformity with God's providence" (*De doc. ignor.,* I, 22). Discursive reason cannot comprehend Providence. It turns it into the antecedent choice of a subsequent event, which God makes in time. Only the intellect clearly grasps Providence as the coincidence of temporality with eternity.

G. *The fundamental difficulty in this thinking* is that although the operation is effected with the help of discursive reason (*ratio*), what makes it incomprehensibly comprehensible is not discursive reason but the intellect (*intellectus*). We still need rational categories, with which to distinguish and to oppose, even where we conceive of them as abolished.

It is a kind of thinking which, each time it expresses itself, falls into an essential contradiction, but in such a way that the contradiction itself reveals the truth "intended." Where a proposition is established as absolute, the mind has strayed into a blind alley of false rational propositions.

The absolute cannot be adequately conceived of in rational categories, but only in the *coincidentia oppositorum*; and yet the moment the absolute itself is expressed in words, it is reduced to rational opposites (as we shall see later: archetype-copy, oneness-otherness, *complicatio-explicatio,* God-world).

Because this thinking is continually becoming rational, it is misleading, for instance, in the conception of two superimposed worlds (the so-called two-worlds theory). Whereas speculative thinking recognizes only unity, that is, the One which is beyond all opposites, the thinker is in fact continually led back to opposites, the one and the multiple, the one and the other.

A rational solution of this difficulty turns out to be impossible. When expressed in such terms, the gap, the leap, the *tmēma,* the unbridgeable gulf, itself becomes an object, a rational idea.

Speculative thinking must remain the thinking of the unthinkable, it must preserve an unresolvable tension. The fundamental concepts remain paradoxical. For example: is the *coincidentia oppositorum* the essence of absolute divine infinity, or is it rather the form in which alone our intellect, through discursive reason, can refer in thought to the incomprehensible? Cusanus seems to tend now in the one direction, now in the other. If the *coincidentia* is seen as the essence of the godhead, the consequence is an objectivization in the sense of something known in the *coincidentia*. If the *coincidentia* is the essence of our intellectual contact with the absolute, the form is that of human thinking of God.

The same difficulty recurs at every point. That which demands that we push beyond the objective, beyond distinctions, comparisons, and oppositions, in order to reach it, reverts to the objective, and is expressed in terms of distinctions, comparisons, oppositions.

The impetus given by the *coincidentia oppositorum* nevertheless leads to something definite. We are repeatedly swept up in a vortex: things are not as I think them in objective terms—but when I think them in terms of the *coincidentia oppositorum,* I am made aware of them as nonobjective reality.

H. *On and on—beyond what? whither?* Speculative thinking leads to points of rest where truth itself seems to be really present. But once stated, the thought does not bring repose and gratification. Rather, the impulse is aroused to carry speculation further, beyond what has been attained and what it was possible to say. In speculation the transcending never comes to an end. If it is supposed that a concept, an insight, a movement of thought confers possession, as it were, of what we have been looking for, this merely means that the goal has eluded us again and will continue to lead our thinking onward. This dissatisfaction with momentary satisfaction, this need to go on despite passing gratification at the completion of a thought, is the dominant feature of Cusanus' speculation. Here is an example:

What is meant by "creator" and "creation"? Cusanus asks God: "If with Thee to see is to create, and Thou seest nothing other than Thyself, but art Thyself the object of Thyself . . . how then dost Thou create things other than Thyself?" (*De vis. dei, loc. cit.,* p. 56).

Our thinking runs into "the wall of absurdity" which is the coincidence of creating with being-created. Yet this is no real difficulty, for with God, creation and existence are the same. "And creating and being created alike are nothing else than the sharing of Thy being among all, that Thou mayest be all in all, and yet mayest abide freed from all" (*ibid.*).

In other words, on this side of the wall is the thinking that tries to comprehend the creating creator; the wall itself is the coincidence of opposites: creating and being created; beyond the wall lies unrestricted infinity, to which no name is adequate, which cannot be seen through the veils of thinking and speaking, which is in no sense a thing to be expressed or comprehended, but which towers infinitely high above all things.

This perspective is characteristic of all Cusanus' speculation: The infinite impels speculative thinking to progress infinitely; it may pause for a moment to rest in silent nonknowledge, but must then resume the movement that no temporal thinking can evade:

"Thus, while I am borne to loftiest heights, I behold Thee as infinity. . . . He who approaches Thee must needs ascend above every limit and end and finite thing. . . . He who ascends above the end, does he not enter . . . into ignorance and obscurity, which pertain to intellectual confusion? . . . The intellect knows that it is ignorant, and that Thou canst not be grasped because Thou art infinity. For to understand infinity is to comprehend the incomprehensible" (*De vis. dei, loc. cit.,* p. 60).

Because God is infinite, He is the goal of our longing. "That which sates the intellect, or that is the end thereof, is not that which it understands; neither can that sate it which it does not understand at all, but that alone which it understands by not understanding. For the intelligible which it knows does not sate it, nor the intelligible of which it is utterly ignorant, but only the intelligible which it knows to be so intelligible that it can never be fully understood—this alone can sate it" (*op. cit.,* pp. 78–79).

This is the paradox of Cusanus' thinking: By its power of attraction the infinite engenders longing. When we accede to this longing, we are brought into the presence of the infinite. Longing and repose coincide.

1. *Why speculate?* According to Cusanus, speculative reason goes beyond discursive reason; because of its explicitly contradictory character, it "understands by not understanding." Yet Cusanus applied himself wholeheartedly to just such speculation; for him it was the only kind appropriate to its subject, "the sweetest of man's delights." Was it superfluous, a mere hobby of the cardinal's leisure hours? One of his last works, in which he once again summed up his speculations, was titled *De venatione sapientiae,* "Concerning the Hunt for Wisdom" (*sapientia* as distinguished from *scientia*). He says that his purpose was "to record the main results of my forays in pursuit of wisdom and bequeath them to posterity; I have always kept them before my mind's eye, and have become more and more convinced of their truth as I grew older."

Cusanus had but one goal, a single idea in which all ideas meet: in his thinking to attain to the One, in which all things are and whence they spring, in which I too have my source. What must a man think in order to come into contact with the incomprehensible? What can he say in order to express the ineffable, to make it communicable? What methods must be devised?

The hunt for wisdom does not bring results that can be possessed in the form of ready-made knowledge; it only discovers movements of thought that we must carry out, intellectual experiences that we must repeat.

Such thinking is a persistent contemplation, the movement of which promotes the awareness of being that sustains life. The state of speculative meditation leads to a consciousness freed from practical concerns, drawing its contents from other sources. Cognition becomes love, and love engenders cognition. What attains clarity in the calm of meditation is what has always sustained life and must ever more consciously sustain all future life. By sounding the depths of infinitely changing becoming, thought enables us to cast anchor.

How should speculative writings be read? We must go along with the movement of the thought, experience it in its truth, participate in it. Only a certain musical ear for ideas can attune us to this kind of thinking, and for a profound understanding of it our ear must be trained.

Philological studies, which draw comparison, ascertain the meanings of words, point out discrepancies, and discuss historical influences, are useful as a preliminary to understanding, but often lead us astray, encouraging rationalistic misinterpretation.

To read works in their chronological order confers a certain biographical insight. But the essential is to grasp at every point the constant presence of the One.

We shall consider three questions in detail: (1) What is the mind which experiences this kind of thinking? (2) What is the faith that sustains it? (3) What kind of truth is inherent in mathematics?

At the heart of each question we find a concept that is not a discursive concept. In this thinking concepts are not defined with logical cogency and are not related to one another, but denote guiding threads whose meaning is disclosed in the course of attempts at speculative thinking. In the present case such concepts are Mind, Faith, Truth.

II. THE MIND

1. *The mind in general*

A. *The image of God, which knows itself.*—If every created thing is an image of God, the human mind (*mens*) is one par excellence. For not only is it His image; it also knows it is His image. Cusanus writes: Man, the living and spiritual image of God, knows when he enters into himself that he is an image of the same kind as its original (*in se intrat et scit se talem esse imaginem, quale est suum exemplar*). He glimpses in himself this original, his God (*deum suum*), whose likeness (*similitudo*) he is (*De ven. sap.*, 17).

Because man's knowledge is merely an image of divine knowledge, it cannot resemble God's. This too he knows. When an animal does not know, it does not know that it does not know. Only man knows that he does not originally, fundamentally know. Through this knowing non-knowledge he finds the way to truth.

When with the help of the method of the *coincidentia oppositorum*, the mind goes beyond discursive reason, passes through the intellect, and arrives at intuition of the absolute truth (*intuitio veritatis absolutae*), it is making use of itself in its capacity as an image of God's mind (*De mente,* 7).

B. *Man as a "second God."*—Conscious of his mind's likeness to the divine mind, Cusanus is filled with powerful self-confidence. He is elated by the spontaneity of his thinking, by the experience of its creative power.

With its infinite capacity for forming images, the human mind is inexhaustible in producing conceptual schemas and in creating ingenious forms. Man does not know how far he can carry this ability to produce images of the infinite: Man is a "second God" (*De beryllo,* 5).

c. *Divine mind and human mind.*—Cusanus' humility is equal to his self-confidence. The human mind is merely an image. A gulf separates it from the divine mind. "Man is God, but not absolutely, for he is man. Therefore he is a human God" (*homo enim deus est, sed non absolute, quoniam homo; humanus est igitur Deus*) (*De con.,* sect. II, 14). The differences between the divine and the human mind are as follows:

All things are in God, but in God they are the models of things. They are also in our mind, but here they are the likenesses of things (*De mente,* 7).

The divine mind creates when it conceives; when our mind conceives things, it shapes its thinking to the forms of created realities (*assimilat*). It produces concepts or intellectual visions, not the things themselves (*De mente,* 7). "Just as the word of God creates essences, so our mind produces copies" (*To Albergati,* 22).

This may be clarified as follows: The multitude of things is the unfolding (*explicatio*) of the enfolding (*complicatio*) of the infinite mind. If we call the world the unfolding of God's enfolding, the knowledge achieved by the human mind is a copy of that original process.

For example, the mind knows number as the unfolding of the One, magnitude as the unfolding of the point, composition as the unfolding of simplicity, time as the unfolding of the present, temporality as the unfolding of eternity. With these copied contents of its thinking, the mind is able to assimilate them to the originals; it cannot know the originals themselves. But in so doing, it copies in every way the unfolding of the divine mind.

Furthermore, God has exact knowledge of things, because He creates them. We do not produce the being of things, hence our knowledge of them is inaccurate, approximate, conjectural. In the divine mind all things subsist in their exact and original truth. In our mind all things are imaged representations of the original truth, i.e., the form of our thinking is conceptual (*notionaliter*).

D. *Greatness of the human mind.*—The power of the human mind, says Cusanus, is admirable.

Although God creates real things (*entia realia*), man creates concepts (*entia rationalia*)—mathematical concepts and concepts of the real things. Further, he creates artifacts (*formae artificiales*), things not found in nature but produced with materials provided by nature: tools, spoons, bowls, pots, works of art.

This high degree of creativity is something to be proud of: "Do not imitate, says the carver of spoons, the form of any natural thing. The forms of spoons, bowls, and pots are products of human art alone. My art, then, consists not in imitating created forms but in producing them, wherein it comes closer to the art of the infinite" (*De mente,* 2).

Though the human mind is only a copy, it is analogous to the infinite mind in its inexhaustible capacity for producing images. What is latent in it has no definite form, but as soon as it is affected from the outside (unlike the divine mind, it needs to be so affected), it can adapt itself to any form and create concepts of all things (*De mente,* 4).

E. *Judgment as mind.*—The "living mind" in us can do more than produce copies. Our experience shows that it speaks in us and passes judgment: This is good, this is right, this is true. It censures us when we deviate from the right. The mind passes "sentence and judgment, without ever having been taught to do so, by an inborn faculty" (*De mente,* 4).

F. *Man as microcosm.*—When man as image of God's infinity discovers the creative bent of his mind, he embraces the whole universe with it. Just as he is a second God, so he is a second world, the microcosm (*De con.,* II, 4).

Man, however, comprises the universe only in a limited human way. Man is a world, but, because he is man, he is not the concrete universe. Therefore he is a human world (*humanus mundus*). Man can be everything, God, angel, beast, lion, or bear, but always in a human way.

Second God and microcosm, the two hang together in man's mind: "The mind sees all things in itself as in a mirror. Man sees all things as made like him. His assimilation of them gives him the living image of the creator of all things and he recognizes himself as made in the image of God . . ." (*De ven. sap.,* 17).

The mind's eminent position leads to this proposition: "Only the mind is an image of God." All other things, of a lesser eminence, are images of God only in so far as the mind reflects itself in them—it is reflected to a greater extent in living beings endowed with sensation than in plants, and to a greater extent in plants than in minerals. "Hence the creatures that have no mind should be called mere unfoldings of God's enfolding, rather than images of it" (*De mente,* 4).

G. *Not to become God, but to approximate God.*—The human mind is the otherness of the infinite One. The more it detaches itself from its otherness and ascends to the simplest One, the closer it comes to perfection. Just how far can the mind go in this sense?

Since the other can be known only in relation to the one, the human mind, because of its otherness, can see itself only in relation to the divine One. Man, however, cannot know the divine One in itself, but only as the One is humanly conceived (*De con.*, II, 16). This signifies: Even when the mind attains the highest degree of its truth, it does not become divine in thus coming closer to God, it only comes closer to the best possible image, which remains separated from the original by an unbridgeable gulf. Yet in this copy—the human mind—we find all things that are God and creation alike.

H. *Judgment and measure have their origin in the infinite.*—Discursive reason thinks the finite in finite terms. It sees the finite as commensurable only with the finite. Finite things can be known only in relation to infinite things. Discursive reason cannot think the infinite adequately; it remains within the domain of the finite.

Cusanus sees, however, that the thinking of the finite becomes true only in the light of the infinite, when discursive reason yields to the intellect. Under the assumption of the infinite, the finite becomes truly known. The mind possesses its faculty of judgment only because it is an image of what is the original of all things. It possesses within itself something toward which it directs its attention, and according to which it can make judgments concerning finite things.

How does this come about? This Cusanus explains with the help of an analogy: If, in addition to rationally determined (dead, as it were) written laws, there were also a living law, it would, as a living law, be able to read in itself the decisions it has to make (*De mente,* 5). Thus discursive reason is limited to the domain of the finite, which in itself is meaningless; but the mind is the activity of intellectual thinking, which does not make inferences from finite propositions, but judges on the basis of the infinite.

The same is true of measurement. Knowledge involves measurement. But all finite standards of measurement originate in and are guided by the standard of the infinite. As an image, the mind is a living standard of measurement; it measures itself by itself (in the same way as a living circle might measure itself by itself). The mind is an absolute standard of measurement, which cannot grow either greater or smaller. It sets itself up as the model of all things, the better to discover itself in all things (*De mente,* 9).

However, the standard of measurement and the thing measured are commensurable only when both are in the same domain. The living or absolute standard is the source and guiding principle of all determined, finite measurements, but it is not commensurable with them.

2. *Cognition as conjecture* (coniectura)

A. *The universal character of the distinction between exact and conjectural knowledge.*—We obtain cognition of things by comparing them and applying a common measure. When we compare and measure them, we find that they are never perfectly equal. Two or more things are never so similar that they might not be infinitely more similar. A difference always remains between the standard of measurement and the thing measured. This shows that perfect precision is never achieved. Our conception of a thing is never so exact that it might not be infinitely more exact.

How do we account for this? Where truth is not seen and thought in itself, but only in and through something else, accuracy is impossible. For example: As a rational thing, the circle cannot be exactly conceived on the sensory plane. Any circle we perceive falls short of the perfect circle we hold in our minds. The same falling short may be noted when we compare any finite knowledge with the divine intellection which apprehends things in themselves.

Our knowledge is always inadequate, and yet, in so far as it is true, it is linked with truth itself. Our knowledge reflects in various ways the distance between what we know and what we are striving to know. Our knowledge is conjectural. "Since exact knowledge of the truth cannot be achieved, every positive human assertion about the true is a conjecture. Therefore our knowledge of the unity of unattainable truth is knowledge in conjectural otherness [*alteritate coniecturali*]" (*De con.*, I, 2).

The categories of our discursive reason permit us to conceive of things only as finite. When confronted with the infinite, which we can neither forget nor yet attain, discursive reason breaks down; our thinking can grasp the infinite only in terms of opposites that no longer exclude each other (as discursive reason demands), but coincide. Within the domain of the finite, however, we can achieve only conjectural knowledge.

The conjectural character of our knowledge is universal, but denotes different things in different domains. Our knowledge comes close to the truth even in sensory experience, and never quite attains the truth even when the finite mind has ascended as high as it can. For then it comes up against "the wall."

B. *The conjectural in cognition and in being.*—Not only cognition but the existent itself is a copy and as such is never exactly commensurate with the original. Cusanus also uses the term "conjectural" for merely approximate being. Neither the existent nor cognition is exact, they are merely "conjectural." All human knowledge is conjectural in relation to truth as such. Conjectural, too, is the reality of the copy in relation to the original.

Thus Cusanus refers to the Church as it is in the world as the *ecclesia coniecturalis* (Letter of 1442, Basel edition, p. 826).

c. *Greatness and limits of conjectural knowledge.*—Conjectures reveal both the greatness and the limits of our knowledge. They constitute the spiritual creative process in mankind. "Conjectures must be produced by our mind just as the real world is produced by the divine intellect (*De con.*, I, 3).

Our conjectural knowledge defines our limits; it separates us forever from the infinite divine knowledge, but at the same time manifests the truth to us. All positive assertions are mere conjectures, but as such they participate in the truth (*id.*, I, 13).

If in man's finite existence absolute truth can be known only through *participatio*, it is not because of any intrinsic flaw in this truth, but because it resides in someone who is not human. Spiritual participation in that incommunicable but most effective light is the very essence of finite human knowledge . . . otherness. Hence conjectures are the form of truth itself—created minds know the truth only in so far as it can be copied (*De con.*, I, 13).

d. *Conjectures and points of view.*—Every conjecture is advanced from a point of view. Its content is seen in a particular perspective. "Because the mortal mind is of finite efficacy and different in every individual, the conjectures of a number of men about the same unfathomable truth are bound to differ in degree and in various other ways. Possibly one man grasps better than another, but no one grasps the sense . . . with unfailing sureness. Accordingly I present what I have to communicate here as my own conjectures" (*De con.*, I, 2).

Cusanus speaks of human existence in all its variety, and here too he speaks in "conjectures." For instance (following the pattern of ancient tradition) he describes the "variety of the inhabitants of the earth in respect of their mental disposition, bodily constitution, form, color, way of life, moral failings." But mankind is not an aggregate of unrelated parts. All countries have produced their famous men in all branches of knowledge, in order that one and the same human nature may be made manifest in various ways (*De con.*, II, 15).

Cusanus speaks of various worlds, the spheres, as it were, of the universe (the choruses of the Pseudo-Areopagite), in their hierarchical order. Each world judges differently in its being-for-itself, and differently in its relation to the worlds above it. No world counts or speaks or acts like the others. Purely intellectual natures (*intelligentiae*) are not numerable like stones or animals, they do not speak like men; rather, each world has its own way (*De con.*, I, 15).

E. *The mind is never satisfied.*—Because the human mind is confined to conjectures, it is never satisfied. It is always trying to go beyond successive conjectures to arrive at a better conjecture, beyond each particular stage or type of thinking to a higher stage. This infinite longing is not despair over ultimate inability to know, but rather a fulfillment in nonknowledge, attainable through the guidance of the infinite.

The human mind alone is characterized by this unceasing striving. It is restless even in repose. All created things other than man desire nothing beyond what they have received, that is, each is content with its particular likeness to God. "But when our spiritual nature recognizes itself as the living image of God, it has the power to become ever purer and closer in form to God, although, being a copy, it never becomes the original, the creator" (*To Albergati,* 7).

F. *What the conjectural is not.*—As the fundamental structure of the truth as we know of it, the conjectural is true because it refers to the truth itself, which resides solely in the infinity of the divine. Therefore the conjectural character of the human mind is not to be confused with arbitrary conjecture, nor with skepticism in the sense of universal doubt; neither is it a relativism that dissolves everything into mere relations, without unity and without direction. Because our finite knowledge recognizes its conjectural character, it implies the presence of the infinite as its standard and guiding principle. The infinite itself, which cannot be known, guides finite knowledge and is present in it directly. Finally, the conjectural, as understood by Cusanus, has little in common with "hypotheses," which require to be confirmed or refuted.

G. *Liberation through awareness of the conjectural character of human knowledge.*—Because the mind is aware of the conjectural character of its cognition and of the things existing in the world, it strives in each domain to come closer [to the truth], to arrive at better conjectures, to deepen its insights. This is a process that can never be completed. But through it the human mind is also liberated from the fetters which are imposed on mankind in every field of inquiry, whenever we lose sight of the conjectural nature of our concepts.

H. *Intelligibility and unintelligibility.*—In modern times the principle that the world is intelligible has been recognized explicitly and implicitly. Modern science has come to the conclusion that some elements of the world are intelligible; it investigates the foundations of these intelligible contexts, and the knowledge it achieves has compelling certainty, although we do not know exactly how far we can go in this direction. At the same time, however, science has arrived at the insight that the world as a whole cannot be an object, nor be made intelligible as such. Scientific superstition has taken the intelligibility of the world for granted and assumed that what we do not yet understand will soon be understood.

For Cusanus intelligibility has a higher meaning, since according to him human thinking consists in copying divine cognition. At the same time, however, he stresses the unintelligibility of the world, since according to him the imititative character of human cognition in relation to divine cognition can can never be overcome. Attracted by divine truth, we achieve knowledge through a process of conjecture. But because our knowledge remains conjectural, we experience the unintelligibility of the world.

I. *The "theory of knowledge."*—It is clear from the foregoing that Cusanus' "theory of knowledge" (to use a term coined in the nineteenth century) is metaphysical from the outset, that is, he does not presuppose some initial void—allegedly involving no presuppositions—as the starting point for his investigation of knowledge. The finite mind is a copy of the infinite divine cognition, understands itself to be such a copy, and on this basis takes cognizance both of its tremendous potentialities and of its insurmountable limits. The subjectivity of human cognition is not self-contained, but transcended in the objectivity of God's creation.

3. Methods and aim

A. *Metaphor as a state of being and as method.*—We must distinguish the following: first, the metaphorical character of everything that has existence for us; second, the mirror images or "enigmatic words" in which we formulate our reflections when we come up against "the wall" that separates our finite being from infinite being; third, the artificial metaphors which we produce in a spirit of play.

(1) In the *structure of being* everything that is, is a copy of the original or a metaphor. The world is the eternally present language of the eternally infinite being of the godhead. The finite human mind is an imperfect copy of the infinite divine mind.

(2) When we think the infinite mind, *we think in "enigmatic images"* produced by the human mind. These, too, are called metaphors. Concepts of discursive reason, sensory intuitions, and other activities of the human mind serve as such metaphors. For example:

Otherness, relation, leap; participation, image; enfolding, unfolding are concepts which first become clear to us in the finite sphere, and which then serve as metaphors for the relation between God and the world, between transcendence and man. But where the metaphor, because it is forever leading us astray, must itself be discarded, we speak in paradoxes whose inherent contradictoriness cancels out their rational, objective content: *coincidentia oppositorum, docta ignorantia.*

Metaphors become paradoxical when a concrete image is used to illustrate an abstract idea. Cusanus says, for example, that God is like an infinite sphere whose center is everywhere and circumference nowhere.

A metaphor is called a "symbol" when only the sign is given and its relation to what it signifies is not explicitly stated. That which is symbolized is entirely given in the symbol without being referred to; it is known symbolically as not known. Therefore, symbolic knowledge is present only as ignorance, a not-knowing which we have to carry ever further, and which is completed only momentarily by means of a symbol whenever our discursive thinking breaks down.

(3) In order to clarify something we cannot visualize, we *invent metaphors* for what we would understand even without them.

Such metaphors are not symbols but guiding threads. Cusanus is very fond of them and well aware of what he is doing when he invents them. Often they become for him more than metaphors—i.e., they become symbols.

Even a child's toy can serve as a metaphor. A spinning top, for example. The faster it spins, the more it seems to be standing still: this shows how the greatest motion is at the same time the smallest, or even no motion at all. Thus in God the most tremendous motion is at the same time perfect rest. Children's games reflect the order of nature, and the latter reflects God (*De possest*).

Although these three types of the metaphoric (the metaphorical character of all things, the mirror images and enigmatic words of our thinking, the lessons to be learned from games) can be distinguished from one another, they come together in the single field of speculative cognition, where the metaphorical relation is a fundamental structure. The experience of metaphorical being and the production of enigmatic images are the substance of speculative philosophy. The invention of metaphors as vivid illustrations is an integral part of speculative exposition.

Inspired by the living truth of metaphorical thinking, Cusanus says: "To grasp the inner meaning we must rise above the power of words [*verborum*] rather than be bound to the peculiarities of names [*vocabulorum*]. These can never be adequate to such great mysteries. And metaphors should serve only to point the way: they have to be transcended, their sensory meaning must be dropped if we are to ascend to simple intellectual knowledge" (*De doc. ignor.*, I, 2). But since no one way is right once and for all—"for what needs to be said cannot be expressed adequately"—it is very useful to say things in many ways (*De mente,* 4).

And so we come to the final step, to which Cusanus never refers as such: The fact that we speak of metaphors when interpreting speculative thought and the appearance of things is itself a metaphor. This follows inescapably: if everything that is, everything we imagine and think, is metaphorical, then this statement itself is a metaphor. Only thinking which grasps the metaphorical character of all thinking results in the perfect state of suspension, which enables us to move freely within every type of symbolism. But as long as we express ourselves in words, we cannot go beyond "metaphor."

In a deeply moving letter to a young monk, written in 1463, a year before he died, Cusanus said: "Keep in mind that in this world we walk in the ways of metaphors and enigmatic images, because the spirit of truth is not of this world and can be grasped by us only in so far as metaphors and symbols which we recognize as such carry us onward to that which is not known (*To Albergati,* 48).

And where is that? "When a man, in whom there is a living image of God, recognizes himself as the living image of his creator, he contemplates his creator by looking into himself, because he is carried onward from the copy to the original." Hence the summons: "Mind the living, spiritual image of God within you. It would not be a living spiritual image if it did not know itself to be an image" (*To Albergati,* 5, 6).

But how did this situation, which even metaphors cannot express adequately, come about? "The Creator of all things wanted to be known, in order to show His glory. Therefore, in His desire to be known, He created rational beings capable of cognition" (*To Albergati,* 3). Another metaphor! Another in the endless circle of metaphors which cannot detach itself from the metaphorical to become real and substantial! (And yet this does come about—the conditions under which speculation as a whole gains content for Cusanus will be discussed in section III, "Faith.")

B. *Degrees of knowledge.*—In his treatment of the mind, Cusanus follows two lines. On the one hand, he describes it as a copy of the divine original. On the other hand, he describes in objective terms the successive degrees of knowledge, leading from sense perception to the intuition of God. He distinguishes three principal degrees or stages: the senses, the discursive reason, the intellect (*sensus, ratio, intellectus*).

The sense organs apprehend real things, those created by God; discursive reason supplies its categories—forms, genera, species; when discursive reason breaks down, the intellect brings us closer to godhead.

Sensory knowledge is inherently confused. As soon as it makes distinctions, reason is already present in it. Reason brings clarity by drawing distinctions, noting oppositions, and excluding contradiction. The intellect leads us to learned ignorance by demonstrating how opposites actually coincide.

Sensory knowledge is entirely positive: it affirms. Discursive reason both affirms and negates. The intellect goes beyond affirmation and negation.

Sensory knowledge does not question. Reason questions on the assumption that either affirmation or negation must be correct. The intellect questions by inquiring into the presupposition of questioning. As questioning progresses, it becomes evident that rational statements invariably presuppose what can be clearly grasped only by the intellect.

An example: Only the absolute One makes cognition possible. The mind cannot formulate any question that does not presuppose this underlying unity. "The very question whether it is, presupposes its being; why it is, the ground; for what purpose, the purpose of all things. Thus, what is presupposed in every doubt must be that which is most certain" (*De con.,* I, 7).

At each stage of cognition, our thinking is true only in respect of the adequacy between thinking and object characteristic of that stage. For example: when we speak about God at the rational stage, which is not adequate to God, "We subject God to the laws of discursive reason, and assert His Oneness, while negating His Otherness. This is what is done by nearly all modern theologians" (*De con.,* I, 10).

But no stage of cognition is self-contained for us; the truth lies in none of them taken singly. Rather, we attain to truth as we ascend and descend the degrees of knowledge. Each stage contributes something indispensable, but its truth resides in the whole of which it is only a part. In the ascending order: "The mind unifies the being-other of sense perception in the productive imagination, it unifies the various images of the productive imagination in discursive reason, it unifies the being-other of rational cognition in simple intellectual unity." In the descending order: The unity of the intellect descends into the being-other of discursive reason, the unity of reason into the being-other of representation, the latter into the being-other of the senses. "Because cognition begins with the senses, it is true not absolutely but only relatively: rational in discursive reason, true in representation after the manner of representation, and in the senses after the manner of the senses" (*De con.,* II, 16).

Each stage strives for autonomy. Thus "the intellect does not wish to become sensory," but to remain "perfect intellect in full activity." And yet it can achieve this activity only by calling upon the senses, "in order to pass from possibility to reality." The slumbering discursive reason must be awakened by the senses, which arouse it to wonderment. "Thus the intellect comes back to itself via a circular movement" (*De con.,* II, 16).

All this activity of the mind, the various stages of which form a cycle, has its purpose and goal entirely in itself. "Just as God does all things for His own sake, in order to be the spiritual beginning and end of all things, so the unfolding of the conceptual world, which is produced by our mind in comprehending it, is present for the sake of the creative mind itself. The infinite intellect is the heart and core of the human mind" (*De con.,* I, 3).

Cusanus is inconsistent in his enumeration of the stages or degrees of knowledge and in the terminology he applies to them. Discursive reason, for example, is sometimes split into the faculty of representation and the faculty of apprehension. And sometimes he adds a fourth stage, a stage beyond thinking, which is contemplation (*visio, intuitio*) and the process of becoming One (*unio*). At this point the question of Cusanus' mysticism arises.

c. *Speculative ecstasy and mysticism.*—1. *Cusanus himself had no mystical experience.* He called the experience of his thinking "a kind of mental trance" (*De vis. dei, op. cit.*, p. 87). The nature of this speculative experience is explained in Cusanus' letters to the monks at Tegernsee.

The vision of the divine is sometimes called "rapture." But those who "regard self-produced images and visionary illusions as true vision" are mistaken. The truth is "an intellectual object" and can only be seen "without seeing."

Nor is it possible, Cusanus says, to speak adequately of the other rapture, that of intellectual vision. He declares forthrightly, soberly: "One man may be able to show another the way which he knows from hearsay to be the right one, even if he has not traveled it himself. But a man who has traveled it in vision can point it out more reliably. If I were to say anything of the kind, it would be rather unreliable. For I have not yet been given the taste of how friendly the Lord is." Thus, Cusanus himself denies having had mystical experience, though he does not deny its reality.

On the subject of his own speculations, this is what Cusanus said to the monks: "The study whose purpose is the ascent of our intellectual mind to union with God is not completed so long as God is conceived in rational terms." Where negation and affirmation (negative theology and positive theology) coincide, there lies "the most secret doctrine of God, to which none of the philosophers has access so long as the principle common to all philosophy is recognized as valid, the principle that things that contradict one another do not coincide." The man who investigates the doctrine of God must "sacrifice himself and plunge into darkness." There he discovers "that confusion is certainty, darkness light, and ignorance knowledge." There, beyond the coincidence of opposites, lies the domain "of the divine hunt," the perilous hunt. This movement is never completed; the plunger is forever being deflected from the true way, into side paths which lead to corrupting illusions.

2. *Experience, not words or logic.*—"We are led on by the eternal and infinite wisdom, which indeed radiates from all things, giving us a kind of foretaste of its effects, such that a wondrous longing impels us to meet it halfway." This is the true life of the intellectual mind, its very own and authentic life.

We sense the "ground and source, through which, in which, and out of which we are and move when we conceive its life-giving power of attraction in nonconceptual insight." But "he who regards as truth that which is conceivable, is removed from true infinite wisdom" (*De sap.*). Hence "those whose judgments are based only on analysis, who speak only in words and not out of inner experience," are not wise; the wise are those who, thanks to such experience, "know all things and to the same extent know nothing at all" (*ibid.*).

All thinking about God to which man's power of apprehension is adequate must remain conjectural, and this is true also of the word of God. In the Bible God speaks in human language. Although, because they are God's, the words are more exact than any others, nevertheless the language remains conjectural.

3. *The "goal" cannot be described.*—The goal, the inner disposition whereby the infinite, God Himself, is present, cannot be described as a "something." It seems to be nowise the same in different persons. It may be adumbrated more or less as follows: it awakens to itself; it becomes maturer or becomes flatter and dimmer; it apprehends itself; it is enhanced through experience of people and things and of itself, all of which point back to an authentic source that is elucidated in meditation; it is never present ready-made—all statements of this type circle around something that is not grasped in them. When we think we have grasped it, it vanishes. "You might adduce countless paraphrases of this kind and so gain some idea of the lofty height at which wisdom dwells. . . . Infinity alone is so high" (*De sap.*).

4. *"Beyond it."*—"Wisdom is experienced only in the awareness that it reaches higher than any knowledge and that it is unknowable" (*De sap.*). Consequently thinking always strives to go further. Whatever may be formulated in a proposition, in a word, is for this very reason not yet the point which thinking strives to attain—a point beyond the formulation, the "absolute ground," "being itself," "what precedes being." And even these expressions are only signs.

The very questions, Whence? Whither? imply an attempt to capture the infinite, and hence are inappropriate. There is no such thing as an ultimate question. Questioning, too, questions beyond every question.

This thinking does not lead Cusanus to mystical experience. And yet his own thinking is continually drawing him on to the point where thought itself can go no further, but can only move in dialectical circles, repeat itself in endless variations. His thinking is forever trying to take off and soar into the unthinkable, the ineffable, failing again and again to do so, and rising to a new attempt.

At this point we encounter two possibilities. Does the forward-impelling thinking that goes from thought-experience to thought-experience in its drive for knowledge resign itself to failure as thinking and as experience, and by that same token find, in the given concrete situation, a motive for transcendence-related activity in the world? Or has God disclosed Himself personally to a man who now falls to the ground, as it were, and overawed by the majesty of His bodily presence, renounces his philosophical freedom? Cusanus often seems to take the first course, but then at other times resolutely pursues the second, combining the two in some way we do not understand.

D. *Love.*—1. *Love is the ultimate criterion.*—What is the impulse behind so perilous a line of speculation? Whither falls the man who plunges into it? How does he wrest himself free from the illusions that lie in wait for him?

By love alone. Although this word has taken on innumerable meanings, and has often been abused, it has lost none of its force and weight. The ultimate criterion for man's motives and goals, guidance and conduct, is his love of God. Of this love every other love is a copy; or, in other words, every other love finds its consummation in the love of God.

2. *Description of love.*—"In the lovable we find endless and ultimately unfathomable motives for love." Happiness in love is mediocre where the loved object is something conceivable and finite. Love is truly blissful only where "the lovable quality in the loved object is beyond all measure, infinite, illimitable, and inconceivable." It is learned, love-inspired ignorance (*De sap.*).

Love is life itself. Obscurely it knows in advance what it desires. Just as the infant in arms thirsts for milk, so the intellect thirsts for wisdom. "It has a kind of foretaste of it" (*De sap.*).

The spirit of love is not of this world. Love is "the power that illuminates the man born blind and enables him to acquire sight through faith, although we cannot say how this comes about" (*De possest*).

3. *Love inseparable from insight.*—But the criterion of love is by no means unambiguous. Love itself often takes deceptive forms. It must not draw self-certainty from mere emotions and delusions (this and what follows, from the letters to the monks at Tegernsee). For there can be no love without insight; indeed, love is clairvoyant.

What is wholly unknown can neither be truly loved nor found in the quest for knowledge. Accordingly, the loving ascent without knowledge is not reliable. "In the guise of a messenger of light, Satan's messenger easily deceives the over-confident, who imagines he has experienced God when he has only discovered something metaphorical." A striving toward love in disregard of the intellect is illusory. If "the highest goal is the beatitude of knowing God," then "knowledge is here identical with love and love identical with knowledge."

We have come full circle. "He who loves God is recognized by God. He who is known by God, recognizes God." Here lies the perfect love "beyond the coincidence of opposites, beyond the containing and the contained," beyond the comprehending and the comprehended.

4. *Love in everything that is.*—Love is omnipresent in the world. It is the "nexus" that holds things together. It is active at every level of reality. It is the spirit (*spiritus*) that sheds its light down to the least ramifications

of the existent, that glows in the *ratio,* in the soul, and finally in all nature. In reality everything is united with everything else. In the same way the soul is linked with the body. The soul forms its own appropriate body just as this particular body demands this particular soul. Accordingly, the physiognomists are justified in making inferences about the soul on the strength of the body (*De con.,* II, 10).

Love, too, is linked with the body. One of his sermons (Basel edition, p. 555) indicates the intricacy of Cusanus' thinking in this matter. He is delighted by feminine beauty. One who "beholds a beautiful woman and meditates on the sight glorifies the Lord and admires the infinite beauty of whose light this earthly beauty is as a distant shadow." But although in this context Cusanus says of such an admirer only: "Beauty does not move him carnally, but moves his mind," he writes a little later: "If the rapture is so great even in the union of bodies, how much greater must be the rapture of the mind's union with wisdom, which is beauty itself." The statement that "even in perishable matter beauty attracts us in its own way as absolute beauty attracts the mind" might apply both to the rapture that is free from desire and to carnal union. One might suppose that here for a moment even in the erotic union of lovers Cusanus recognized the beauty of the world—the reality of living things as a reflection of eternal beauty. But this is not the case.

The flesh is covetous and everywhere at odds with the spirit. The choleric are easily angered, the sanguine are inclined to dissipation. "The flesh is like an overheated pot, which seethes and bubbles. The soul is continually throwing wood on the fire—namely, living nourishment which it finds where it may. Thus it keeps the fire going: with beautiful colors through the eyes, lovely melodies through the ears, tastes through the mouth, scents through the nostrils. . . . All flesh is corrupt and impure. Because the soul is warped and partial to the flesh, it is corrupted and becomes bestial."

Whenever, on the basis of his philosophical views, Cusanus asserts the excellence of the world and all created things, he immediately goes on to remind us of the fundamental corruption of the flesh. There is no way of reconciling these two views. In all its manifestations at every level, love, because it is a copy of the divine, has the character of truth and goodness. But the flesh, like all worldly things, was corrupted by mankind's original sin. On the one hand, the world is glorious and beautiful, on the other Eros is the work of the Devil. There is no connection between these two ideas.

Although Cusanus assures us that love permeates nature and matter down to their least ramifications, he does not grant it a capacity for spiritualizing earthly reality. If eroticism is excluded, what is left? A love which is powerless because it is without an object, hypocrisy? No, something entirely different—a love of God which draws its inspiration from God's love for every individual within the framework of the living Church, as realized in religious orders, in religious ideas and institutions, in a religious authority, directed away from, not toward, mankind and the world, and toward the beyond.

We can detect in Cusanus an atmosphere of remoteness from Eros, an atmosphere in which the grandeur and misery of the human condition, its tragic involvement, seem to pale. The possibility of great love in this world, rooted in, but not limited by, Eros, was beyond his horizon. Far from carrying him away, such love did not even arouse his wonder. Confronted with reality, he fell back at once upon traditional views and evaluations: the superiority of asceticism, marriage as the sole legitimation of Eros. For the sake of another, different afterworld in the beyond, he casts a veil over what is eternal in Eros here and now. He devaluates the reality of existence in the world by absolutizing the ascetic way of life. Asceticism has been practiced by men in all high cultures as an authentic possibility of existence, but it is an excess, not a fulfillment of the human reality. It proclams the world to be sinful. Such a judgment actually keeps us from glimpsing the true yawning gulfs that threaten and that we cannot close; there can be no human self-realization if we turn aside from the dangers that confront us. Openness to risk and danger yields to the fixed idea of a total sinfulness produced by the Fall, which can be wiped out only by the redemption of mankind through the operation of heavenly grace. Thus Cusanus takes an attitude of shallow realism toward everything that happens to be as it is in this sinful world.

Cusanus' attitude toward Eros is matched by his evaluation of science. His occasional affirmations of a boundless will to knowledge stand side by side with a total condemnation of scientific curiosity. In his view, science has value only in so far as it leads to the knowledge of God. Consequently, he does less than justice to the authentic will to knowledge, which seeks to penetrate everywhere, which recognizes no limits, which discovers no totality and no harmony. He never experienced the kind of knowledge that can lead to an indictment of God and to the destruction of pious illusion. He would have condemned such knowledge as blasphemy, this in the name of a world-negation which is itself blasphemous, a product of religious bigotry.

III. FAITH

Introduction

A. *Formal transcending.*—Under the impact of Cusanus' philosophical thinking we are apt to forget that he was a Christian and a prince of the Church. He takes us into the realm of Plato, Plotinus, and certain Asian thinkers, the realm of great speculative metaphysics.

Speculation of this sort, which we may call formal transcending, is not an end in itself. Its only purpose is to illuminate the realm inaccessible to thinking, the realm that derives its content from what we call "faith."

The conceptual structure of formal transcending is often dismissed as laborious, pompous nonsense, continually repeated in the convolutions of thought. Speculative philosophers are attracted to this kind of thinking because it opens the door to infinity. The attraction is strongest when the thinker is captivated by the infinite itself. He seems then to hear its voice.

The goal of formal transcending, the Archimedean point situated outside everything, is insubstantial, a mere point. In itself it provides no support. Such thinking must receive its weight from elsewhere. What is the source of this something which is not only experienced as limit but, though for all object thinking it is nothing, takes hold of us by virtue of the attractive power of being itself?

It is that from out of which and with which we are given to ourselves. Does it dawn upon us in an act of infinite trust? But what do we trust? Is it the fundamental experience of love? But what do I love? Is it what speaks to us in ciphers from the infinitely remote realm that we try to reach by transcending? But where is that which speaks to us in ciphers? Is it clarified in a faith which, in Nicholas of Cusa, understands itself as the intellect, the image of infinity, and hence trusts itself? But on what ground does the intellect conceive of itself as the image of infinity? Does this awareness come to us directly as the language of divine revelation? But what revelation is convincing, let alone demonstrable, to all men?

Trust, love, the language of ciphers, our awareness that our intellect in its infinite movement is an image of God—all these are subjective states of mind in men to whom an objective reality has been disclosed. But although these states of mind can easily be named, they cannot be pointed out from outside. Like transcendence itself, the existential source cannot be defined in objective terms.

B. *The fundamental Christian-ecclesiastical attitude.*—Cusanus considered his thinking to be Christian and in accord with the teachings of the Church —this he never doubted. Christ, the Trinity, the sacraments, the Church, the hierarchy, the dogmas—these constitute the point, situated at a depth he cannot fathom, to which all his thinking is referred.

Time and again he tells us that God is beyond the reach of the human intellect. "No ascent, however high, can enable us to see God from the natural standpoint otherwise than in an enigmatic image." The seeker's vision is obscured by mist. How nevertheless can he gain a glimpse of the invisible? Never unless God "makes Himself visible in the real world by revealing Himself" (*De possest*).

We in our weakness cannot help ourselves. When man has abandoned hope in himself, convinced that he "is sick, as it were, and entirely unable to obtain what he longs for," he turns for help to the revealed God.

But there is only one such revelation: that of Jesus Christ. God the Father discloses Himself in the Christ. Having begotten His Son, God dwells in Him bodily (*corporaliter*) for He has assumed a body in which He "has remained the perfect God" (*Exc.,* IX, 637; Scharpff, p. 484).

If, contrary to Cusanus' intentions, we were to separate his philosophy from his faith, we might underestimate the earnestness both of his philosophy and of his Christian faith.

c. *Independent speculation and Christian faith.*—Perhaps Cusanus' philosophical thinking is independent after all, in the sense that he employs cognitive methods that do not spring from Christian faith though they support it and throw light on it.

Is not speculative thinking, when it is not merely a tiresome intellectual game, always rooted in some faith—the pieties of the ancient Greeks, the Asiatic religions, or Christianity? Cusanus assumes—and on this point he is obviously mistaken—that this faith is everywhere one and the same. He takes it for granted that the revealed faith of Christianity is the only true one, which all other men espouse without knowing it, and which they will profess once they have understood themselves properly.

For Cusanus, speculative philosophical thinking and the Christian faith merge into one. We can spend a long time in his company, studying his meditations on many subjects, without ever encountering specific Christian dogmas. We can follow him perfectly well in his attempts to transcend discursive reason through the paradoxes of seeking and yet never finding, of touching in nontouching, of knowledge in ignorance, of proximity in distance. Inspired by his grandiose human self-confidence we may well make his ideas our own, without ever thinking of Christ. And yet from his point of view, this is quite inadmissible.

Is such a procedure justified? For the purposes of our own present philosophical realization, assuredly, but not from the standpoint of adequate historical understanding, not if we wish to provide a historical exposition. To him everything was Christian, to us it is not. To Cusanus the implications of his faith were fully realized in the Christian religion; to us, what he expresses in Christian formulas often holds a truth that has no need of Christian wrappings. Actually, the independence of reason characteristic of a philosophical faith is as inseparable from Cusanus' thinking as are its Christian underpinnings.

d. *Philosophical writings and sermons.*—In studying Cusanus we must make an effort to share his understanding of revealed faith. This faith is explicit in all his writings with the single exception of *De staticis experimentis,* which seems to be little more than a technical note and is in my opinion unworthy of the fame it has achieved. The truths of Christian revelation are an integral part of Cusanus' thinking. To consider his philosophical writings separately from his sermons is to obscure the great thinker's over-all conception.

His sermons are permeated with philosophizing. But in selecting the philosophical material of his sermons, he asks himself: "What is edifying?" —he does not expound philosophical speculations for their own sake. In the margin of difficult passages, especially those that might induce doubt or misunderstanding in the faithful, he often notes: *"non aedificat."* But his philosophical writings always treat, along with other subjects, of Christian beliefs. Both categories of works are animated by the same spirit, though traditional religious conceptions, including some that are very odd, play a far larger part in the sermons.

1. *What is faith?*

Cusanus replies as follows (primarily in his sermons).

A. *Faith and reason.*—Even when the human mind is only moderately endowed with reason, it is able to believe. If it has no reason at all, it cannot believe, for then it cannot think, and hence cannot assent.

Just as nature reveals light to our vision, and just as a truth strikes us as evident, so the pleasant and the useful disclose themselves to our will. All this takes place spontaneously and implies no merit on our part. We can speak of merit only when the nonvisible, the improbable, the indemonstrable, the redemption that is not disclosed spontaneously by our nature, is believed by virtue of faith.

Faith produces conflict in the mind. The mind assents necessarily to what has been proved. But faith must struggle. The improbability of its content clashes directly with discursive reason. Without courage in the struggle that faith must wage, there is no victory.

Because of its weakness, discursive reason looks for points of support in demonstration and proof. Because of its inherent strength, faith needs no external support. Discursive reason that asks for proofs is like a money-lender who demands security for a loan. The heathen demand such security before they are ready to believe. Christians believe in God's revelation without it.

The believer's self-understanding is called the knowledge of faith. Only by reflecting upon faith do we achieve clarity about it. In thinking about his philosophical faith, man comes to understand his experience of his fellow men, of the world, and of fate.

B. *Faith and will.*—"Faith is a kind of thinking that is associated with assent" (*cum assensione cogitare*). Because the will is free, it lies in our power to believe or not. God has conferred upon us this capacity for faith—the ability to grasp revelation when we hear it. In its pride, reason will not believe what it does not understand. The humble man, however, does not understand unless he believes. Adam and Lucifer fell because they tried to live by their own knowledge. He who believes in the Resurection and in life everlasting—beliefs which reason and experience refute, rather than confirm—must necessarily let this reason die away. "He must become as a fool and a slave who renounces the freedom of his reason and willingly lets himself be taken captive. This is the greatest combat, not against flesh and blood, but against proud, presumptuous reason." The ability to believe is our greatest virtue (*maxima nostrae animae virtus*); it is the power of the will, God's greatest gift (*donum*).

c. *Faith is more than hearing and less than seeing.*—To see God would be to come face to face with Him. Merely to hear the Word is not yet to believe. Faith is more than hearing, but less than seeing. To believe what we have only heard is to assent to what we have not seen.

Faith is the light of the soul. "Just as the eyes see the stars only thanks to the light they emit, so we gain knowledge of the divine only in the light of the divine." The light of the living faith surpasses "the natural light of the senses and even of the intellect, as we see in the sacrament of the Mass, where the senses are vanquished by faith." In this faith the visible "coincides" with the invisible.

d. *The power of faith.*—Faith surpasses nature by what it itself is and by the goal it has in view. It also surmounts the power of nature, for nothing is impossible to the believer. Faith raises us above every limitation.

The believer knows what he wants. His knowledge of God is both his strength and his power (*potentia*). "He who knows what he desires to know, and who is what he knows," has achieved "the peace that passeth understanding."

2. *Revealed faith and philosophical faith, theological and philosophical thinking*

When we read what Cusanus says about faith, we are not unmoved. Although his faith in revealed religion is alien to us, he seems to say things in which we can recognize our own capacities for faith. How is this to be interpreted?

In order to go beyond discursive reason, Cusanus proceeds in two ways: he appeals both to the dogmas of the Church and to the philosophical *intellectus*. He never discusses the relationship between the two. All we can do is note what he actually does in his thinking.

An example: In most of his works he discusses the Trinity, through which he sees the original godhead and the world as its copy. But he does not always refer to the dogmatic formulation of the mysteries: he arrives at his conclusions through the pure *intellectus* whose logical movement is incomprehensible to discursive reason. Actually such dialectical thinking presupposes the conclusions toward which he is progressing. It is set in motion by anticipation of the gratifications it goes in search of. It does not compel the assent of discursive reason, but it is convincing to the intellect. It marks a point of culmination, a momentary exaltation. But then, that which has been conceived in terms of philosophical speculation, and which Cusanus regards as consistent with the thinking of the Greek philosophers, is suddenly identified, as though this were the most natural thing in the world, with the Father, the Son, and the Holy Spirit. This twofold approach is a general feature of Cusanus' thinking:

a. It is not theological thinking. For he does not interpret the articles of Christian faith on the basis of the Biblical "word of God." He does not employ the language of dogmatic theology. On the contrary, his thinking takes the form of a philosophical thinking accessible to all men, Christians and non-Christians alike.

His speculations aim from the outset to arrive at the point where the dogmas, the Trinity and the Incarnation, for example, take on their true meaning. In his treatment, the articles of faith seem to coincide with his philosophical ideas.

b. His philosophizing does not presuppose particular articles of faith, but it does imply a fundamental attitude of faith, which he explicitly calls Christian. Because Cusanus regards his mind as a copy of the divine original, philosophical faith and revealed faith are for him identical. In the Bible man is described as "made in the image and likeness of God." In philosophy this serves as a cipher of human self-awareness.

What we call "the duality" of his thinking was to him no such thing. He does not recognize multiple sources of faith, but only the one, the Christian. He recognizes no philosophical faith. Not being in search of one, he neither rejects nor accepts this possibility.

The interest in faith inherent in such a fundamental attitude is not the same in the philosopher and in the religious believer. Nor is the foundation of faith that gives the existential impulse to speculation by any means the same in all the great thinkers, although they are often in agreement on specific points.

Because Cusanus assumes that Pythagoras, Plato, and Proclus are essentially in agreement with revelation, his ideas are developed so undogmatically—and for long passages without reference to Church dogmas—that a modern reader can easily forget he is reading a Christian author. It never occurs to Cusanus that his philosophical ideas and his theological ideas might conflict. To him philosophy was not a rational substructure support-ing the higher, the mystery. Reflection on the mystery of revelation was itself philosophy.

At the same time Cusanus insists that "understanding in freedom" is essential to this kind of thinking. He tells us what this is. A man who does "what the intellect orders him to do," does not obey in the manner of a slave; a slave is one who "is compelled for fear of punishment to obey a law he does not understand because it contains something secret" (*Exc.*, V, 499; Scharpff, 412). The free man is the man who has achieved maturity, who is capable of understanding. Although Cusanus' freedom illumines the mysteries of faith in its own way, it does not dispel them by intellec-tual ingenuity nor reduce them to a bloodless, purely logical freedom from contradiction.

The freedom of this thinking becomes apparent when we compare it with the rationalistic, unfree thinking of John of Segovia (Haubst, Fromherz). At first Cusanus' ally at the Council of Basel, John turned against him when Cusanus went over to the papal party, though he kept up friendly relations with him until the end of Cusanus' life. John of Segovia was a man of rationally fixed principles, and for this reason he never departed from the conciliar line. After the conquest of Constantinople by the Turks in 1453, his sole interest became union with Islam. He believed that such a union (in the most literal sense) could be achieved without delay if the Moslems were confronted with rationally compelling proofs of the dogma of the Trinity! Nicholas of Cusa also worked for peace and religious unity, but bore in mind the needs of the moment. When the Church was being threatened with a new schism, he sacrificed logical con-sistency to combat the immediate danger. In the face of the Moslem threat, he wrote a colloquy of the sages of all nations in Heaven before the throne of God, dealing with eventualities in the distant future. He had no illusions about the possibility of a Christian crusade against the Turks. Reliance on logic drove John of Segovia to advocate an unrealistic course of action, both when he championed the conciliar principle and when he imagined that rationally correct arguments on the Trinity would overcome the mili-tancy of Islam. Both he and Nicholas of Cusa were convinced of the power of the mind, but where John of Segovia bogged down theoretically and practically in his slavish devotion to rational logic, Cusanus incorpo-rated rational logic in his dialectical logic. John of Segovia was unwittingly drawn into a vacuum by the superstitious belief, ever recurrent over the millennia, in the absolute power of proof in all things. As though either religious mysteries or political conflicts could be settled by disputations! It would seem that John himself began in the end to waver on this score. Cusanus may have been perplexed in given concrete situations, but he was never uncertain about the truth of his philosophical thinking.

3. *Speculative metaphor (cipher) and revealed bodily presence (spatio-temporal reality)*

A. *The twofold character of Cusanus' thinking.*—Cusanus is perfectly straightforward whenever his faith in the Church is speaking: The certainty of faith surpasses all things (*omnia certitudine superat*).

From the ambiguity of ciphers he passes to the certainty of sensory knowledge. From the historicity of his existential reality, he passes to the historical reality of space and time. In Christ God assumed a body, in which He dwells bodily (*corporaliter*) in all His glory.

Cusanus developed, in philosophical terms, the necessity of a unique human being, who, as the consummation of the human and thereby of the world, is the reality of God. The speculatively necessary place of the Greatest is occupied by the historical "fact"—Jesus Christ. What the speculative intellect thinks it understands, faith sees as real: the Man-God.

B. *The turning point.*—Cusanus regards all metaphors as provisional. In order to attain to the highest unity, we must discard everything that can be thought or imagined, and hence we must also transcend all figures of speech.

His ideas lead up to a point where they become a sort of metaphor and yet strain to surmount figurative language. This occurs when to the question, What is the infinite One, he replies: "Itself." Or when he thinks the highest unity and says that it can be conceived only as triunal—as unity, equality, connection, and in other categories—he no longer regards his thoughts as images or metaphors or conjectures, i.e., to be conceived in human categories, but rather as thoughts which directly grasp the being of God. And when all the categories have been transcended in the *coincidentia oppositorum,* that which is actually being sought suddenly turns up again, in categories. The unintelligible becomes intelligible in categories.

On the pathway to the highest we must transcend all finite things in the *coincidentia oppositorum,* but where are we led from there? Merely to the furthest limit, "the wall," past which we can go no further? Or into the obscurity of Nothingness, the objectless darkness, from which everything that is finite nevertheless takes its scale of measurement? Or to the light which arises in this darkness? But how does this come about?

In two ways: the categories of our thinking cease to be categories and grasp "the One itself." The thinkable ceases to be merely thought, God becomes incarnate.

C. *Liberation through speculation and reimprisonment in the content of faith.*—Cusanus carries out the process of intellectual liberation that is characteristic of all great metaphysics. But in him liberation does not content itself with metaphor. His speculation, which has just broken through every barrier and overcome every difficulty to bring us face to face with the infinite, is recaptured and fettered to dogmatic views or mysteries. Whenever this occurs, there is a break in the continuity of thought. His logical-alogical thinking opens up immeasurable spaces, which are gradually filled with ciphers (enigmatic images, metaphors, signs). As these ideas become available for specific contents of the revealed faith, the openings are sealed up again.

D. *Superstition.*—To see the absolute as an object or to make an object into an absolute is superstition. For this reason we also speak of scientific superstition when, on the basis of scientific findings, something is conceived of as Being itself, or when science is expected to answer mankind's every question. Scientific superstition is an alarming modern attitude fraught with disastrous consequences. Cusanus had no knowledge of this phenomenon.

Here we are referring to another superstition, this one age-old. We encounter it whenever, as above, a content of faith, instead of being clarified by the language of ciphers and so oriented toward the infinite, becomes the object of a sense perception or an object in categorial thinking. Superstition arises when the language of ciphers is transformed into a fixed corporeal thing.

Cusanus was one of a long line of Christian thinkers, faithful to the teaching of the Church, who resisted the inroads of superstition whether from inside or outside the Church. He condemned many practices of the Church of his day: "When consecrated things are used for purposes for which they are not intended, we have superstition. For example, when holy water is used as a remedy against sickness or to increase fertility. The same holds true of the light of the Easter candle, of baptismal water, and other things: bathing on Christmas Eve and Shrove Tuesday to combat fever or toothache . . . begging the intercession of St. Valentine in a case of epilepsy . . . carrying a cross around the fields in spring to ward off storms. There is superstition, too, in certain offerings laid upon the altar, such as stones on St. Stephen's day and arrows on St. Sebastian's day" (*Sermons,* pp. 158 ff.). Firm adherence to the simple faith, as laid down in the teachings of the Apostles, is quite enough. The rest is of no consequence, mere human invention. Superstitious practices lead to idolatry (*Sermon,* Scharpff, p. 484). They intrude on meditation and mystical experience, so fomenting fraud, self-deception, and self-indulgence in the form of spurious visions.

Cusanus never draws a clear distinction between faith and superstition. He does say, however: "It is superstitious to accord divine honors to persons other than God, indeed, it is idolatry" (*Sermons,* p. 197). But how are we to distinguish God in His corporeal form from an idol? Nor does he state clearly how superstition arises. The "human inventions" referred to above,

he says, are inspired by the Devil. Evil as well as good spirits induce
thoughts and images in the mind (*Sermons,* p. 195). Thus the origin of
superstition is accounted for by another superstition.

However, Cusanus dismisses this whole domain—superstition, demons,
the Devil—as of superficial importance. "We must recognize that the Devil
cannot penetrate the innermost sphere of the rational soul and be inwardly
present to Being; only God can do that. . . . Only He who created the
human mind can enter it. . . . And because the Devil cannot do this, he
does not know the secrets of the human heart; God alone knows them.
No creature can know the secrets of conscience" (*Sermons,* pp. 192 ff.).

4. *Whence comes the content of faith?*

Just as every man acquires understanding and self-knowledge with the
help of his mother tongue, so he acquires his faith with the help of traditional
beliefs (i.e., the philosophical as well as the revealed faith) in living communication with his fellow men, in practical experience, and by reading. Cusanus
grasps the miraculous character of language and writing. "Through the
written language the dead speak with the living, the absent with the
present—a truly divine masterpiece" (Scharpff, 411).

No one understands what another has written unless he penetrates
the author's meaning (*intentio*). This is possible only when the spirit that
moves both of them—speaker or writer and listener or reader—is one and
the same. The Bible bears witness to "the word of God." Since man was
made in the image of God, he can understand God's language, the natural
language of the world, and the supernatural language of revelation. He
understands the divine words of the Holy Scriptures thanks to "the light
of the Word that already dwells in him." But—for the same reason—"He
who has not the same spirit as Jesus cannot understand the Gospels."

Hence the radical manner in which Cusanus founds faith solely and
exclusively upon revelation. For example, when the believer asks in what
way Jesus was borne by the Virgin, and how one and the same God can be
Father, Son, and Holy Spirit, his faith replies: "We know this for certain
because the Gospels tell us it is so" (*To Albergati,* 42). Again: "The
authority of the Gospels is incomparably superior to everything else that
can be thought or uttered" (*ibid.,* 47). The word of the Bible is proof against
all doubt, because it is not man, but God, who speaks to us in the Bible. The
word of God cannot be false.

Cusanus would deny the validity of such an objection as the following:
What is asserted as a reality in the world, yet goes against all experience
and standards of intelligibility, has to be false as a statement of fact;
consequently there can be no such things (in the sense of corporeal things
in the world) as the conceiving of life through the Holy Spirit (which is

not a biological reality), the virgin birth, the resurrection from the dead of a man who, after a short stay on earth, ascends to Heaven. Cusanus forestalls all such objections: Because nothing is impossible to God, questions such as these as to how events attested by believers actually came about are irrelevant. To human thought, many things are inconceivable. Human cognition is confined within modes appropriate to human understanding, but this is not true of God. Therefore, the man who does not believe that God is capable of acts unintelligible to man "is making a judgment about himself rather than about God and is utterly in error" (*To Albergati,* 43).

The revealed faith to which Cusanus subscribes without reservation is based upon the Scriptures, the word of God, the Church, the body of Christian tradition. Philosophical faith, on the contrary, though also based on traditional views expressed in a variety of works, both sacred and profane and assuming many contradictory forms, assimilates freely this philosophical tradition. The speculative metaphors (ciphers) speak to philosophical faith in the medium of its rationality and essential love for freedom. This possibility is outside Cusanus' horizon when he speaks as a Christian, though perhaps not when, hardly aware of what he is doing, he speaks of man as an autonomous being, as a rational individual, different from all others, and attuned to the language of all things—whenever, that is, he philosophizes freely.

5. Authority and originality

A. *Unquestioning submission to the Church.*—In dedicating a work to Pope Pius II, who formerly, when he still bore the name of Enea Silvio de' Piccolomini, had called Cusanus his teacher, he wrote: "I submit to your judgment all I have ever written or ever shall write, and myself as well, without reservation, as behoves a believer who will never in any matter be in disagreement with Your Apostolic Throne." Although the words are traditional, they are perfectly sincere in this case. The philosopher's submission lacks any touch of self-castigation, such as it might have had if he had felt that there was any conflict between his philosophy and the teachings of the Church; his faith in the One Truth was never shaken. As a matter of historical fact, he was always left perfectly free to think as he wished.

B. *Criticisms of authority. The layman. Faith is the beginning of knowledge.*
—He was amazingly outspoken in criticizing the authorities (primarily in the dialogues on the layman). The layman (*idiota*) becomes the vehicle and discoverer of the truth, who defends it against the book learning of the theologians. The truth is to be found in the streets and market places, not in the circles of the learned.

The layman remonstrates with his erudite interlocutor: "Your insights depend too much on the prestige of writers and their doctrinal opinions. You live on the nourishment others supply, not on food that is naturally suitable to you. The man who walks in the ways of wisdom bears witness not merely to what he has been told, but also to what he himself has experienced. It is not enough to know what has been written about wisdom. Rather, we must ourselves arrive at insights, achieve knowledge at first, not at second hand."

The figure of nature and the world as a book to be read, as distinguished from the books composed by men, goes back to the Church Fathers. The significance of the "layman" is a *topos* that became familiar to Cusanus during his stay with the monks at Deventer. He invested it with freshness and force.

His anti-authoritarianism is not directed against the Bible. Nor is it directed against book learning as such, the value of which he does not deny: "I do not say that there is no wisdom in books. But I do say that books are not its source." Cusanus' respect for experience reflects a will to get back to the source. He sees the source of all knowledge in the thoughts and acts of men going about their business in the market place, in the way they count, measure, and weigh, in the activities of artisans who create works after the models in their own minds. Cusanus was himself a great reader and left a large library; many of the volumes are crammed with marginal notes in his own hand. His *idiota* is thoroughly familiar with the ideas of the philosophers. It is in the name of authentic appropriation that Cusanus opposes merely learned wisdom. What books awaken in us must be freshly tested for ourselves in our own experience—whether in the world or in our own soul, in the experience of faith and speculation.

Nowhere does Cusanus voice even the slightest criticism of the authority of revelation. But he does insist on our need to grasp its message directly; we must not simply pay it lip service, in the absence of understanding. In the authentic life of the spirit, the authority of revelation is unshakable wherever matters of faith are concerned. In this connection, Cusanus repeats Augustine (*fides praecedit intellectum*) and Anselm (*credo ut intelligam*). In one passage (*De doc. ignor.*, II, 11) he writes: "Faith is the beginning of knowledge (*fides est initium intellectus*)." And again: "The man who wants to arrive at an insight must have faith, for without it he will get nowhere." Hence, "Where there is no true faith, there is no true knowledge."

c. *Not even in germ a heretic.*—Certain of Cusanus' statements might have been declared heretical, as had been the case with some of Meister Eckhart's. But no danger threatened Cusanus, prince of the Church, who had rendered extraordinary political services to the cause of papal power and had labored for Church unity. An attack on him by Wenck, a professor at Heidelberg, might have led to his condemnation. Cusanus was stung into refuting the passionate pamphlet of this rationalistic scholastic—the only time he ever did such a thing.

However, the Church paid no attention to Cusanus' ideas. In the nineteenth century, a few Catholic theologians took up the old attack again and amplified it, but the Church remained silent. His thinking fell into oblivion. After 1565 (date of the Basel edition of his works), neither the Church nor any monastic order arranged for a new edition. The Heidelberg *Akademieausgabe* (begun in 1932) was initiated by non-Catholics.

Cusanus himself had no heretical leanings. His sincere quest for the truth was inseparable from his determination to submit to the judgment of the Church—the visible, existing Church of his day. Entirely foreign to him was the sort of radicalism that stops at nothing in its conflict with the world as it is, envisages the possibility of revolution, and compels the world to transform itself. He did not fight for the truth as such, only for the truth within the Church. He did not champion the faith of the New Testament against its corruption by the Church, which claims a monopoly on Christianity and imposes its faith by brute force when it has the means of doing so. Cusanus was not a revolutionary; his own reform activities were carried on within the Church, on orders from his superiors.

D. *"Esoterism."*—He feared that wisdom, by giving rise to misunderstanding, might impair the faith of the multitude. He has the layman himself say: "I am not sure that it is right to lay bare such great mysteries and to disclose such bottomless depths so casually" (*De sap.*). He expressed the wish that "Books for the understanding of which the multitude is not prepared be removed from public places" (*Apol.*, p. 25). And yet the truth that is thus to be kept hidden is for Cusanus at the same time the truth which man has the innate capacity to understand. The layman utters the truth, and the same layman expresses concern over its possible harmful effect.

The distinction between a knowledge accessible to all and a knowledge accessible only to initiates is an old one (in India as well as in the West). According to Cusanus, propositions which acquire their true meaning only in the light of "knowing ignorance" are capable of being misunderstood, because, once formulated in rational terms, their meaning becomes fixed. This was how certain of Meister Eckhart's propositions, which Cusanus defends, came to be condemned as heretical. People unprepared to understand such things should not read them. But whom are we to call unprepared? The multitude? The merely learned? After all, what the layman stands for and is momentarily inclined to keep secret, is the truth which is directly and fundamentally accessible to man as man. Cusanus was aware of the ever-recurrent problem involved, but did not solve it any more than any other thinker has done.

6. Faith and obedience

Faith based upon revelation demands obedience. "When we opt for faith we submit to the Word, we willingly surrender both our reason and our will" (*Sermon,* Scharpff, 482). Such a statement is surprising: for, as we have seen, Cusanus demands that we should understand authentically, that we should make insights our own, that our thinking should not be second-hand.

Cusanus would presumably reply: Faith resides fundamentally in obedience itself. "Obedience" does not imply that we come by our faith at second hand. Faith in obedience to the Church is authentic as such. The truth is one. True philosophy and true Christian faith cannot be at variance. In theory, submission to the dogmatic decisions of the Church cannot involve any conflict. Nicholas of Cusa never experienced actual conflicts and we can hardly doubt that, had any occurred, he would have submitted to the Church.

Religious obedience of this kind is not obedience to one's own conscience, but definitely and explicitly consists in an obedience to the Church as automatic as the monk's obedience to his superior. Cusanus justifies such obedience: "Where there is obedience, there is love of God. Love of God makes man as pliable and obedient as wax subjected to the action of fire" (*Sermons,* p. 144). Hence, obedience to it "is meritorious, even though the man who commands obedience is blameworthy. Obedience is the more meritorious when your superior demands it on an unjust ground" (*ibid.,* p. 143).

IV. TRUTH IN MATHEMATICS

Cusanus composed twelve works dealing explicitly with mathematics (between 1445 and 1459). They show what great importance he attached to mathematics.

A. *Infinity.*—And yet Cusanus is really interested in only one aspect of mathematics: infinity. At no point does he address himself, like a professional mathematician, to solving mathematical problems as such. In the best professional judgment he was a mathematical dilettante. He confines himself to problems such as the relation of a circle's circumference to its diameter, of the circle to the square, of the arc to the chord. Since in each of these problems, one member of the pair is incommensurable with the other, they all involve the notion of infinity. He was unable to solve any of them.

If we suppose that a circle is extended indefinitely, we arrive at an infinite circle, in which arc and chord coincide. An infinite circle would be an infinite straight line. The sum of three angles of a triangle is equal to two right angles. If we make one of the angles progressively greater, so that it approaches in magnitude the sum of two right angles, the apex of the triangle will move ever closer to the base, and finally the sides of the triangle will coincide with the base.

The infinity of the figures in which the opposites of circle and straight line coincide is seen by Cusanus as an expression of God's infinity. He quotes Anselm, who likened God's supreme truth to an infinite straight line, and others who likened Him to an infinite triangle, an infinite circle, an infinite sphere. According to Cusanus, all these conceptions are correct, and for all their seeming divergence essentially identical.

We cannot visualize a circle as a straight line, but, Cusanus says, the intellect can readily conceive it as such. The intellect comprehends the coincidence of opposites, which leads by various paths to the same goal, whatever our starting point in the finite may be. Just as the differences between geometrical figures are equalized, all dissolving in the one infinity, so all finite things are equalized and absorbed in the infinity of God. And just as the plurality of finite geometrical figures is grounded in infinity, so are all finite things grounded in the infinity of God.

B. *Progression and leap.*—Progression toward an infinity that can never be attained becomes, when consciously effected, an amazing experience. We move on and on, beyond each successive limit (of number, line, space, or causality). No beginning or end is ever attained.

Something entirely different, however, may happen. The never-ending progression or regression (the *progressus* and *regressus in indefinitum*) becomes intolerable, we feel that we are out of our depth. At such times we are prepared to believe that Aristotle was right in saying that whenever such a *regressus in indefinitum* turns up, our point of departure must have been faulty. The necessity of an end comes to be regarded as an argument against infinite process. Infinity is impossible to conceive of.

Or the problem is solved by a "leap." The infinite (in the sense of a *progressus in indefinitum*) suddenly becomes the completed infinite. Cusanus believes that this completion is achieved in the *coincidentia oppositorum*. The indefinite progression signifies an endless intellectual activity; its completion signifies a fiction that cannot be grasped as reality. At this point Cusanus' train of thought changes direction: thus understood, infinity is the ground out of which arise all finite figures as limitations.

Both trains of thought became symbols for Cusanus. The first symbolizes how the human intellect ascends to God: just as in the *coincidentia oppositorum* contact with mathematical infinity is established, so in the thinking of the *coincidentia oppositorum* as a whole the intellect makes contact with God. The second course symbolizes the descent from infinity to the finite: just as the longest, infinite line contains all other lines, so the absolutely greatest, absolute infinity, contains all finite things.

c. *Mathematical infinity and the infinity of God.*—All these mathematical ideas—the indefinite progression of the series of numbers and figures, and the leap into the infinite—are intended as symbols. But infinity is also the essence of the divine Being. Cusanus searches for the purest mathematical symbolism as a way of giving us an intimation of God's infinity. He proceeds by the following stages: First, "Since all mathematical signs are finite, we must regard mathematical figures, with all their possible variations, as finite." Second, "The finite relations must accordingly be transposed into infinite figures." Third, "These relations of the infinite figures are transposed into infinity pure and simple, which is independent of any figure" (*De doc. ignor.,* I, 12).

The finite figures cannot be proper symbols—only the ascent from finite to infinite figures is a symbol. Mathematical infinity becomes a symbol of absolute infinity. As finite mathematical figures are to infinite figures, so all finite things are to the infinity of God.

In mathematics, which may be regarded as the science of the infinite, infinity can be grasped only to the extent that specific concepts of infinity (indicated by special signs) are employed for the solution of specific problems. But behind each symbol "for the infinite" that enters into mathematical operations, there always remains another infinity that is beyond our grasp.

How mathematical infinity can become a symbol of divine infinity is the constant concern of Cusanus' speculation. Infinity in a problem of mathematics is not the same thing as infinity conceived of as object of metaphysical speculation. The former serves as a metaphor for the latter.

Infinite approximation in geometry (for example, in the "nonmeasurable" relations between polygon and circle, diameter and circumference, arc and chord) is used as an image of something entirely different—the way knowledge approaches the infinity of the godhead. Because geometrical operations can be visualized, they provide us with analogies illustrating how the mind proceeds from knowledge of finite things to knowledge of the infinite God. The "infinite" mathematical figures become the image of divine infinity "by transposition" (*translative*) (*De doc. ignor.,* I, 16).

d. *Mathematics a symbol of divine creative power.*—The lengths to which Cusanus carries his mathematical symbolism are most fully disclosed in passages where not only numbers or figures or single operations, but the whole process of mathematical cognition is seen as a copy of divine cognition. In mathematics we know exactly what our reason produces, and we know it with complete precision because we ourselves have brought it forth. Thus mathematical reasoning is the most appropriate symbol for the divine mind, which produces the things themselves (not merely intellectual schemata) and hence knows them as exactly as we know the mathematical figures we ourselves construct. "Since nothing in our knowledge is certain save for mathematics," mathematics provides "an enigmatic image for the hunting out of God's work" (*De possest,* Opera, 259; *et illa est aenigma ad venationem operum Dei*). Mathematical knowledge is the only exact knowledge, and in it the mind knows itself and its powers. Because it is a copy of divine knowledge, the godhead reveals itself in it (*ibid.*).

The copy is not so much the numbers and geometrical figures as the activity of our mind in producing them. Cusanus denies that such mathematical entities could have "another, still more real being over and above the mind" (*De beryllo,* 32). The truth they embody originates in the human mind, and they owe their character of certainty to its creative power, not to some other world. (Indeed there is here no alternative. A self-subsistent ideal world of mathematical objects discovered by investigation, and such a world constructed by the mind, are aspects of one and the same thing. What we produce we also discover. What the mind creates is valid as such.)

E. *Number.*—"Without number there would be no distinction, order, proportion, harmony, or even the multiplicity of things in general" (*De doc. ignor.,* I, 5). "What does not fall under quantity or magnitude can be neither conceived nor visualized" (*De possest,* tr. 32). Since all our cognition is bound up with quantity, magnitude, number, figures, "number constitutes the method of cognition itself" (*De mente,* 6). "Number is the archetype of all our intellectual concepts."

Quantity is inseparable from finitude; whatever quantity we deal with, we can always conceive of more or less. Discursive reason can give names to things only because quantity (or "number") is one of their characteristics. If number were something infinite, the greatest would coincide with the smallest, and all determinations would be null and void. For it amounts to the same thing to say that number is infinite or to say that it is nothing at all (*De doc. ignor.,* I, 5).

What is the origin of number? Mathematical number is a creation of the human mind. But even as such, it is a copy of divine number. The latter is inconceivable to us; we call it "number," just as we speak by a remote analogy of the divine "mind" (*De mente*). Just as the mind as a whole is a copy of the divine mind, so the mind's creations are copies of divine creation. Mathematical number is a copy of the archetypal divine number, which is the ultimate source of number as we know it.

The actual plurality of things, however, is different from the abstract plurality of number. In our *cognition* of things, plurality is our human contribution. For only the mind enumerates. There is no such thing as number in itself, in abstraction from the work of the mind (*De mente,* 6).

But the reality of the things which to us appear in the plural lies in the divine mind. God is the original Creator of the real world of the human mind, which is a copy of His mind. (That the archetype of real things in the Creator's mind is number is proved by the beauty inherent in all things; for beauty consists in proportion, and proportion rests upon number; *De mente*.)

In brief, Cusanus says: In the Creator's mind, the first pattern of things is number, the archetypal number inconceivable to us. But the first pattern of our knowledge of things (of the conceptual world created by us in the likeness of things) is the number of our discursive reason (*De doc. ignor.*, II, 13). The human mind accomplishes three things with the help of number. First: It gains insight into the mathematical world it creates. Second: Number enables it to know finite created things. Third: With the help of number our mind obtains a glimpse of the godhead whenever, guided by purely human imitative notions of number, it rises to an intimation of the archetypal divine number.

F. *The importance of mathematics for philosophical speculation.*—Cusanus is interested in mathematics for several reasons:

(1) "Everyone knows that in mathematics truth is grasped with greater certainty than in the other liberal arts" (*Compl. theol.*, cap. 2). Because of their certainty, mathematical propositions serve as guides to philosophy in its own investigations (*De doc. ignor.*, I, 11). But above all: The most certain knowledge—for it is produced by the mind itself—is the best copy of the divine mind.

(2) In constructing figures and numbers we effect a transition from the sensory, not, to be sure, to the supersensory, but to the nonsensory. A triangle perceived by the senses is never identical with the mathematically conceived triangle. All sensory perception is subject to fluctuation. The mathematical object has stability (*De doc. ignor.*, I, 11). The mathematical object frees us from attachment to the merely sensory. Practice in contemplating mathematical forms and in operations leading up to their construction teaches us how to deal with nonsensory things, and is thereby a preliminary step to dealing with the supersensory.

(3) Mathematical insights serve as symbols. Figures and numbers become signs of a cognition that is no longer mathematical, but metaphysical. Mathematical relations and mathematical constructions become an image and likeness of the divine creation. Cusanus appended a *Complementum theologicum* to his mathematical writings. His aim is to show that through intellectual vision in the mirror of mathematics, the truth we seek in all that is knowable is reflected—and not merely in remote similarity but in a kind of radiant proximity (*non modo remota similitudine, sed fulgida quadam propinquitate*) (Basel edition, p. 1107).

The great tradition of mathematically oriented philosophy goes back to the Pythagoreans, to Plato and the Neoplatonists. Proclus believed that without mathematics no knowledge of the divine is possible. Cusanus shared this belief.

G. *Relations between mathematics and philosophy.*—Today we can sharply distinguish: *First:* Pure, free development in the field of mathematics, without regard for empirical reality or applicability to natural science. *Second:* Mathematics in the natural sciences, which presuppose the mathematically graspable order of material things, and progress in knowledge to the extent that mathematics supplies the means or, conversely, to the extent that empirically measurable phenomena make possible the application of previously developed, but hitherto "useless" mathematical insights. This is done in full awareness of the fact that such a method achieves knowledge of the real world, not as such, but only in a certain perspective, in which other realities are deliberately disregarded. *Third:* The symbolism of numbers, in which the mathematical mind becomes a metaphor for the divine mind, or numbers, proportions, and figures are looked upon as symbols for divine realities.

Cusanus is often clear about the relation between mathematical knowledge and mathematical symbolism, but not consistently. Like many other thinkers, he seems to have been misled by two currents of thought:

(1) Modern philosophy was powerfully influenced by mathematics, which became its model and whose methods it applied. This had disastrous results when attempts were made to mathematize philosophy. In some cases the independence of philosophy was in effect preserved (e.g., in Spinoza), in others philosophy was led astray. The radical difference between mathematics and philosophy began to be apparent with Descartes but did not become completely clear until Kant. To the German speculative metaphysicians (Hegel, Schelling) the difference between their kind of cognition and mathematics was self-evident. Kierkegaard had nothing to do with mathematics. Cusanus still took mathematics as his guide and failed to achieve fundamental clarity.

(2) The other current of thought is the mysticism of numbers. To be sure, Cusanus' fundamental thinking is purely speculative: it actually creates metaphors and employs them as such, without deception. Only occasionally does he relapse into the ancient mysticism of numbers and produce schematisms whose lifelessness is in strange contrast to the authenticity of his fundamental speculative ideas.

The tremendous appeal of mathematics for philosophers rests upon certain facts that never cease to astonish us. Among these are: the self-evident character of mathematically construed relations; the fascinating "beauty" of mathematical insights, which seem to be governed by a hidden purposiveness; the difference between indifferent observations and fascinating mathematical insights—a difference which the mathematicians may not be able to justify objectively; the capacity of the human mind, on the basis of self-posited assumptions, to perform operations which lead to the discovery of ever new splendors; the applicability of mathematics to nature, in so far as it is governed by measure, number, and weight—a (partial) coincidence, which is anything but self-evident, between mathematical laws and the laws we discover in nature, the fact that the same laws and the same order are to be found in both.

All this provides an inexhaustible source of philosophical wonder. How can this be? Why is it so? The answers arouse further wonder. No final solution has been arrived at. Cusanus lived in just such an intellectual climate, which began with Western philosophy and is still very much alive today.

H. *Was the Creator of the world a mathematician?*—Cusanus writes: "In creating the world, God made use of arithmetic, geometry, music, and astronomy, arts that we also make use of today in studying the relations between things, elements and motions" (*De doc. ignor.*, II, 13). This does not mean that the world was created by a mathematician. Cusanus is speaking allegorically, momentarily putting the imitative human mind in the place of the original. He is aware that the whole of mathematics is a production of the human mind, which was created by God and endowed by Him with its productive faculty. Hence mathematical thinking is human thinking. Man, not God, is the mathematician. "The things of mathematics are neither a What nor a How, they are merely signs which our reason has discovered for itself, and without which it could not do its work of building and measuring" (*De possest*).

The assumption of natural science that no matter how far it progresses it will always discover a mathematical order in things does not do away with the fact that we see, feel, understand, and distinguish forms which remain inaccessible to mathematics. The most we can say is this: no definable limits are set to the mathematical investigation of reality. The proposition, "We are trying to investigate the mathematical order of the world *ad infinitum*," does not entail this other proposition, "The world in its entire reality is subject to mathematical laws." In brief: The methodological assumption under which we attempt to progress as far as we can must not be interpreted as a theoretical anticipation of our knowledge of the world as a whole.

I. *From speculation to mathematical science.*—Two tendencies are implied in the idea of attaining or even of approaching the infinite through the *coincidentia oppositorum*.

First: Cusanus' real intention is to "go beyond"—i.e., his goal is the absolutely infinite, which is God. He looks upon his mathematical and physical conceptions as metaphors or signs or enigmatic images of this infinite. Herein lies the meaning and the achievement of his philosophizing. Is it futile because the most it can promise us is clearer awareness in nonknowledge? In my opinion, the infinitely progressing elucidation of nonknowledge is enough.

When Cusanus seeks to approach the infinite through the *coincidentia oppositorum,* mathematical operations serve as metaphors. Moreover, when infinity is seen from the point of view of the finite, the experience of the limits of the finite casts some light on the finite. But in no way is the infinite conceived of as a methodological tool for the scientific investigation of the finite.

Second: The special feature of Cusanus' mathematical symbolism is that this line of reasoning is turned around: What, in the *coincidentia oppositorum,* was intended only to bring us closer to the knowledge of God, is now conceived as the source of mathematical knowledge in the world. The aim is no longer to use mathematics as a guide in metaphysical speculation, but to further mathematics itself. What was originally a philosophical method is now expected to lead to mathematical discoveries. "It is my intention to use the coincidence of opposites for the improvement of mathematics" (*De math. perfectione*).

In going beyond the opposition between curved and straight lines in geometry, beyond the opposition between motion and rest in physics, and beyond all other such oppositions, Cusanus is attempting to attain the infinite, where all opposites are united and from which they are produced. In mathematics this would lead to a knowledge that grasps mathematical infinity through various signs and operations. What "lies beyond" would be made knowable in the world. Cusanus hoped that his principle of the *coincidentia oppositorum* would prove methodologically useful to this end, though his own efforts to make it so appear to have been in vain. He arrived at ideas of mathematical possibilities and anticipations of a future mathematics, but he failed to find the crucial step which, indeed, is objectively unrelated to his speculative assumptions.

Part Two: The Whole of Being

Nicholas of Cusa does not construct a self-contained system of being and empirical existence. Such a system is precluded by his type of thinking, in which intellectual operations yield only images and metaphors, strike out now in one direction, now in another, and are consummated in nonknowledge.

For this reason Cusanus' writings do not form a system in which particular works, subjects, or ideas take a permanent place. Cusanus is always beginning afresh. In its speculative movement his thinking goes back to the sources again and again. Whenever it begins to disclose a tendency to schematization, we must distinguish, according to his own standards, between the living speculation and the system of knowledge that may result from it. Sometimes his speculation produces conceptual schemata that stand in the way of the speculation itself.

For this reason a systematic exposition of his ideas on being would fail to do him justice. It is possible to select passages from his writings and shuffle them around until they seem to fall into a system. But to do so would be unrewarding. There would still be many discrepancies, because the arguments and the terminology of different works fail to harmonize as parts of a systematic whole. There are schemata in his thinking, but there is no construction of a systematic whole. His speculative mode of thinking opens up experience. To be communicated this experience has to be objectivized. Accordingly it will be worth our while to supply some explicit objectivizations.

This we shall attempt from several points of view. Our exposition will necessarily be disjoined; we shall not attempt to deduce a single systematic whole from one or more arbitrarily chosen principles. The "one idea" that shines through constantly cannot be grasped directly. In our exposition of the "whole of being" we shall resort to paraphrase, as we did in connection with the "fundamental ideas."

In his early work, *De docta ignorantia,* Cusanus adopted a threefold division: God, the World, Christ. We shall follow this division.

I. GOD

1. *Dialogue on the hidden God*

In a dialogue (*De deo abscondito*) between a heathen and a Christian the following argument is developed:

(1) The heathen: What do you *know* about the God you worship? The Christian: All that I know is not God, and all that I grasp conceptually does not resemble Him. He is above all things.

Then nothing is God? Is God nothing?—By no means. He is not nothing. The name of nothing is nothing.

If God is not nothing, is He then something?—Not at all: God is all things rather than any one thing.

How very strange! You maintain that God is not nothing, yet is not any one thing. But this is beyond the grasp of all reason!—God is above nothing and above any one thing. Nothingness obeys him, so that something comes into being. He surpasses all that is and all that is not, and both obey Him. He is not any of the things which follow from His omnipotence.

(2) Can God be *named* at all?—He is ineffable, because all namable things are insignificant in comparison with His inconceivable greatness. But He can be named over and above all things, since He is the original ground of all things namable. He who confers names upon others cannot Himself be without a name.

Then is God both ineffable and effable?—That is not the case either. He is neither named nor not named, nor is He both named and not named. Nothing that can be said is adequate to His sublime infinity, which lies above every possible idea of Him.

(3) Then God cannot be subsumed under that which *is?*—He cannot. —Then He is just *nothing?*—He negates these contradictory designations, so that He neither is nor is not; similarly, it cannot be said that He *both* is and is not, or that He is *or* is not. None of these statements attains to the source which precedes all that is utterable (*De princ.*). He is the fountainhead of all the springs of being and nonbeing.

The heathen mulls this over: Then God is the fountainhead of all the springs of being and nonbeing? He is told in reply: No! and is surprised: But those were your very words!—Whereupon the Christian says: I spoke the truth when I affirmed it, and now too I speak the truth when I deny it. For if there are any springs of being and nonbeing, God is prior to them all.

(4) Is not God the *truth?*—No, He is prior to all truth. Nor yet is He by any means something different from the truth. He is infinitely far above and prior to everything we conceive of as truth.

(5) God, who is free from every sort of determination characteristic of created things, cannot be discovered anywhere in the domain of creation. All composite things in the world and every individual composite thing are what they are only because of Him; He who is not Himself a composite thing remains unrecognized in this domain. In the eyes of all philosophers, God is the hidden God.

2. On speculation

Nothing can be said about God—and there is no limit to what is said about Him. Hence the thesis: No statement is applicable to the One. For every statement implies otherness or duality. No name applies to that which is self-posited. Even the term "the One" does not really apply to it (*De princ.*). Whether we call it "the One," the "Non-Other," "Capability as such," the "source," or something else, such names will always be inadequate. Cusanus writes: "The unnamable source of the namable source cannot itself be named source. For it is anterior to all that is namable and surpasses it" (*De princ.*).

Yet so peremptory a thesis is not allowed to stand in the way of a speculation in the course of which infinitely many things are said about God; rather, it serves to clarify the sense of such speculation. We learn what takes place when speculation ventures the impossible and what it produces when it breaks down—how our thinking deepens as it comes closer to the hidden God, and makes us feel the overwhelming reality of what is hidden—how what eludes the thinker attracts him ever more strongly.

Although the inability to make statements is taken seriously, the result is not silence. Impressive images and categorial connections occur time and again in the course of conceptual operations which lead to that abyss in the sight of which all statements and existence itself become for the first time transparent.—Also the statements of negative theology are made retroactive and are freed from the "non." Positives and negatives are alike transcended.

The speculative ideas go in pursuit of what is hidden in concepts which, though they cancel one another out when clarity has been attained, do so in such a way that, in the light they produce, the world is transformed for the thinker and the thinker himself is transformed.

The supreme art of pure thinking consists in giving lucid expression to speculative experience in the sequence of propositions. Often in the last two and a half thousand years such thinking has seemed to die out in the Western world, but has repeatedly reasserted itself. It has often been choked off by underbrush, shot through with the weeds of habit and idle fantasy. And it can also degenerate into rational schematisms.

3. *Examples of speculative attempts to approach God*

A. *Beyond the* coincidentia oppositorum.—We repeat Cusanus' most cherished idea: God is inconceivably conceived in the coincidence of opposites. His infinite abundance is attested by the infinite differences which become one again in the coincidence of opposites. Being and nonbeing, the greatest and the smallest, Being and Potential Being, past, present, and future, all coincide.

The speculative "hunt for wisdom"—or for God—is unsuccessful so long as the rational principle—"Everything either is or is not"—is observed. Because God is anterior to this principle—which is valid only within a limited sphere which God surpasses—those who remain under the sway of this principle cannot possibly find God (*De ven. sap.*, p. 13).

The magical phrase *"coincidentia oppositorum"* can either be dismissed as nonsense or extolled as dialectical profundity. With reference to the absolute to which the idea is supposed to lead us, it remains ambiguous. At times it seems to mean: God is the coincidence of opposites. At other times the idea is only a springboard from which we are supposed to leap in order to touch the absolute—no one can tell how. But whoever makes the leap falls back to his starting point. We are left this side of "the wall."

This ambiguity hints at a reality the truth of which comes to life only within ourselves through our thinking, yet which is not present merely because we think. Thought is a sort of speculative knocking at the door, a pounding away at some insurmountable obstacle. It is still a far cry from gratification at having reached a long-sought goal.

B. *The non-other* (non aliud).—Cusanus calls God the *non aliud*. This means: Without being other, God comprises everything within Himself. The world is otherness (*alteritas*) because whatever is in it is either one thing or another.

But the *non aliud* and otherness must not be allowed to freeze into rigid opposition. For all things are in God. There is nothing outside Him, and in Him nothing is different from anything else. He is perfect identity with Himself. "If infinity could ever exist, and something else exist outside it, then neither infinity nor anything else could exist" (*The Vision of God*, *op. cit.*, p. 62).

What is not in God is not in itself either. Otherness is not a positive principle. Otherness derives its name from nonbeing (*alteritas dicitur e non esse*).

If the *non aliud* were set in opposition to *alteritas* (an opposition we cannot help stating the moment we talk about anything at all), we should miss the point. The speculative attempt must break down as such in the rational statement: only then is its full truth disclosed. Were we to overlook the breakdown of rationality and interpret the statement literally, we should be saying something that can never apply to God. For the statement as such makes the infinite finite and turns God into a determined concept.

But God, who is indefinable rationally, is the definition of Himself and of all things. Therefore we find Him nowhere more clearly than in non-otherness. But non-otherness is not the opposite of otherness, for otherness is "defined" by the fact that non-otherness is anterior to it.

God has no opposite. He is non-otherness, which is opposed neither by otherness nor by nothingness, for He is also anterior to nothingness and defines it. This is why Pseudo-Dionysius says that God is all in all and nothing in nothing (*De ven. sap.*, 14).

c. *"Potentiality"*: (1) *The category.*—Possibility is distinguished from actuality. Possibility denotes either logical or real possibility. Real possibility implies potentiality (*potentia*), which is a power (*potestas*). In Cusanus' speculation these categories are interdependent.

(2) *Ascending speculation.*—In the world of otherness, possibility is separated from actuality, potential being from actualization. What is in the world is just what it is and yet can always be other than it is. This is its inconstancy. To man, however, this limitation of his actuality by possibility also signifies his freedom to set in motion his actuality—which is

inadequate, which has already escaped him, but which is destined to take wing—thanks to the horizons opened up by possibility.

Not so God. Here is perfect actuality. Every potentiality has become actuality, everything that can be has already achieved being. Here, what can be and what is are indistinguishable. Cusanus coins a new term to designate this particular *coincidentia oppositorum*: *possest*. Only God *possest* ("can-is") because He is actually what He can be. God cannot become anything that He has not been for all eternity (*De ven. sap.,* 13).

In one of his last works *De apice theoriae* ("The Pinnacle of Theory"), Cusanus takes another speculative step forward. The capability that cannot be surpassed by any limited entity, he now calls "Capability as such"; without it there can be no capability of any kind. Every other faculty presupposes Capability as such. Nothing antecedes, nothing is stronger, more solid, more essential, more glorious than Capability as such, the capability of the first ground and the first source, the capability of every faculty. And in another passage he says the same thing: Nothing can be anterior to Capability as such, nothing better, nothing more powerful, more accomplished, simpler, clearer, better known, truer, more adequate, more constant, more accessible. Because it is anterior to any and every determined faculty, it can neither be nor be named, neither felt, imagined, nor understood.

Capability as such is not potential being or living or understanding, it is not potentiality qualified in any way. It is precisely the potentiality of potential being and living and understanding. Every qualified faculty is an image of Capability as such. Thus ability to be is an image; ability to live is a truer image than mere ability to be, and a still truer image is ability to understand.

(3) *Capability as such in the mind.*—All things are manifestations of Capability as such, and nothing else. But one of these manifestations is pre-eminent: "The living, discerning light that is called the mind contemplates Capability as such within itself, and at the same time sees itself as its image." Ability to see is the mind's highest capability. This is illustrated in parables:

Just as a traveler forms in advance an idea of his destination, such that he can direct his steps toward the desired goal, so the mind can see in advance the goal of its aspiration. If it could not see from a distance the goal of rest and joy, how could it ever attain that goal? The faculty of sight is directed toward Capability as such, which in all its splendor is alone able to satisfy the mind's longing. Another parable: "Just as books were composed to enable the spirit to disclose itself, not under compulsion, but because the free and noble spirit wishes to reveal itself, so Capability as such proceeds in all things."

Capability as such—than which nothing can be more powerful or better, and to which nothing is anterior—now seems to Cusanus far more appropriate to the Godhead "than capability (*possest*) or any other term designating that without which nothing can ever be or live or understand."

(4) *Light or darkness?*—At this point in his speculations Cusanus arrives at a proposition that seems to reverse the sense of his previous thinking. On being told that nothing is clearer, truer, and more easily understood than the term "Capability as such," the disciple says: I find nothing more difficult than something that is always sought and yet can never be entirely found. Cusanus replies: "The clearer the truth, the more readily it can be grasped; formerly, however, I thought that it was more easily found in darkness." But it would be wrong to speak of a real reversal. What we have here is not a new attitude, but the paradox inherent in the coupling of the terms "light" and "dark." Precisely when darkness is deepest, another, inconceivable light is born, a light that can be attained only by passing through the darkness.

(5) *Reason for Cusanus' enthusiasm.*—The enthusiasm with which Cusanus speaks of "Capability as such" may seem surprising. With the help of this category he believes that he has attained in a unique manner that which, to his mind, cannot be named in any way.

This is the astonishing thing about all categorial speculation: seen from the point of view of discursive reason, it disintegrates into an idle playing with words. If there is truth in speculation, it is discernible only through the echo it arouses in man's Existenz at times when the wonder of our being here and now is not allowed to seep away but driven into unfathomable depths. The questions and answers give rise to a form of truth which becomes more intense and more present as, amid the tension between vain solutions and insolubility, answers give rise to new questions.

(6) *Posse facere, posse fieri, posse factum.*—Cusanus' speculations about "Capability" supply him with the possibility of conceiving the world under the aspect of a tripartite division: *posse facere, posse fieri, posse factum* (the faculty of creating, the faculty of coming into being, the faculty of having come into being.

Capability as such is the faculty of creating (*posse facere*). It creates the world, namely, the world that can come into being (*posse fieri*). This faculty does not have its source in itself. Anterior to it is what is eternal and cannot be created, Capability as such, which is all things that can be. The faculty of coming into being could not arise of itself. Whence would it arise? It presupposes a having-been-created.

Because it has been created, the faculty of coming into being has a "beginning," but not in time, for it is simultaneous with time, which was created along with the faculty of coming into being.

The created faculty of coming into being, which is so to speak initial in relation to beginningless eternity, is itself constant and permanent and does not come into being. In it lie all things and every individual thing as it will be when fully unfolded.

What has developed out of the faculty of coming into being—the phenomena in the world—is of two kinds. First: the things that have come into being but in doing so have fulfilled their potentiality, for example, celestial and spiritual nature (the *prima facta*), that is to say, the sun, the moon, the stars, and the angels. These remain constant, just as they are. Second: the things that have come into being but without fully realizing their potentiality. These are forever defective, unstable, changeable. In these things the process of coming into being has never fully attained its limit. In the world as a whole the faculty of coming into being is fully actualized, for there is indeed nothing that is greater than the world; but the things that have come into being in the world are always singular and perishable.

The eternal (*aeternum*) is everything that comes into being, although it does not itself come into being, but rather is the principle and end (*terminus*) of every thing that can come into being. On the other hand, the faculty of coming into being is ever enduring; it has its end (or reaches its pinnacle) not in itself, but in eternity (*De ven. sap.,* especially 37–39).

The eternal, the creator, or Capability as such cannot become nothing or other than it is, because it is prior to nothingness and the ability to come into being (*De ven. sap.,* 39).

D. *Origin.*—In *De principio* Cusanus discusses the meaning of the proposition that God is origin. Origin here does not mean origin of the world (creation). Before the world came into being, in eternity, God was origin and origin of the origin, and that which originated in both (*De princ.,* 11).

Cusanus elucidates: "Everything that is seen in eternity is eternity." The origin in eternity cannot exist without that which originates in eternity. But eternity is not some sort of extended duration, it is wholly simultaneity, even at the source. We have an intellectual intuition of the origin that has no origin and the origin of the origin (*De princ.,* 10).

E. *Being and nothing.*—The origin must be itself, through itself. For if we failed to understand that it is, we could not understand that there is anything at all (*De princ.,* 18). Here Cusanus implicitly asks the question: Why is there something, why is there not nothing? At this question no abyss opens before him—God discloses Himself. We understand that something is because God created it. But where does God come from? This question Cusanus does not answer, for at this point the thinking of something ceases. Yet thinking itself does not cease. The answer lies in the speculative movement of Cusanus' thought.

Even before he comes in view of the abyss, of the possibility that nothing is, he has led us away from it. He says: The Origin, Absolute Being, must be One. "If this be eliminated, the intellect concludes that nothing can be" (*De princ.,* 7). Because this conclusion simply does not come under consideration, the One is at the source, the One God demonstrated.

Cusanus then asks: Since nonbeing is, which comes first, being or nonbeing? He answers: Nonbeing presupposes being. Without that which is negated there can be no negation. Where there is negation, that which is negated has been before. A logical proposition is here applied to being itself, nothingness cannot be of itself. It comes after being. It receives its nonbeing from being.

Negation implies that what is negated is not eternal. Therefore only that which is posterior to the eternal—and this without exception—can be negated. Accordingly negation of the eternity of being is impossible.

Nonbeing cannot of itself enter into being. But everything that is posterior to nonbeing has been produced from nonbeing not by nonbeing, but by being which is prior to nonbeing. If being came after nonbeing, it would have been produced by nonbeing or would have originated in nonbeing. But nothing comes from nothing.

Nevertheless, Being, the eternal being of the creator, contains nonbeing. Nonbeing is everything that can be. Because everything that exists is produced by eternal being from nonbeing and is still tainted with nonbeing as limitation, perishability, destructibility, this production is called "creation" —*creatio ex nihilo* (*De possest,* toward the end).

Retrospective.—The speculative impulse never comes to a stop. It continues to push beyond everything that can be said and defined in the saying —for everything utterable, every actual thought, is thereby finite. Even the infinite, once uttered and become an object of thought, has been made finite.

To carry out the transcending movement, we must think. When our mind has gone beyond the thinkable, it seems to us for a moment that we have arrived at the deepest insight, but then, once we have formulated it in words, we are disappointed and our impulse to go beyond is reawakened. Thus speculation is the means of finding the real goal, which lies far beyond all images, ciphers, definite ideas, the harbor where we can cast anchor and come to rest.

In all transcending thinking, we transcend only our ability to think. The transcendent remains ambiguous for us. For this reason, the modes of "beyondness" turn up time and again at crucial points in speculative thinking: beyond being (*plus quam ens*), beyond being and nothingness, beyond substance, beyond the one, in short beyond each successive conceptualization.

Only a very few terms seem for a moment to designate the absolute accurately enough to require no movement "beyond." The "infinite" is one of these; yet each successive form of a determined infinite is transcended as the mind moves toward an ever-receding infinite. The "itself" is another such term (Being as such, Capability as such, the Origin as such, the One as such), but this "as such" is more a pounding away at something that has

arrested our thinking than a fulfillment. In our ability to think, we remain
in relation to God and do not think God. When we call Him "Himself" we
do not think God Himself.

The "beyond" is meant to be more than a merely negative statement
about God. It carries us "further than" the "not" (God is not this and not
that). Hence the paradoxical expression: To know through nonknowledge.
In disregarding everything else, we come close enough to the transcendent
to touch it in some inconceivable way (and we touch it by thinking, not by
ecstasy and not by the mystical *unio,* not by abolishing the subject-object
dichotomy).

In transcending thinking we arrive at a point beyond all ciphers. Our
thinking outdoes itself. It is unseemly for thought to stammer, but not to
outdo itself in full lucidity and in so doing to become certain of itself and
of that which it seeks. In the extreme situations of human life, when Existenz
becomes actuality, we say "the rest is silence." Not so Nicholas of Cusa, a
Christian believer in revelation.

4. From speculative thinking to acceptance of Revelation

Cusanus addresses God: "I behold Thee . . . and I know not what I see,
for I see nothing visible" (*The Vision of God, op. cit.,* p. 58). Do such
meditations content him as assurances of the reality of God? God is real,
but in a unique, incomparable way, not like the real things in the world, not
as a hypothetically discovered reality, not as an object of thought. He is
"neither an abstraction of the discursive reason nor a blending with things"
(*De doc. ignor.,* II, 3). Is Cusanus brought closer to the reality of God
through thinking?

When we read his speculative texts, in which he operates with ideas
accessible to all men, borrowed from the philosophers of pagan antiquity,
it is possible to forget that they were written by a believing Christian.

Faith can scarcely be distinguished from speculation when he writes:
"It is not our task to get closer to the inaccessible." God Himself "turned
our faces toward Him so that we may seek Him most zealously." When
we do this, He discloses Himself to us in all His majesty (*De doc. ignor.,*
II, 13).

Whenever Cusanus comes across questions that resist investigation (e.g.,
immortality), he takes it for granted that no man can know such things
unless he has been instructed in them by God (*De doc. ignor.,* II, 12).

He leaves no doubt as to the direction of his speculations. When we have
attained the highest insight, freed from all representational images, when all
that exists has fallen away, we discover God as the One who cannot be
understood. Our mind catches a glimpse of Him in shadow or in fog,
in darkness. The speculative vision veils the hidden God in mystery. If

He Himself does not dispel the shadows with His light and reveal Himself, He remains totally unknown to those who would search for Him through intellectual insight. "All we have said amounts only to this, that we should like to understand how He surpasses all understanding." But the "vision which is so easy, and the only one that fills us with bliss"—the vision of that which surpasses all understanding—"was promised to all believers by the truth itself, the Son of God, if only we will follow in His footsteps and cleave to the path He showed us in His words and deeds" (*De possest,* end).

To Cusanus the content of his speculation coincides with the content of revealed faith as interpreted by the Church. To us this is ambiguous. In studying him we participate in a thinking which he intends to be universal, authentic, independent. Yet in nearly all his writings we come to a point in his reasoning—a point that is never so marked by him—where a sudden break occurs, and where independent thinking gives way to the contents of revelation.

As long as his philosophizing is related to age-old philosophical speculation, which Christianity calls pagan (though it is not pagan at all, but marks the highest refinement of speculative thinking), we recognize his greatness, especially where he expresses a new self-awareness of man. Viewed in the context of more than a thousand years of philosophy, his speculations are meaningful, quite apart from their references to Christ.

Now it is true that such speculations cannot, by their very nature, be self-resolving. What gives them their real weight and at the same time supplies their motive power comes from elsewhere. We are reminded of this by those of Cusanus' teachings in which we cannot follow him.

God (the eternal, the infinite, the One, He Himself) is "touched without being touched" in the course of speculation. He is experienced in the thinking of the human mind which understands itself as a mere image. He is seen in the world taken as the visible splendor of His invisibility. But the revelation through which God spoke in the flesh, as Christ, at a specific place and a specific time, is of crucial importance.

Revealed faith says: After the creation of the world, the "Origin" spoke in time, to the Jews ("Hear, O Israel, thy God is One") and to all men through Christ, the Logos. He was present in the flesh. To the question, Who art Thou? He answered: "Even the same that I said unto you from the beginning" (John 8, 25). Jesus says: "Then shall ye know that I am" (John 8, 28). Cusanus comments: Only he who owes his Being to himself can say truly, "I am" (*De princ.*).

But does the language out of the "Origin," which is Revelation, adequately express this Origin? No, for this language is human, not divine. In Cusanus' own words: "Human statements about the divine are inaccurate. But concerning that which Christ said about the divine in human language—since men can grasp it only in the human way—we must assume that the statements in the Gospels, which are couched in human terms, are more accurate than any others; for in them the word of God speaks about itself" (*De princ.,* 18).

5. *Example of a conceptualization of Revelation: the Trinity*

In nearly all of Cusanus' works, trinitarian thinking occupies a very important place. Now we shall try to determine what his starting points were in this connection, intuitively and conceptually, and discuss some of the recurrent figures he employs.

A. Unitas, aequalitas, connexio.—The greatest infinite One is triune. For oneness implies equality (with self) and the bond between oneness and equality (*unitas, aequalitas, connexio*). This inner articulation of the divine Being is to be thought of without recourse to "otherness." In this sense "equality" does not, for example, signify equality between two entities, a One and an Other, each equal to the other, but identity with self. Similarly, the bond between oneness and equality is not a bond between different things, but oneness itself.

We are thus asked to apply categories such as oneness and otherness, difference and equality, separation and combination, to that which is devoid of otherness, difference, or separation—in other words, to that which is rationally unthinkable. We are supposed to carry our thought into regions where thought cannot go, i.e., regions where we are not supposed to make distinctions. And yet we have constantly to do just this if we are to conceive a one that is not one, an equality that is not an equality between two, a nexus that does not link several entities.

This is expressed as follows: Oneness is anterior to the one and the other, and to the number one; equality is anterior to equality between different entities, also to inequality; the nexus is anterior to the act of linking. That which in graspable thinking is anterior or presupposed, is obtained again in transcending the domain of the thinkable, where all is otherness, distinction, and combination (*De doc. ignor.,* I, 7).

To conceive of a triune oneness we must transcend all concepts. We must renounce everything that comes from the senses, the imagination, and discursive reason, if we are to achieve the simplest, most abstract insight, namely, that all things are one. In terms of this insight, the highest One can be conceived only as triune (*De doc. ignor.,* I, 10).

B. *Why not four in one? The triangle.*—It might be asked: Why three in one, why not four or five in one? That the latter alternatives are out of the question is demonstrated with the help of a mathematical figure. The simplest element in any polygon is the triangle. The triangle is the smallest polygon: no polygon can have fewer sides. Since the smallest coincides with the greatest, the greatest polygon is the infinite triangle. It contains all polygons. The quadrangle is not the smallest polygon, and hence it cannot coincide with the absolutely greatest. The greatest triangle is the simple measure of all triune things (*De doc. ignor.*, I, 20).

The first figure is the triangle. All other figures can be reduced to it, but the triangle cannot be broken down into figures having two angles or one angle. "This shows that the beginning of mathematics is triune" (*De possest*). The origin is the simple. The simple is that which is not One any more than it is triune, and therefore is One. In the enigmatic image of the triangle it is seen as the triune God (*ibid.*).

c. *Number.*—It seems impossible that three should not be a number. "When anyone says one, one, one, he is saying one three times. . . . Yet he cannot say it three times without the number three, even if he does not name three. When he says one three times, he is repeating the same without numbering it, for to number it is to make the one other, but to repeat one and the same thing three times over is to make plurality without number." Therefore the plurality that is seen in God is a numberless three, an otherness without otherness, an otherness which is identity (*The Vision of God, op. cit.*, p. 83).

d. *How the Trinity is reflected in all things.*—As the Trinity, threeness is reflected in all things, and all things are reflected in it—objects, events, and activities.

The unity of cognition comprises the knower, the knowable, and knowledge. He who knows most is also he who is most knowable, and marks the highest degree of knowledge.

The trinity of love includes the lover, the lovable, and the bond between the lover and the lovable. Love is in essence triune (*The Vision of God*, chap. 17). What is experienced in finite love is experienced most fully in infinite love. The infinite capacity to love and the infinite capacity to be loved are one in the infinite bond of love. The triune God is perfect love.

e. *The Christian Trinity: Father, Son, Holy Spirit.*—Concepts do not come alive until they are visualized. There is no Trinity until we see it as God the Father, God the Son, and God the Holy Spirit.

God the Father begets the Son, and the Holy Spirit lives and breathes in them.

The Trinity comprises Him whose selfhood presupposes no ground, Him whose selfhood presupposes a ground, and Him who presupposes the two others.

The one God is all-powerful in the triad. He begets Himself in the Word (*logos*) which is the Son, in whom He sees Himself and all that can come into being through Him. The Holy Spirit is the bond between them and produces that which is love of God.

F. *Critical observations.*—We cannot fail to notice what deep satisfaction Cusanus derives from his recurrent trinitarian thinking. All we can ask is, why?

(1) Speculative conceptions lead to mental experiences, the test of which lies in their formal purity. We do not contest the possibility of such experiences (on the contrary: we believe them to be philosophically irreplaceable and to have been so ever since they made their first appearance in the West with Anaximander), but their truth is surely to be determined by a criterion which cannot be a fixed and universally valid standard. Where discursive reason breaks down, we have recourse to figures of thought which speak to us or remain empty or become distorted, and which one of these is the case can scarcely be decided on objective grounds. The crux of the matter is not correct reasoning but an existential act of appropriation, rejection, or transformation. Such an act does not have the universal validity of a rational statement. Only their existential repercussions endow such experiences with meaning.

Opposed to trinitarian thinking is the kind of philosophizing that forgoes any attempt to penetrate the inner life of transcendence. Such a penetration appears incompatible with the elucidation of Existenz in the area of ciphers. From the point of view of such elucidation, there is no transcendence in itself, but only transcendence for Existenz within the all-encompassing. An alleged "penetration" of transcendence results in a narrowing of Existenz. We must abandon such presumptuous attempts, which aim at more than man can achieve, if philosophy is to lead us to the broad horizons actually open to us. Trinitarian thinking signifies a limiting of man's capacity for experiencing transcendence.

(2) From the outset Cusanus' speculative trinitarian thinking is devoid of independent philosophical energy and leans on revealed faith, which in the Trinity created an uncommonly rich dogma of its mystery. Those who do not share this faith can only shrug their shoulders and acknowledge their inability to understand.

(3) The more Cusanus' thinking is directed toward the godhead as such, the more his philosophizing, like any other speculation, loses itself in the pure light produced by the breakdown of categories, a light in which there is nothing more to be seen. The moment representations, intuitions, conceptual constructions reappear, he is no longer concerned with the godhead but with God as viewed by man on the basis of experience in the world. Ideas, representations, images—i.e., guidelines—are always in danger of being inadvertently mistaken for God. God is thus hedged around with limitations, however magnificent these may seem as

ciphers. Then a point may be reached where, in the collapse of prevailing errors, men, drifting without guidance on the seas of perplexity, lose all notion of transcendence.

Cusanus' thinking discloses a world drenched in the brilliance of God; it does not succeed in drawing the hidden God out of His hiddenness, save in terms of the revelation in which Cusanus believes. His philosophical powers are no doubt more fully disclosed in his ideas about the world, which is illumined by his experience of transcendence. But the two belong together—his speculation on God and his speculation on the real world.

Cusanus' vision of the cosmos is simple, beautiful, and grandiose. We shall outline its main features.

II. THE WORLD

1. *The cosmos*

The relation between God and the world, as conceived by Cusanus, is dominated by this fundamental idea: The bottomless gulf between the infinite and the finite is bridged by the idea that the finite participates in the infinite. Plato speaks of participation (*methexis, participatio*), of how indefinite Becoming participates in the eternal Ideas. Participation means to be an image, i.e. to be informed by an Idea. Everything that the world is or that is in the world is, in so far as it is, an image of the original Form.

It is an age-old thought: The phenomena, said Anaxagoras, are what we see of the nonmanifest. All the sages agree, writes Cusanus, that the visible is in truth a part of the invisible. The Creator can be known from the creatures as in a mirror or as through a riddle, not through inference from the known to the unknown. Our gaze passes over the definiteness of the world and discovers the indefiniteness of original Being. Only to this gaze is the essence of the world itself disclosed.

The definite, and hence the limited and restricted—by virtue of the fact that it is, by virtue of what it is and how it comes into being—is a copy or image and participates in the original, which remains hidden even when it manifests its presence by the very fact that it is being copied.

All ideas about the relation between God and the world involve an insoluble difficulty. The principle: "There is no common measure between the finite and the infinite" (*finiti et infiniti nulla est proportio*) seems to exclude any link between the two. Between the infinite and the finite there is neither a measurable distance nor any transition. Between the eternal idea and Becoming there lies an unbridgeable gulf, whether we conceive of it with Plato as a "cut" (*tmēma*) or in terms of the Biblical *creatio ex nihilo*.

Must we, then, conclude that God's infinity and the cosmos of finite things are totally unrelated, one being above the other? The very fact that both are referred to in such a proposition introduces a minimal relationship into their unrelatedness. Cusanus' speculation is entirely focused on this relationship, in an effort to do justice to its reality.

The God-World relation cannot be conceived in the manner of a relation between finite things in the world nor yet as a relation between two worlds. The very category of relation, which is a category of discursive reason, must take on new meaning. With this category we arrive at a relation that cannot be compared with any relation in the world.

A. *Infinity of God and infinity of the world.*—The absolute infinity of God has its counterpart in the infinity of the world as an image. But how? Is not everything in the world finite? God's infinity and the world's finitude remain infinitely far apart.

The infinite God might have created an infinite world. But the world, because its possibility as such is not absolute, could not actually be infinite, could not be greater or other than it is. Since the limitation of its possibility originates in God and the limitation of its actuality in contingency, the world, which is necessarily limited, is finite through contingency (*De doc. ignor.*, II, 8).

This finiteness, however, has a special character in Cusanus. Ascent to the absolutely greatest or descent to the absolutely smallest is impossible. Rather, in relation to every given finite thing, there is always a greater or a smaller (*De doc. ignor.*, II, 1). This results in another kind of infinity of the finite world: we can always go further in the world. This is the endlessness of the world. God's infinity is the archetype, perfection as infinity. The infinity of the world is an image of God's infinity—it is mere endlessness.

Therefore the universe as a whole is neither finite nor infinite, but both at the same time. It is infinite in the sense that it cannot be greater than it is and hence is unlimited (*interminatum*). It cannot grow ever greater *in actu*. Nor is there anything actually greater that limits it. But it is finite in the sense that its actuality is restricted (*contracte*) (*De doc. ignor.*, II, 11).

The infinity of God is complete—"Thou, God, art the End of Thine own self" (*De vis. dei,* chap. XIII). The infinity of the world is incomplete, it has no end.—God is infinite because He is what He has. The world is endless because it is in a state of constant insufficiency. "The infinite source is absorbed only finitely, so that all created Being is in a sense a finite infinity" (*De doc. ignor.*, II, 2).

B. *The world as otherness* (alteritas).—Otherness consists of the one and the other (*alteritas constat ex uno et altero*). Oneness (*unitas*), however, is anterior to all otherness (*unitas natura prior est alteritate*). It is also called *unitas aeterna*. It is not a number. It is called the *non aliud* (the non-other), it is the godhead.

Discursive reason cannot conceive this oneness because it is bound to the one and the other. There is nothing outside this oneness. It is anterior to *alteritas,* hence *alteritas* is not its opposite. This "opposite"—without which discursive reason cannot conceive anything—is *unum et alterum* (the one and the other). The misleading expression (*unum et alterum* as the opposite of *unitas*) is linguistically unavoidable to discursive reason. Because discursive reason invariably thinks in terms of relations, it inquires into the relation between *unitas* and *alteritas,* and with this very inquiry leaves the plane of knowing nonknowledge, which is that of speculative thinking. Still, speculation is obliged to make use of the expressions it condemns.

The world is not Origin, but otherness. Nevertheless, each of its realities is related to the origin through which it is. It is image, copy, expression, representation, mirror, or whatever other name we may give this fundamental relation.

Related to the Origin, "the world perceived by the senses is a form of the world not perceived by the senses, and the temporal world is a form of the eternal and nontemporal world. The formed world is a copy of the unformable world." It is "form of the unformable and representation of the unrepresentable" (*De princ.,* 35).

The world is not the truth, but its origin is the truth. Therefore nothing in the created world is exactly true; the created world cannot grasp the truth in its exactness (*De princ.,* 37).

The world in its relation to the Origin is inconceivable to discursive reason. This is why discursive reason perceives only contradictions: the one origin from which all things receive their own nature "is neither different from them nor identical with them." The world's otherness seems completely separated from its origin and then again completely connected. Even though "the Creator is not identical with the creature, yet He is not so far removed as to be different." Cusanus quotes St. Paul (*De princ.*): God is "not far from every one of us: For in Him we live, and move, and have our being" (Acts 17, 27 f.).

The connection between otherness and the Origin is attested by oneness in otherness. The world is neither the absolute One nor the scattered Many. It is oneness in the manifold of infinite multiplicity and variety.

What is in the world, as well as the world itself, does not derive being from itself, but originates in the eternal One. The eternal One cannot impart a diminished Being. Hence, difference, multiplicity and the divisibility it entails, perishability and imperfection do not originate in the One or in any positive cause, but only in otherness and contingency. The more unity there is in created otherness, the more it resembles God (*De doc. ignor.,* II, 2).

The absolute oneness of God cannot, as such, be in the world. But all oneness of the world and in the world is a copy and originates in the Creator, whereas difference and multiplicity originate in otherness.

This line of argument starts from a graspable, definite sense, which is supplied in advance. What is first taken as a determination in the finite is then turned into a symbol and finally transcended toward indeterminability, whence we are expected to glimpse the infinity of authentic being and so gain insight into the metaphysical essence of the world. Such reasoning carries three implications. *First:* We cannot think anything without distinguishing between the one and the other. This fact becomes a symbol for the essence of the world as *alteritas* in relation to the Origin. *Second:* We think the oneness of a whole as the relation of the parts to a totality. This becomes a symbol for the absolute, intrinsically harmonious oneness, which has nothing outside itself. *Third:* We think the one as number. Just as the series of numbers is produced out of the one, so the multiplicity of things is produced out of oneness, and the world out of God. The one and the numbers become symbols for the production of the explicit from the implicit.

c. Complicatio *and* explicatio.—With the help of analogies, Cusanus elucidates the relation between God and the world in several ways.

In every case, this relation becomes ambiguous (when interpreted rationally), and true only when it is grasped in knowing nonknowledge. Thus the infinite is present in the finite and at the same time separated from it by an unbridgeable gulf. God is present in creation (immanent) and yet as Creator separate from His Creation (transcendent).

(1) Complicatio *and* explicatio.—Regardless of the gulf, Cusanus conceives the relation between God and the world as a relation between enfolding (*complicatio,* also *implicatio*) and unfolding (*explicatio*).

The infinite oneness is the enfolding of all things (*complicatio*). The world is unfolding (*explicatio*). God is enfolding in so far all things are in Him; He is unfolding in so far as He is in all things (*De doc. ignor.,* II, 3). The world of the finite makes explicit in multiplicity what is implicitly one in the infinite.

The notions of enfolding and unfolding occur in several analogies. One is the number from which all numbers are unfolded; the point is the one from which lines, surfaces, and bodies are unfolded; rest is the enfolding of which motion is the unfolding; the now is the enfolding of time, from which the successive moments in time are unfolded; identity is the enfolding of difference (*ibid.*).

Just as the One, the point, rest, the now, identity, enfold that which is produced from them, so from the absolute oneness of the infinite is unfolded the manifold of the finite.

(2) *Absolute and contracted.*—The absolute of the godhead reappears as the contractedness or concreteness (*contractum seu concretum*) of the world. God is absolute Being, the world is contracted Being. Because this concrete world receives from the absolute everything it is, everything that is predicated absolutely of the absolute must be predicated of the contracted contractedly (*De doc. ignor.,* II, 4). Everything that is said of the absolute may also be said of the world, but in an entirely different sense: thus the

infinity of the world is "contracted" (*infinitas contracta*). The absolutely greatest becomes the contracted greatest, the eternal becomes the endless duration of the one-after-the-other, the simple the totality of a compound, the one the unity of the many, identity the equality of the different.

(3) *The one God and the universe.*—Because there can be only one God, there can also be only one world. God, as the simplest One, is in the one world. He is, as it were, at the center of the world, in all things, and things in their multiplicity are through the mediation of the one world in God (*De doc. ignor.*, II, 4).

(4) *On the meaning of analogies as guidelines.*—Here as throughout Cusanus' work, analogies are guidelines, not cognitions. They serve to make the unintelligible intelligibly communicable. The how of this enfolding and unfolding is beyond discursive reason. We cannot understand how the multiplicity of things is produced by the divine mind, since God is the infinite oneness. God seems to be multiplied, as it were, in things, and yet it is impossible that the infinite and supreme One should multiply itself (*De doc. ignor.*, II, 3).

D. *Degrees:* (1) *Cusanus rejects the traditional view of a hierarchically ordered cosmos with intermediate beings.*—The idea of the cosmos as a hierarchy of beings, suggested by Plato and fixated by Aristotle, was current throughout the Middle Ages. The earth is the center; ascending from the sublunary sphere one attains to the spheres of the moon and the planets, then to the pure celestial spheres of the fixed stars, and finally to the Paradise of the godhead; descending one arrives in the interior of the earth, in Hell. Dante gave the most beautiful picture of this hierarchically ordered cosmos in his poem describing his journey "down" into the innermost circle of Hell, and then "up" again through each successive sphere to Paradise. This view of the cosmos divided into layers, inhabited by intermediate beings in a gradual progression from the world to God, was rejected by Cusanus in his speculation. He presents a radically different picture:

(a) At every level we remain in the world; the different modes of being and modes of cognition relate not to the cosmos but to our existence in the world.

(b) The cosmos is infinite. It has no center. The earth, or sublunary sphere, and the celestial bodies are not ordered hierarchically according to their nobility and purity. The cosmos is homogeneous.

(c) We are constantly soaring toward God or falling away from Him, but we are "immediate to God"—there is no mediation. There is only a leap over the unbridgeable gulf: the gulf between God and all created things. This conception, which has been recurrent from Plato down to the present, allows the question, What is man? to be answered in accordance with man's existential answer to another question, Does he live in awareness of this leap, or does it not exist for him?

This sharp distinction between God and the world, the infinite and the finite, leaves room for no intermediate beings. Cusanus speaks of angels and demons in the traditional way, but as existing within creation, not as intermediate beings between man and God.

(2) *Levels of God's creation.*—Rejecting the hierarchically ordered cosmos does not imply rejection of the idea of levels or degrees. In creating the world, God created the levels of being in the world. No individual thing can be all things, for then it would be God. Consequently God created levels to which all things are assigned (*De doc. ignor.*, II, 5). Every created thing is held to be perfect in its kind, that is, according to its place in the hierarchy of beings. The world is one. Nothing is separate, everything falls within the system. Hence nothing is superfluous, everything is part of the whole which could not exist without this multiplicity.

Development in the world leads to progress *ad infinitum*. Only between God's infinity and the imitative endlessness of the world is there an unbridgeable gulf, not within the world. But within the world, it is only in relation to God's infinity that all things are seen in their proper proportions, at their right places, in hierarchical orders.

(3) *Levels of reality.*—Cusanus puts forward several hierarchical schemata. They do not contradict one another, but they vary the picture. Examples:

(a) The ascending series begins with elemental matter, existence without order, chaos. The minerals represent a somewhat more highly ordered stage. Then comes organic growth, and within it, living creatures endowed with senses, the faculty of representation, reason, and intellect (this is the highest level, for it is the closest image of the eternal wisdom) (*De sap.*, I).

(b) The series: God, intellect, soul, body (*De con.*, I, 6). Here the schema is as follows: God: beyond the opposites, Truth itself; mind: intellect and discursive reason, the oppositions of reason transcended in the intellect; soul: unfolding of the unity of the intellect and reflection in it; bodies: the final unfolding which no longer contains anything else.

The schema of the soul is as follows: As the light of intelligence descends into the dark realm of sensibility and sensibility ascends to it, two intermediate stages between the two are produced in discursive reason (*ratio*): the faculty of comprehension, which is closer to the intellect, and the faculty of imagination, which is closer to the senses. Thus we obtain the four elements of the human soul. Their truth lies solely in the whole (*De con.*, II, 16).

Sensibility apprehends only sensory data, but in a confused way; it does not discriminate (even in connection with sensory data this is done by discursive reason); it does not negate, for to negate is to distinguish; it merely asserts the presence of sensory data, but it does not assert this or that. Discursive reason uses sensibility as a tool (*De con.*, I, 10).

(c) The schema of the real world is presented in the form of an image: Two pyramids (one on a base of oneness, the other on a base of otherness) interpenetrate so that the apex of each touches the base of the other. On one side is light, on the other darkness. Or: The world is situated between God and nothingness. This image shows that the progression of oneness into otherness is simultaneously a progression in the opposite direction, from otherness into oneness. The two contrary movements are disclosed in every existent in the world, in all things. A realm of light and a realm of shadows interpenetrate (*De con.*, I, 11 f.).

(d) *General notions.*—The world is concrete in the changing individual entities that come into being and pass away, and abstract as the plurality of general notions (categories, universals). The human mind produces these abstractions as instruments by which to approach the cognition of things. This immense domain of the general is a creation of the mind, but as such it has a timelessness of its own. It has no intrinsic reality, but remains within the human mind between the absolute actuality of God and the actuality of individuals, which is the only real actuality in the world (*De doc. ignor.*, II, 6).

E. *Motion in the world.*—Nothing in the world can be devoid of movement; all things share in the movement of being or of thinking. Cusanus distinguishes three kinds of movement: *First,* the ever-present circular movement starting with absolute oneness, descending through all beings in the world, down to the levels of intellectual, rational, and sensory nature, and then back to absolute oneness. In this movement the light of the supreme heights reaches down to the lowest, darkest depths. As we ascend to the successive levels, we find everywhere some residue of darkness, though less and less as we ascend, until it is entirely dissolved in the utter purity and radiance of God (*De con.*, I, 11 f.). Thus there is a two-way movement in the reality of the world.—*Second,* the rectilinear movement in the production of the other, which never turns back upon itself.—*Third,* a movement of inner tension and opposition: "A natural impulse and a contingent impulse goad and drive each other on, so that we have uninterrupted production and destruction, production of the one being, destruction of the other" (*De con.*, II, 7).

Motive power permeates the entire universe. This power is called nature. Cusanus calls the movement of the universe a created spirit, without which nothing is unity, nothing can subsist. This movement brings about the loving union of all things. No individual thing moves entirely like any other, but each in its own way shares in movement, so that we have one universe (*De doc. ignor.*, II, 10).

F. *Why existence? The idea of the Creation.*—Cusanus never asks, Why is there anything at all, why is God? Rather, he asks, Why is the world? Imitation, otherness, enfolding and unfolding, levels of reality—all these notions are attempts to grasp what the world is. From this follows the question: Why is the world? The answer is the idea of the Creation.

The idea of the Creation is itself a metaphor. God conceived in eternity the idea that he would create. Since nothing had yet been created, He could have created something else that we cannot conceive. "The eternal divine mind, with perfect freedom to create or not to create, to create in this way or in another way, determined His own omnipotence from eternity, according to His will" (*De ven. sap.*, 27).

Seen in rational terms as the divine will pursuing an end, the act of Creation may be interpreted roughly as follows: God creates the world out of kindness, because He wants to be generous; or He does so in order to see Himself in His creations and to be seen by the created intellect; or in order to glorify and exalt His own eternity.

Elsewhere, when the metaphors express absence of purpose, the creation of the world is conceived as the unfolding of that which is enfolded. In this process "the concrete infinity descends in an infinite way (incommensurably) from the absolute. The whole universe was brought into being by an emanation of the concrete greatest from the absolute greatest, and this applies to all beings that are parts of the universe as well as to the universe itself" (*De doc. ignor.*, II, 4). In another context Cusanus describes the emanation in the manner of Plotinus, as a flow toward the world and back from the world: "In the absolute One is the beginning of the flowing out and the end of the flowing back; in the sensory one the end of the flowing out and the beginning of the flowing back coincide."

All such images must be discarded when the unbridgeable gulf between God and the world, between infinity and finitude, is resolutely asserted in keeping with Cusanus' fundamental idea. Here we interpret his meaning as follows: Because the world does not flow (emanate) from God, does not develop from Him, it is not, as world, a process of the godhead. God is not the seed from which the world grows, God is not a God in process of development. Rather, the world, as a creation, is endlessly changing in time, cutting across time but oriented toward God as an image to its original. It is always turned toward the original in its endless movement, and yet it is always the same and always a new reality. The world itself, as change, is not a development in time with a beginning and an end. Its existence remains essentially the same from the Creation to the end of the world. The ciphers of the Creation and the end of the world are an intimation of the timeless actuality of the infinite eternity, in which all temporality, which has neither beginning nor end in time, is transcended.

G. *Noncomprehension and further examples of the incomprehensible.*— Reason does not comprehend things that lie beyond the domain of the finite. Our noncomprehension is manifested in conceptions that are absurd from the point of view of discursive reason. But by apprehending these absurdities, reason prepares a springboard from which we are enabled to attain the other kind of comprehension.

The nature of the world (of the concrete, *contractionis*) cannot be known unless the absolute original is known. Not only in our knowledge of God, but also in our knowledge of the world, we must never lose sight of a non-comprehension which lies within our comprehension (*De doc. ignor.,* II). Discursive reason cannot comprehend such matters as the following:

(1) God is totally free from ill-will (*invidia*), and yet the beings He created disclose such features as divisibility, difference, plurality, imperfection, perishability. Whence do these come? They cannot have a positive cause. They have no cause at all, but are contingent (*contingenter*). But who can comprehend the Creation, if it must be conceived at the same time as necessary and as contingent? Created beings, which are neither God nor nothing, seem to be situated somewhere between God and nothingness. Yet they cannot be compounded of being and nonbeing. Thus it seems that they neither are nor are not. Discursive reason, which cannot transcend opposites, does not grasp the being of created things (*De doc. ignor.,* II, 2). "All we can say is: The plurality of things is produced by the fact that God is in nothingness" (*De doc. ignor.,* II, 3).

(2) If God is all things, how can we conceive that created beings are not eternal, since God's being is eternity itself? In so far as creation is the being of God, it is eternity, but in so far as it is subject to time, it is not of God. Who can comprehend that creation is from eternity and nevertheless in time? (*De doc. ignor.,* II, 2.)

(3) Who can comprehend how God can be revealed to us through visible creatures? God cannot be manifested in concrete signs, for such signs inevitably require other signs to explain their meaning, and so on *ad infinitum.*

(4) Who can comprehend how the infinite One becomes multiple or how God unfolds Himself in the plurality of things? If you consider God in so far as He is in things, you imagine that things are something in which He is. But this is an error, because the being of a thing is not a separate being, but is derived from the being of the Greatest. Without God things are nothing, just as number is nothing without the One. How God enfolds things in Himself and unfolds them is beyond our understanding (*De doc. ignor.,* II, 3).

2. Cosmological ideas

A. *Image of the infinite. Center and periphery.*—The old metaphor "God is an infinite sphere whose center is everywhere and whose periphery is nowhere" is not an analogy applied to the world, but an apt description of its imitative character.

Because the cosmos is an image, it is infinite, but its infinity is of the imitative kind, which denotes endlessness, the possibility of always going further. In time, eternity is endless duration. In space, the infinite is the endless; in the division of matter, it is the impossibility of ever arriving at the smallest part. Neither the greatest nor the smallest, neither the most distant boundary in space nor the smallest particle of matter, neither the beginning nor the end in time is accessible to us. When we conceive of the world as having been created simultaneously with time, we speak metaphorically of a beginning and an end *of* time, not *in* time. The cosmos is not infinite in the same sense as God, nor can it be conceived as finite, since no boundaries confine it.

Thus the cosmos has no center and no periphery. If it had a periphery, it would be bounded by something else. If it had a center, it would also have a periphery, which it does not have. If the cosmos had a center and a periphery, it would have its beginning and end in itself; outside it there would be something else, empty space, for example. As a copy, the cosmos cannot be contained between a center and a periphery. For God alone is both the center and the periphery.

The earth is not the center of the world and the fixed stars do not constitute the periphery of the physical cosmos. Neither the earth nor any other place is the center of the cosmos.

B. *Measure, motion, direction are relative.*—Every measure is relative: in the world, measure and the measured are necessarily different. But there is no absolute measure, and because there is no absolute measure, no measurements are completely accurate. Astronomy makes the false assumption that the movements of all planets can be measured by the movement of the sun. But no two points are exactly congruent in time and space, hence our judgments about the celestial bodies are far from accurate (*De doc. ignor.,* II, 1).

Every motion is relative. No motion can be the absolutely greatest, because that coincides with rest. Everything in the cosmos must be in motion, though not uniformly so. There are no fixed poles of the sky. "Since we can perceive motion only in relation to something motionless, to a pole or to a center, we (falsely) presuppose the latter when we measure motions."

Every direction is relative. Wherever a man stands, he believes himself to be at the center. The antipodes have the sky above them, just as we have. But what is "above" to the one is "below" to the other.

C. *The earth.*—And now our own planet, the earth. Since everything in the cosmos is in motion, obviously the earth too is in motion (*De doc. ignor.,* II, 11). Because nothing in the world is mathematically exact, "the earth is not spherical, although it tends to a spherical form."

Since in the world there is no greatest single perfection, motion, or form—for the world is the oneness of the many, homogeneous in space and time, and no place in it is superior to any other (i.e. it is not the hierarchical cosmos of Aristotle, Ptolemy, and the Middle Ages)—it follows that "this earth is not in any sense the smallest or lowest part of the world" (*De doc. ignor.,*

II, 12). Nor is the earth's darkness a proof of its inferiority. If we were on the sun, we should not perceive the sun's great brightness, for the brightness would be above us, as the region of fire is for us. If we were outside the earth, we should perceive it as a bright star. "The earth is a noble star, which receives light, heat, and influences from all the other stars." But these influences are not evidence of its imperfection, because, being a star, it in turn influences the sun. The influence is reciprocal. No star can subsist without the others. The earth is as adequate a dwelling place for men, animals, and plants as the other stars are for the living beings which inhabit them. "We conjecture that no star is uninhabited."

What Cusanus calls "the world" is not just the world that is visible to us. The one world contains many worlds invisible to us. We imagine that all things refer to us and exist for us. But countless stars, far greater than the earth we inhabit, have not been created just for this earth, but for the glory of their Creator. The philosophers fail to grasp this when they interpret everything solely from the point of view of the world visible to ourselves, as if this earthly world were the crown and summit of all God's works (*De ven. sap.*, 22).

D. *The smallest parts.*—The infinite is present also in the smallest. "We cannot arrive at the demonstrably simplest elementary units, which are entirely *in actu,* because there is no absolutely Greatest or Smallest in respect of the gradually different, even though discursive reason believes that such exist" (*De con.*, I, 12).

The term "element" does not denote the same thing to the senses, to discursive reason, and to the intellect. What the senses regard as the elements (fire, earth, water, air) are, to discursive reason, composite (*elementata*), universal first products of the elements. "What sensibility holds to be an element, is to discursive reason a composite, and what reason regards as an element, the intellect regards as a compound" (*De con.*, II, 4).

3. *The eternity of the world*

The world is eternal, but it is not eternity itself. It is eternal by virtue of its participation in eternity. "The eternal world" is the world that cannot end, that endures forever.

The world did not begin in time, but time began with it. Hence we can say both that the world has a beginning and that the world has no beginning. For the world was not preceded by time, but by eternity (the term "preceded" has no temporal connotation here). The world is neither eternal absolutely, of itself, nor has it a beginning in time. Time itself has no beginning in time.

Cusanus carries this formulation still further. Time has its ground in the world, not the world in time. The "duration" of the world does not depend on time. For when the motion of the sky and time ceases, the world does not cease to be. But if the world came to an end, time too would come to an end (*De ludo globi,* I).

The following statement by Meister Eckhart had been declared heretical: "When God was and when He begat His Son, who is as eternal as Himself and equal to Him in everything, at the same time He created the world as well." Cusanus defends Eckhart's position.[1] God and the world were in the same now of eternity. For the world did not begin in another now of eternity, but in the same now in which God is. "The assertion, Eternity is, was never true unless the assertion, The world is, was true at the same time."

Such formulations—like all speculative thought—are absurd to discursive reason, because the representations which unavoidably guide such thinking cannot be visualized. We speak in terms of time, although the things we speak of cannot be represented under the category of time. This is made evident by the questions which discursive reason, unguided by speculation, asks:

Where was God before He created the world? The question is absurd because it presupposes a time and place when they did not yet exist. The appropriate answer is: God never "was" anywhere; "was" is a statement about existence in time. Why did God not create the world earlier? The question makes no sense, for "earlier" and "later" designate differences in time; accordingly, He could never have created anything "earlier" or "later."

Such questions are suggested by the terms we use to express our rational representations. The proper way to deal with them is not by condemning them as "foolish" or "blasphemous," but by systematically elucidating the speculative mode of thinking.

4. Individuals

Only individuals really exist (*De doc. ignor.,* III, 1).

A. *Necessary particularity.*—Every existent thing in the world differs from every other existent thing; we find no two or more individual things so alike that they might not be infinitely more alike. Absolute identity between them is impossible (*De doc. ignor.,* I, 3). "No entity can be entirely identical with any other entity at any one time" (*ibid.*). "There is nothing in the universe that does not enjoy a certain singularity, which is not to be found in any other being" (*ibid.*).

---

[1] Josef Koch, *Sitzung der Heidelberger Akademie der Wissenschaften, Cusanus Texte* I. *Predigten.* 1937, pp. 51 ff.

B. *Every individual is the whole of the universe.*—The world is one, and one in such a way that everything is in everything. In every created thing, the universe is that created thing. The universe exists "concretely" (*contracte*) in every individual thing.

Each thing is the whole world in a limited form, as participation in the whole, as mirror of the whole, as drawn into the whole by interaction. "All things are in all things, and each thing in each thing" (*De doc. ignor.,* II, 5). Since the universe is concretely in things, each actually existing thing is a concrete representation of the universe. To his friend, Cusanus says: "Everything universal, general, and special 'Julianizes' in you, Julian, just as harmony 'flutes' in the flute, and 'cithers' in the cither" (*De con.,* II, 3). Since each individual existent cannot actually be all things, because it is limited, it limits all things in itself.

Like the universe as a whole, each individual is immediate to God (*De doc. ignor.,* II, 5). God turns His face to every individual. Cusanus illustrates this idea by referring to the self-portrait of Rogier van der Weyden, which seems to be looking directly at the viewer no matter where he stands, and to follow him with its eyes wherever he moves; even when several viewers move in different directions, the eyes of the portrait still seem to be looking at each of them. Similarly, God gazes upon all beings simultaneously and sees each of them in particular (*De vis. dei,* Preface).

C. *Uniqueness and irreplaceability.*—Every created thing is as such perfect in its own way, even though it may seem inferior or superior in relation to another created thing. "Since God communicates Being, which is received in such a way that it could not have been received otherwise, every created being rests in the perfection it received from divine Being, and does not desire to be another creature, as though it could thus attain to a higher perfection, but prefers the being it received from the Greatest as a gift of the godhead, which it strives to preserve without impairment and to bring yet closer to perfection" (*De doc. ignor.,* II, 2). Everyone is pleased with himself, though he admires others. "In his homeland, his own birthplace seems by far the most beautiful place and the same is true of local customs and the local dialect" (*id.,* III, 1). "Each actually existing thing finds its peace in this, that everything in it is itself, and itself in God" (*id.,* II, 5).

The human spirit cannot desire to be angelic, because the human spirit cannot desire not to be. "Since he cannot be another spirit unless he ceases to be what he was, his desire is enclosed in his being. Therefore he not only does not desire to be different, but is happy in that he cannot be different. Indeed, to have one's own being means to have being by participating in the divine" (*Exc.,* Basel edition, p. 696). Hence Cusanus exclaims in one of his sermons: "Take, O man, all things that come your way as the gift of God and speak in admiration. . . . God gave me Being. . . . I, who was nothing, am through His omnipotence that which I am. . . . He has left me weak and sickly in order to display His strength. He has let me fall into sin in order to show me His mercy" (quoted in Billinger, pp. 43 ff.).

5. Summary: The significance of Cusanus' world

A. *The earth no longer the center of the world.*—The case of Cusanus proves that removal of the earth from the center of the world did not necessarily shake Christian faith. Actually, the new view originated in a change, consistent with the Christian faith, in the traditional ideas about the created world.

Nietzsche wrote: "Since Copernicus has removed the earth from the center of the world, man has found himself, as it were, on an inclined plane; he has been rolling ever faster away from the center—whither? into nothingness?" But what has the position of the earth in the cosmos to do with man's position in Being? Nothing at all, unless he is subject to the superstition that God is present in the flesh—a superstition which, to be sure, has deep historical roots.

By his thinking adherence to the Christian faith, Cusanus shows us that the shifting of the earth from its central position (Cusanus believed the center to be everywhere and nowhere) does not affect the position of man, for man is still aware of his place in the totality of Being. Long before Copernicus, Cusanus undermined the idea that the earth is the center, and did so far more radically than the astronomer. (Copernicus still believed the sun to be the center, not only of the solar system, but also of the cosmos.) At the same time, however, Cusanus, unlike Nietzsche, saw man in his unique greatness, as not in the least diminished by this change.

In Nietzsche the astronomical conception becomes the symbol of an entirely different and very important experience: that of an existential nihilism which has been steadily growing in modern times under the cover of superficially retained traditions. The idea that astronomical and other scientific discoveries determine man's faith instead of serving him by broadening the horizons of his knowledge presupposes a general intellectual flattening. But in Cusanus we are dealing with ideas which from the outset transcend the narrow-mindedness that chains men to matter, to a material cosmos, and to technical skill.

B. *The infiniteness of the world.*—(1) Toward the close of the Middle Ages, for the first time since Greek antiquity (whose example had been forgotten), Cusanus broke with a finite conception of the world, such as we find expressed with poetic eloquence in Dante's poem. Only gradually, with Copernicus, Kepler, Galileo, Newton, and Einstein, did empirical science follow up this radical speculative break-through.

The modern conception of the world as infinite is of religious origin; it can be traced back to the idea of an infinite God. The created world came to be seen as the copy of God's infinity, as another, "limited" kind of infinity. The infinite greatness of God required the infinite greatness of the world.

Cusanus does not develop his conception in the spirit of scientific research, which leads us inevitably to abandon all efforts to grasp the world as a whole, in favor of the critical cognition of reality. Nor is Cusanus related to Giordano Bruno, who looked upon the world's infinity as an absolute, and identified the infinite world with God.

(2) It has been said that Cusanus' idea of the infinite was the first expression of the modern sense of life—that its impact has been felt for centuries, that Giordano Bruno, Baroque art, the Romantic movement, all drew inspiration from it. Because this view confuses two radically different ideas of infinity, it is so vague as to be meaningless. It disregards the presence of the idea of infinity in the Middle Ages, even, for example, in Dante's seemingly finite conception of the world. Moreover, Copernicus did not operate with the concept of the infinite; he remained within the Aristotelian-Ptolemaic framework of a finite world.

(3) To be captivated by the infinite can mean two different things. In the world, it is the impulse to go ever further, beyond every limit. It signifies a progress that refuses to stop anywhere. To be captivated by the infinite is something entirely different when the idea inspires us to ascend from the finite to the infinite, from the given world to that which is prior to or above the world, from the awareness that we are chained in the finite (and we remain so fettered even when we progress endlessly within the world) to freedom in the infinite. Cusanus glimpses the infinite in the finite, in that which the finite presupposes: this "pre" is the absolute measurement, the condition of every finite measurement. It becomes possible to experience God's absolute infinity in the world itself, when God's infinity is seen as the original of the imitative endlessness of the world.

The fundamental attitude of insatiable curiosity in finite progress is not abandoned, but placed in a higher perspective. The fundamental attitude of a life in the infinite becomes a guide over the roads and pathways we find in the world, which lead endlessly in all directions. While essentially different, progress and spiritual aspiration must be combined if progress is to be a path upward rather than a servitude.

(4) The fundamental human situation implies both the urge to the infinite, which draws man on ever further toward penetration of the ground of being, and the urge to the finite, in which he feels more secure because he is at home. Both are ciphers for man's openness to transcendence, but cease to be so when they lead to mere endlessness or imprison man in the worldly finite.

Progress in the conquest of the cosmos is ambiguous. Is it—as in

Dante's Ulysses—hubris and sacrilege, or is it a heroic effort to a break through to authentic humanity? This is a question Cusanus does not ask.

c. *The impossibility of a closed world.*—In terms of worldly knowledge, the world cannot be closed in. Cusanus does away with every fixed point in it, every variety of the absolute. To those who strive for a graspable picture of a finite world, Cusanus shows the relative character of all knowable worldly things. Through intellect we gain the insight "that it is impossible to circumscribe the world, to assign to it motion or figure, because it will appear to us a circle within a circle, or a sphere within a sphere, having nowhere center or circumference" (*De doc. ignor.*, II, 11).

d. *The splendor of the world.*—God made the world as perfect as it could be. Therefore it is very perfect (*De ludo globi*). Though it is an image, the world is illumined by the splendor of God.

"In God is everything, outside Him nothing." He alone is "center and circumference of the universe." Hence we know the world only in God and in relation to God. Just as the splendor of the world, though it is only an image, celebrates God's splendor, so our knowledge of the world is a true reflection of God's own knowledge.

I know that the world is very beautiful "because it reflects the highest goodness, the wisdom, and the beauty of the most high God" (*De ven. sap.*, 2). Cusanus refers to the Greek *kosmos*. The world originates in the ineffable eternal beauty. The world is the making visible of the invisible God. The world unveils its Creator, so that He can be known as in a mirror, as in a riddle (*De possest*).

God wills "that the marvels of the universe should move us to admiration. Yet the more we admire them, the more He conceals them from us." No created being has the power to manifest what it really is, for without Him who is in all beings, any one being is nothing. Asked what and why and for what they are, created beings can only answer: "We are nothing by ourselves, nor can we answer your question, for by ourselves we have no knowledge of ourselves. We are all mute. He who created us speaks in all of us, He alone knows what, how, and for what we are. You who seek to know something about us, ask the ground of our being, not ourselves" (*De doc. ignor.*, II, 13).

e. *The individual.*—Cusanus discovers the great, simple, transcendent justification for each individual's right to an irreplaceable value, a unique essence, a role in life—the right to be the particular individual he is. Every individual may love himself and must necessarily love every other individual when he sees him as he really is. For the universe is in every individual, each of whom is, as it were, a copy of one of God's words.

III. CHRIST

A. *Christ and the world.*—By giving Christ the privileged position of a God incarnate, Cusanus vitiates his conception of the world as a plurality of individuals, none of whom is the absolutely greatest, none supremely perfect. He expounds in speculative terms what in fact is merely his dogmatic belief. If the concretely greatest exists, he reasons, it must be something more than concrete. If the concretely greatest were an individual, this individual would have to contain all truth and reality within himself in supreme perfection. He would have to transcend all concreteness, to be its climax, limit, end (*terminus*). Neither would he be purely concrete, for he would be more, namely, God, nor, in so far as he is concrete, would he be God. He would be simultaneously concrete and absolute, creature and creator in one. Such a combination is entirely beyond our rational powers of comprehension.

B. *How the essence of the Man-God is misunderstood.*—According to Cusanus, it would be false to conceive of the Man-God as the union of two persons which had been separate before and are now united, Man and God. He could not be a union at all, for He is a self-contained individual person. "This marvelous union is more sublime than all thinkable unions. Therefore we must conceive of this concretely greatest as God, but at the same time creature, and as creature but at the same time Creator, Creator and creature, without admixture or composition. Such a union is beyond all our concepts" (*De doc. ignor.*, III, 2).

It would also be false, according to Cusanus, to conceive of Jesus Christ merely as a man outstanding in certain respects, more accomplished than other men, as Solomon surpassed all in wisdom, Absalom in beauty, Samson in strength. Since, in respect of accomplishment, the variety of points of view produces different judgments, "accomplishment" in this sense receives praise from one point of view and blame from another. And since the majority of men, scattered throughout the world, are unknown to us, we cannot say who is the most excellent of all. We are not even in a position to gain complete knowledge of a single one of them (*De doc. ignor.*, III, 1).

C. *God as man.*—Since mankind (*humanitas*) could not in supreme perfection exist in any other way, Christ's humanity (also called *humanitas*) must be rooted in divinity. The perfect, actually existing rational being, Jesus Christ, can be rooted only in the divine intellect, which alone is all things in actuality. Since the supreme intellect marks the culmination (*terminus,* limit, end) of all intellectual nature, it must, like God, be all in all.

This very greatest, which is man and God in one, can only be one—can only be one man. For were He not unique, He would not be the greatest.

This one man, who is God, possessed a body appropriate to His spirituality. He was not begotten in the natural way. The Holy Spirit, which is absolute love, formed a living body out of the Virgin's blood. The Mother of God was necessarily free from whatever might have impaired the purity of such a birth: she had never known a man and she was free from carnal desire.

The one Man-God is a physical event in time. He is historical. But He is also eternal. "The man could come forth from the virgin mother only in time, from God the Father only in eternity!" (*De doc. ignor.,* III, 5).

But the temporal birth required a special time: "the fullness of time." When this time came, the Man-God was born, but He remained hidden as such from all creatures.

What we call the immaculate conception and nativity "was not effected in temporal sequence, as in the case of human conception, but in a single moment of supra-temporal activity" (*De doc. ignor.,* III, 5).

D. *Why did all this take place?*—God enveloped the eternal Logos, the word, His only-begotten Son, in human nature, because we could grasp Him only in a form resembling our own. Thus He revealed Himself to us in accordance with our capacity to receive Him (*De doc. ignor.,* III, 5).

Two mysteries are associated with this revelation of God in Jesus Christ—that of the Cross and that of the Resurrection.

The Death on the Cross. "The smallest coincides with the greatest, the most ignominious death of the righteous with the glory of everlasting life" (*De doc. ignor.,* III, 6).

And: "The voluntary and so undeserved, cruel and ignominious death of the man Christ on the Cross, was the eradication, gratification, and purification of all the carnal desires of human nature."

For each man this means: the closer he comes to perfection through steadfastness and courage, through love and humanity, the closer he comes to Christ. "In the real Christian there is in fact only Christ." The Christian must put behind him all the things of this world. "In such withdrawal into himself he sees Christ without recourse to enigmatic images, because then he sees himself in detachment from the world, as one who has taken on the form of Christ" (*De possest*).

The Resurrection (*De doc. ignor.,* III, 7): Christ died in order that human nature might be raised with Him from the dead to life everlasting, in order that the mortal body might become an indestructible spiritual body.

Immortality can be attained only through death and the overcoming of death in the Resurrection. If Christ, as God, had never died, He would have remained mortal. Had He never died, He would not have been able to win immortal life for human nature. Consequently, He had to be freed from the possibility of death through death itself. Only through the Resurrection did immortality become real.

In its temporal manifestation, the truth is symbol and image of the supra-temporal truth. The humanity of Jesus was destructible since it was confined to time; it was indestructible in so far as it was freed from time, above time, united with the godhead.

No man could be raised from the dead before Him, because human nature had not yet attained its highest point (*ad maximum*) in time. No one was capable of this until the advent of Him who said: "I have the power to give my life and to take it back." Because Christ rose from the dead, having undergone the full course of destruction in time, all men are assured through Him of everlasting life—though not all will share in the glory of the godhead, but only those who share in Christ through faith, hope, and love (*De doc. ignor.*, III, 8).

Part Three: Nicholas of Cusa and Modern Science

Among the precursors of modern science were the Paris nominalists, the Italian artists (such as Leonardo) who made discoveries in their workshops, the astronomer Copernicus, etc. One of the founders of modern historical science was Lorenzo Valla, who proved the spuriousness of the so-called Donation of Constantine. Ought we to place Cusanus among such pioneers? He never carried out a systematic empirical investigation, he never made a single real discovery. To this extent he has no place in the history of any one science. Nor was he interested in a universal scientific method, such as eventually came into being. But he occasionally had penetrating insights and put forward tentative hypotheses. Above all, he developed aspects of speculative thought which can, in retrospect, be related to modern scientific theories. Finally, he broached the fundamental problem of the meaning of science, a problem which has continued to haunt us down to the present day—which, indeed, has only today become really urgent.

1. Did Cusanus help to found modern science?

A. *Natural science: experiments with scales.*—Only one work of Cusanus', the *De staticis experimentis* ("Experiments with Scales"), contains no speculative or theological discussion. This treatise is commonly regarded as scientific. The leading idea is that systematic, uniform methods of determining weights should be devised. Everything that can be weighed should be weighed, either directly on scales or by indirect methods. Once the weights have been determined, comparison of the results will permit inferences to be drawn concerning things that otherwise remain hidden. This will prove useful in practical matters—in medical diagnosis, for example, for testing the genuineness of materials, for investigating the elements of matter.

This sounds scientific; but let us look into the matter more closely. Cusanus urges that extensive tables of weights be drawn up for purposes of comparison. He proposes a number of experiments to this end, some practically feasible, others fantastic. One thing is clear: these descriptions of experiments are not the work of a man who handled real things. They do not reflect the ideas of a man who thought with his hands. In all likelihood Cusanus never performed any of his experiments. Often the descriptions say nothing of how to carry out the experiment and do not even enable us to visualize it.

The great theme of the treatise is really this: The world of the finite, which by its very nature consists of the more and the less, should be studied by counting, measuring, and weighing operations. The question of weights should be given special attention. In this connection Cusanus anticipates a line of development that was to prove extraordinarily fruitful. But he does not follow up his own suggestions. He lacked the essential element of modern science—the development of mathematical theory in conjunction with controlled observations based on accurate weights, measures, and computations. He does not anticipate measurement as a criterion for confirming or refuting a predictive hypothesis. Not until such a method was evolved did science become exact science and embark on steady progress. Cusanus gives us mere tabulations of weights (to no definite purpose), along with an assortment of imaginary experiments, designed to make *ad hoc* inferences possible. These are a mixture of shrewd anticipation and nonsense. All this does not come to very much, because he did not actually put any of his proposals to the test. The book has been noticed because of its theme and was once reprinted in the sixteenth century, but it does not seem to have inspired or stimulated any actual research.

B. *Astronomy.*—We have referred to Cusanus' astronomical views, some of which anticipate later scientific findings. All are based purely on speculation or unverifiable hypotheses. Not a single observation is adduced as proof. Cusanus may very well have owned astronomical instruments, but there is no hint in his writings that he ever used them. His speculation on the nature of the cosmos as a copy of the divine Original has nothing in common with astronomical investigation based on observation and measurement.

c. *Mathematics.*—Cusanus' mathematical ideas have also been discussed above. His intentions in this connection are quite clear. He writes: "The smallest possible chord would have no *sagitta* [the distance between the chord and the apex of the arc], hence would no longer be smaller than its arc. Thus, chord and arc would coincide if we could reach the smallest possible in such things. The mind apprehends this as necessary if it knows that neither arc nor chord, because they are quantities, can simply be the actually smallest. For the continuous is always divisible. But in order to attain knowledge of their relationship, I make use of my mind's eye, and I say that I 'see' where the arc and chord are equal, namely, when both are as small as possible" (quoted after Jonas Cohn). Although Cusanus developed ideas such as these, which were to lead in the seventeenth century to the infinitesimal calculus, he himself made no such discovery.

D. *Study of documents and critical history.*—Cusanus had experience of documentary research in archives and libraries, and of historical investigation. He discovered a manuscript of Plautus' in 1426. Before Valla, he recognized the spuriousness of the Donation of Constantine (*De conc. cath.*, III, 1), but did not prove it. He was in direct touch with the texts of the ancient philosophers (he read the Greeks in Latin translation). Nevertheless, we cannot regard him as a critical historian or philologist.

E. *Political thinking. Comparison with the* Defensor pacis.—How antiquated Cusanus was as a political thinker becomes clear when we compare him with Marsilius of Padua, who wrote a century earlier. Marsilius' *Defensor pacis* is a work of secular thinking comparable to modern "political science," whereas Cusanus' *De concordantia catholica* is a speculative work which interprets secular phenomena as an image of divine harmony. To Marsilius, God is a *causa remota* and as such has no place in science. He confines himself to the real phenomena, the secular causalities, and judges them by secular standards. How the will of God asserts itself is beyond rational grasp; the political thinker confines himself to the earthly origin of political power. Cusanus, on the other hand, conceiving of political relationships as "representations" of divine originals, interprets and evaluates them on that basis.

According to Marsilius, the secular power of the Church is incompatible with its own spiritual goals and is therefore harmful. The state should serve human welfare in this world, and though it is possible to maintain that one of its tasks is to appoint priests in order to prepare the citizens for life in another world, it is also possible to hold that priests as a class have no place among the classes which make up civil society. According to Cusanus, the highest task of the state is to guide the citizen to eternal salvation, and accordingly to see to it that the subjects profess the true Catholic religion. Marsilius, on the other hand, is completely unconcerned with the defense of inviolable individual freedoms, but champions the sovereignty of the people, whose organ is an elected government. In his view, for example, measures against heretics are justified when they are demanded by the people and the state. The Church is subject to the sovereignty of the people, i.e., to the state, which should determine the number of clerics required and should guide citizens in their choice of occupation, according to their various abilities. Both Marsilius and Cusanus advocated reforms of state and Church alike; both desired to put the Church-state relationship on an orderly basis. But Marsilius thought along purely intellectual lines and, with the principle of popular sovereignty as his point of departure, ended up by championing the omnipotent state, so anticipating the anti-liberal ideas of a later day, such as were first fully developed by Hobbes. Cusanus had in mind the political realities of his own day, he himself was politically active, and his thinking is permeated with the idea of man's dignity and the freedom of his spirit in view of its perpetual bond with God.

F. *I know only what I can make.*—Modern thinking is characterized by one proposition: I know only what I myself can produce. This has a twofold sense. To Vico (1668–1744) it signifies that we human beings can know adequately and certainly only what human beings have produced, so that history is to be regarded as the one sure science above all others. To scientists it signifies: My knowledge consists not in retrospective understanding, but in productive activity; what I construct, what I bring into existence from my own blueprints—that is what I know.

Cusanus seems to have been the first to hit upon the proposition. To be sure, he does not apply it to empirical knowledge. But in his speculations, he looks upon our entire intellectual activity as the image and likeness of God's activity, as a kind of creation. God knows the real things because He has created them out of nothing. We know intellectual things because we ourselves produce them, namely, the mathematical and rational concepts which help us to approach the real things. Since we are not truly creative, we produce all this in an unreal space, but in such a way that, in real space, we can produce a new reality from a given reality, which we shape according to our creative intellectual patterns.

This sounds so modern that Cusanus has been regarded as a precursor on this score. But what he has in mind is a metaphysical conception of the mind, grounded in the godhead. On the basis of the self-experienced spontaneity of thought, he interprets things already done. His conception does not lead to practical "producing."

G. *Knowledge and power.*—God's knowledge and God's will are interchangeable concepts. What God knows, He wills. His knowledge and His will are not two separate things. Rather, His knowledge is also the reality of that which can be. In Him perfect knowledge and omnipotence coincide. In human knowledge—an image in the medium of otherness—knowledge and will are separate. But man aspires to the original knowledge. "To share in this knowledge is immortal joy." Here is an example of a knowledge which is also will and hence power: The grammarian would be extremely pleased if he could discover a simple rule that would enable him to understand the whole of grammar in an instant; similarly the rhetorician would be delighted if he could find a little word that would at one stroke make him a better orator than Cicero (*Exc.,* Scharpff, 492). A perfect mind, whose knowledge was identical with power, would be omnipotent.

At first sight, such statements may have an ultra-modern ring. In fact they are not modern at all. "Knowledge is power" today means: Thanks to technological knowledge, I can achieve my ends through means available in the world. To Cusanus "Knowledge is power" means something else: Knowledge transforms man, actualizing his potentialities. He does not merely possess knowledge and the possibility of applying it—he himself has become the knowledge that he himself puts into operation.

H. *Novelty and progress.*—Modern science sets a high value on novelty, and great importance is attached to priority in time. The scientist feels that whenever he discovers something, no matter how insignificant in itself, he has contributed to the progress of his discipline. Does Cusanus share in this attitude?

Cusanus is aware of the novelty of his fundamental idea. He says that he has revealed things hitherto unheard of (*De doc. ignor.,* II, 11). In one of his mathematical works (*De geom. transmut.*) we read: "The ancients, gifted with a strong spirit of inquiry, brought many hidden things to light," but "in some of the higher disciplines they did not achieve all their objectives." Is this an early expression of the modern idea of progress? Further on in the same work, we read: "The best preserver of all things so decreed in order that the divine faculty of cognition in us should not become stunted, but should be directed toward that which is still hidden, yet accessible to knowledge. . . . We devote ourselves passionately to exploring the darkness, in order that we may the more peacefully enjoy the strength of our mind."

These words do not connote the modern idea of progress, but the activity of the mind, its perpetual quest as it has been carried on in every age. The latter-day notion of progress signifies: I am taking a step forward, which my predecessors made possible, and my successors will in turn take a step beyond this one. I am destined to be surpassed by future generations, which will in turn be surpassed in the course of an endless progression; the final goal is not knowable. Cusanus means something entirely different. The eternal truth is present here and now; by following the path allotted to me I share in it, and I have the constant gratification of being in it. On my way, I am at the same time at my goal. When Cusanus seems to come close to the idea of progress, as in the above-quoted remarks about the ancients, he is not implying the modern (and true) idea of an advance in our knowledge as a whole. Cusanus' happiness in his knowledge is not comparable to the modern scientist's certainty that he has made some lasting contribution, however small, to the progress of knowledge. Cusanus is concerned not with an endless progression, but with a deepening of speculative thinking in individuals. Summing up his ideas in a late work (*De ven. sap.*), he writes: his aim is to move men keener than himself to deepen their understanding, be it ever so slightly (Preface). In other words, Cusanus expects his successors to make a fresh start and to be stimulated to deeper thinking by his thinking. "On my way" does not imply taking part in an objective, temporal progress. Rather, cognition is the eternal presence of the truth in time. "Man's creative activity has no goal other than itself. Mankind never goes outside itself in its creations. It creates nothing new; what it creates was already in it before" (*De con.*, II, 14).

Philosophical speculation penetrates deeply into the truth. Each philosophy is an original and unsurpassable achievement; speculation does not progress in the manner of the sciences. This would be possible only if there were a single current of true speculation, which discovered universally valid truths and aspired to arrive at the totality of these truths. If this were the case, earlier false philosophies would be outstripped by later true philosophies. But it is not the case. When in his treatise, *On the Hunt for Wisdom,* Cusanus says: "I have made progress," his meaning is that his later treatises expand and supplement his earlier work, that he has devised new forms and concepts relative to the method of transcending. But this "progress" actually consists of his own version of the same speculations on which—as Cusanus himself recognized—all the great philosophers before him had embarked (especially Plato, Proclus, and the Pseudo-Dionysius). In his work he aspires merely to enrich the method of exposition, to devise new comparisons and modes of intellection, to replace some of the old categories with new ones.

The historical sequence of the speculative systems is very different from the progress of knowledge in the world, which has become autonomous. In that sequence, the early thinkers no doubt supply later ones with intellectual instruments, but the transcendent content is each time original and unique. In the progress of knowledge, however, everything that is correct is preserved as part of the steadily growing store of knowledge of the world. Now and then Cusanus evokes the idea of progress, but actually he means a renewal of the speculative impulse, and it would be a mistake to interpret his statements as anticipating the modern idea of a progressing science, in the sense of a steady enrichment of universally valid knowledge.

Thus Cusanus can hardly be regarded as a founder of modern science.

2. *Speculative method and experimental method. So-called "anticipations"*

A. —In Cusanus the essential is not the will to knowledge, but the symbolic power of the knowable, considered as a copy of the divine. Speculative ideas are mirrored in the empirical world.

He does not discover methods of actual investigation, his suggestions for possible methods are formulated so vaguely that we cannot tell whether they are workable or not; he never develops, works out, or applies methods of investigation. His thinking is dominated by speculative methods.

Actually—though Cusanus did not suspect this—his fresh approach to the ancient themes of metaphysical speculation carried him even further away from the attitude of a mathematician, scientist, historian, or political thinker. What was dominant was his fundamentally religious attitude, his experience of the world illumined by transcendence. As though imprisoned in his own symbolic thinking, he seems to draw justification from the fundamentally "conjectural" character of all reality and knowledge of the world.

B. —In creating images, Cusanus broadened the intellectual horizon and so helped to lay the foundations of modern science. But his motives are not really scientific. The way in which scientists set about methodically, step by step, to achieve the solution of a factual problem is alien to him. He fails to understand that all scientific investigation must proceed from particular assumptions to particular goals. He still believes that it is possible to form an over-all scientific view of the cosmos; he lacks the modern scientist's awareness that we can investigate only objects in the world, not the world as a whole. Although Cusanus has some surprising ideas, he does not solve any scientific problems. Still, his mind blazes trails into unexplored territory where marvelous possibilities seem to loom. He appears to be on the brink of science.

"Speculative anticipations" should never be confused with actual anticipations of scientific discoveries. Scientific discovery is achieved solely on the basis of a cogent, verifiable method which needs no philosophical justification. Cusanus' so-called "anticipations" are not cognition but a playing with ideas, a mixture of truths arrived at by accident and of inextricable fallacies.

C. —Cusanus believed that he could deduce empirical knowledge and methods of investigation from his speculative methods and insights. The speculative infinite becomes for him an object of mathematical calculation, and his speculative "measuring" is identified with empirical measurement. God's infinity, of which the world is an image, becomes the endless cosmos.

Historically speaking, a number of scientific insights have originated in metaphysics. Copernicus accepted the Aristotelian picture of the world, merely intending to improve upon it, and yet, thanks to his stubborn adherence to an idea, he made real discoveries concerning the solar system. Inspired by the metaphysical belief in a cosmic harmony, Kepler evolved verifiable theories, and it was by applying the vast fund of astronomical measurements collected by Tycho Brahe that he discovered his laws of planetary motion. Yet metaphysics plays no part in the work of their successors; the scientific achievements which originally derived from metaphysics carried on independently of their origin and continued to develop by their own power.

3. The meaning of science

A. *Science is a whore.*—Cusanus condemns the indiscriminate curiosity of discursive reason; to him knowledge has meaning only when guided by the intellect to wisdom in God: "Just as carnal lust finds its consecration and appeasement only when channeled in the sacrament of marriage, so love of knowledge finds its appeasement only when channeled in true union with the Bridegroom. So long as the mind indulges without restraint in vain knowledge, it no more finds the object of its natural desire than does a man who cohabits with every whore. There can be no true marriage with a fickle woman, only with eternal wisdom" (*Exc.,* V, 473; Scharpff, 492). This comparison of the urge for knowledge with sensual lust condemns neither, but is intended to show that the one achieves its true purpose only in the sacrament of marriage, the other in faith. Discursive reason in itself is barren because, for all its passion, it is endless and empty. It dissolves all things into a multiplicity without constructive unity. It attains truth only in the transcendent, which is objectively called "God," and subjectively "faith." Mere discursive reason can momentarily stir up overwhelming desire, but it remains fruitless. The pleasure it gives is vain and swollen with pride, it produces no divine joy.

Thus science is a whore (when not guided by its ultimate purpose); it is knowledge of God (when guided by its true purpose). Though these statements originate in faith, the question implied in them is still timely. But our answers are different and more complex.

B. *Cusanus and modern science.*—To Cusanus, knowledge of the Whole encompasses all particular knowledge. Modern science pursues particular goals. It is characterized by an irresolvable tension between the fragmentary and the idea of unity.

To Cusanus, knowledge is completed a priori. It is realized in time, in the unending process of the conjectural. Modern science is fundamentally incomplete. Because it is aimless as a whole, it is without end or meaning.

To Cusanus, experiments are means of exposition. Measurements are always approximate; this is justified by the idea that all human knowledge is conjectural. Modern science strives for ever greater accuracy, degrees of in-accuracy being themselves objects of investigation.

To Cusanus, technical application is a matter of secondary importance. It is symbolic of the mind's creative power. To modern science, technical application leads to the creation of a new technological world. This technology in turn serves to promote the advance of science.

To Cusanus, knowledge is certain of itself as an image of the divine original. Modern science strives to find its own limits. Having reached a limit it is, on the one hand, driven to put further questions, whereby, time and again, it surpasses new limits; and on the other hand, it runs into questions it cannot answer.

To Cusanus, the whole is eternity manifesting itself. Modern science changes with the object to be known in an interminable process whose movement affects both object and method.

To Cusanus, the world and knowledge of the world rest upon God and are sheltered in God. To modern science, the being of the world has no roots, and the world is fragmented. The will to knowledge can take the form of rebellion against God.

Cusanus does not share the *sapere aude* (dare to know) of the great modern scientists; he is confident in a foreordained serenity. To him, scientific cognition is a continuously gratifying activity entailing no threat to the peace of the soul. Cognition involves no risk; it is the happiness of encountering God in the reality of the world.

c. *The question of meaning in modern science and in Cusanus.*—Did Cusanus have any intimation of what a science pursued entirely for its own sake could become? Probably not, for modern science sacrifices all metaphysical motives to the pursuit of universally valid insights.

When it is not aimless, having lost all sense of its own meaning, modern science is guided by some principle that cannot be justified on the basis of rational science. Such a principle imposes no limits upon science, but makes science aware of its particular methods and their factual limits. It is in the very choice of themes and methods that the principle discloses itself, though indirectly, by liberating the will to knowledge. For those engaged in scientific pursuits, this principle is the unconscious source of sense and purpose. But what is this principle? Only in modern science has the meaning of science become a great problem, one that does not admit of scientific solution. Kant made an essential contribution toward its clarification with his doctrine of the regulative Ideas and his insights into the radical difference between systematic knowledge and scattered information about facts.

Discursive reason, the logic of contradiction, and rationalism as such can at any time become ends in themselves, laying claim to the status of absolute knowledge; modern science is only one of several historical cases in point. When Cusanus inquired into the meaning of science, this was what he had in mind, not the problematic character of modern science. Today the question is often obscured by the sheer weight of technological developments, but for some thinkers it has taken on unprecedented urgency.

To Cusanus, the technical ability conferred by knowledge is a splendid, noble thing, because it is a copy of the creative mind. Man's creation presents an analogy to divine creation. For Cusanus, however, "technique" was still the age-old artisanal technique, not the entirely new structure of scientific techniques which have systematized the spirit of invention.

Cusanus is also aware of the noncreative use to which the mind can be put: cognition becomes dependent when it subordinates itself to utilitarian ends, when it becomes a mere servant and is thereby cut off from its own origins. "In order to live comfortably by this-worldly standards, men everywhere use their minds only as slaves, with whose help they acquire possessions, praise, and honor—we see this in the arts, both liberal and mechanical" (*To Albergati,* 27).

D. *Knowledge as the loving imitation of God.*—Cusanus has a simple answer to the question of the meaning of science. Human knowledge is a copy of divine knowledge, hence it is the apprehension of a truth that can be apprehended only in and through itself. We are in the truth when the object apprehended and the man who apprehends have both come within the self-sustaining closed circle.

We cannot arrive at the truth from outside it. We arrive at our knowledge of man, or stones, or other objects, by distinguishing different forms and behaviors. We assign names on the basis of such distinctions. But this activity of discursive reason never penetrates to the essence of things, it merely shows how they are related externally, according to the circumstances, as grasped by measurement and other determinations. A man who believes he can attain truth in this way does not know what truth is.

A wise man is, rather, one who knows how ignorant this mode of knowledge leaves him. But such a man also knows that without the truth he does not attain to being, life, or insight. Therefore, as he becomes aware of his ignorance, he longs with his whole being to stand in the truth. But he cannot achieve this through external, discursive knowledge (cf. the treatise *On the Hidden God*).

Cusanus is guided by the idea of a perfect knowledge, which only God possesses; man imitates it, his knowledge is an image of the original divine knowledge. True knowledge is knowledge of God. All the roads of knowledge, including the knowledge of ignorance, lead to knowledge of God. The meaning of all knowledge of the finite is the experience of the infinite as revealed in the finite. Knowledge of the finite is not self-contained, is not grounded in itself. The purpose of science is to serve this true knowledge.

The supreme happiness of the man who pursues knowledge is to recognize himself consciously as God's image and to recognize images of God in all things that exist but are not conscious of being images, i.e., to experience the one great harmonious order of the whole in the objects known and in the process of cognition itself. He blissfully contemplates "all things in the truth which is his only love" (*De con.*, II, 6).

Such knowledge is love and the knowledge of love. "He who has no loving knowledge stands in ignorance. Therefore the mind, if it is to live, must know love, which can be known only by loving" (*To Albergati*, 12).

E. *Science, philosophy, theology.*—To avoid confusion, we must distinguish the very different senses in which we have been using the terms "knowledge" and "science."

Modern science is a body of cogent knowledge which is grounded in a conscious methodology, which not only lays claim to universal validity, but actually is universally valid. Modern science has no universal method, but only specific methods, evolved for specific purposes on the basis of explicit assumptions. It is universal in the sense that there is nothing which from a certain point of view might not become its object. It is not universal if universality is taken to imply a possible knowledge of all things in their totality. Modern science cannot justify its own purpose. Cusanus would call it a knowledge purely of external things, relations, modes of behavior, forms.

Cusanus had not learned (any more than any other philosopher before the nineteenth century, except for Kant) to distinguish scientific knowledge in this sense from philosophical and theological cognition. An enormous intellectual domain which makes use of the sciences but itself has no scientific character is called "philosophy"; within the framework of the revealed faith, it is called "theology."

The source of philosophical insight is a faith which is expressed by methods of thinking characteristic of philosophy. To Cusanus, this faith coincides with revealed faith. Today we make a distinction he did not make. We call science the thinking which is aimed at a cognition of objects in the world and based on rationally defined assumptions. We call philosophy the thinking based on rationally ungraspable assumptions concerning human Existenz. The thinking based on revealed faith is called theology.

F. *Faith within science.*—All three of these types of thinking seem to be present in Nicholas of Cusa. But in him they almost merge into one. He was not aware of modern science, nor was he aware of the autonomy of philosophy. Only by taking cognizance of what distinguished it from modern science did philosophy become clearly aware of its autonomy. Furthermore, Cusanus failed to see that the distinction between philosophy and theology is essentially different from the distinction between science and theology. He uses the term "science" in the old sense, as the unity of scientific, philosophical, and theological cognition.

In the light of the foregoing, we recognize the validity of Cusanus' contention that the purpose of science, indeed of all cognition, cannot be brought to thinking awareness without philosophy. The situation in Cusanus' thinking was very different from what it is in our own. To him, all knowledge of the world culminates in the knowledge of God, and moreover, he conceived of his knowledge of the world itself as dependent upon the knowledge of God. To his mind, finite things are comprehensible only through awareness of their grounding in the incomprehensible. The ideas through which we approach the infinite without comprehending it are for him the starting point of true cognition of comprehensible things in the finite world.

Although Cusanus does not distinguish between cognition of reality and the philosophical reading of ciphers, his cognition contributes in fact to the clarity of the ciphers, and derives its meaning from this function.

Very nearly down to our own day, the majority of creative men (in science, history, philosophy, and politics) have probably been believing Christians. Few, however, have explicitly interpreted the language of the world, in so far as they were trying to investigate it, as the language of God. Striving to preserve the purity of science, they were careful not to let their faith influence their theories or their observations. They sought God not in mere feeling, but through the knowledge of things. Cognition was sustained by feeling and in consequence thinking became clearer to itself. The loss of this fundamentally religious attitude and its concomitant spirituality has brought about a transformation in science itself. In our technological age, science is in danger of losing itself in innumerable factual findings that are no longer mastered intellectually, and in techniques evolved by specialists unaware of anything outside their own specialties. Although modern scientific progress depends exclusively on technical specialization, the particular sciences nevertheless point to a greater whole. We feel its presence in the scientist and in his achievement, but it is not an object of cognition and is not explicitly recognized. When this greater whole is lost sight of, specialized scientists, for all their subtely of mind, become stunted both in matters of knowledge beyond their domains and spiritually in their own lives. The same fate seems to await a science which strives to become an end in itself, not only in respect of methods and certainty, but also in respect of its meaning. The fact that it cannot be an end in itself is attested by the growth of scientific superstitions as substitutes for a lost faith: positivist, naturalist, and spiritualist fictions, equally devoid of transcendence and of the scientific spirit.

A man of purely scientific outlook might say: Why not stay within the graspable bounds of the real world? Here lies our only certainty, because it is valid for everyone. The world is to be understood in itself and only through itself. What eludes our knowledge, we shall one day know; if it is unknowable, it is of no consequence to us, because for all practical purposes it is nonexistent.

And yet, thanks to science, it has been becoming ever clearer that the world cannot be understood on the sole basis of science. Because perfect factual accuracy is unattainable and because at every point we come up against the infinite as against a limit, the world itself offers no ground of certainty. There are discontinuities, "leaps," in nature and in history. When we enter the domain of the infinite, paradoxes arise which science cannot tolerate. Everything that escapes empirical observation though existentially present in time—the unconditional in ethical action, the experience of extreme situations, the greatness and nobility of man—can be elucidated, but not in terms of a thinking grounded in universally valid scientific knowledge.

Even if we do not accept Cusanus' ideas in their specifically Christian formulations, the great question they raise in regard to the meaning of science is more acute today than ever before, because today the meaning of science has been called into question more radically than at any other time.

Part Four: Man's Task

I. THE INDIVIDUAL

A. *To be oneself.*—Cusanus addresses God: "Thou makest reply within my heart, saying: Be thou thine and I too will be thine [*sis tu tuus, et ego ero tuus*]." This is his fundamental experience: I should be myself. Not until I have come to be myself can I experience the reality of God. God's first gift to us is the freedom to be ourselves: "Thou hast left me free to be mine own self, if I desire [*ut sim, si volam, mei ipsius*]." If I am not myself, God is not real for me. But the freedom to be oneself is not self-created, it comes from God. Freedom means: I must be myself if God is to be mine. Because He has left me free, He does not constrain me. He expects me to choose to be my own (*ut ego eligam mei ipsius esse*). "This rests then with me, and not with Thee." But what rests with me is nevertheless awakened by God: "If I hearken unto Thy Word, which ceases not to speak within me and continually enlightens my reason, I shall be mine own, free" (*The Vision of God, op. cit.*, p. 32).

Here we stand with Cusanus at one of the summits of philosophical thinking: my attitude toward myself in the face of the transcendent. But one thing gives us pause: Cusanus is speaking in general terms, not about actual personal experience. He did not strive unremittingly to become transparent to himself—an experience that is both disquieting and revealing. This is perhaps why his actual life (which will be discussed in Part Five) does not come up to the level of his self-certainty. The truth of his magnificent statements would have been deeper had he ventured to apply it to himself, to the historicity of human Existenz, which is always individual and unique. Cusanus is too sure of himself, too bland in his general statements. And yet they are a magnificent formulation of man's task.

b. *Individuality and selfhood.*—To be an individual is not yet to be oneself. Every real thing in the world is an individual thing. But man is the only creature whose mind is conscious of being a copy [of the divine] and thus man alone can become himself. The will to be oneself signifies the will to be this individual in his uniqueness and not another, to be true to one's own God-created individuality and to accept it fully. Yet with this self-restriction the individual who is in process of becoming himself comes closer to eternity.

Of all existent things man has the distinction of not merely being an image, but also of knowing himself to be one. Because he knows this, he can rise toward the original, can make the copy more real. His cognition is participation in divine cognition and thereby rises above the abyss of radical otherness. Because the original is infinity, the copy can be seen as an infinite movement of the productive mind: because the copy knows that it participates in the original, this movement is upward. The infinite is present as the life of the finite.

c. *The leap.*—If man, whose thinking in the world is finite, does not lose himself in forgetfulness of his situation, he has an ineradicable urge to soar from the finite to the infinite, from the shifting soil of the finite to a firm support in the infinite. But the springboard for this leap is the world itself, and we do not gain elevation above the world by leaving it.

Cusanus' speculation elucidates this soaring movement. Through nonknowledge it arrives at concepts which are unlike the concepts of finite thinking.

The abyss of nonknowledge serves as a bridge and yet remains an abyss. In the world all cognition is comparative. It takes us ever further, without arriving at the infinite. We cannot attain to the infinite by moving closer. The leap from the finite to the infinite can be effected only by the leap from discursive thinking to intellectuaal thinking (from the *ratio* to the *intellectus*). We swing ourselves over the abyss, and leave the whole realm of the finite behind.

This, however, is not accomplished by extravagant imaginings, but by thinking. Unlike discursive thinking, which tolerates no contradiction and attempts to eliminate it by posing finite alternatives, intellectual thinking, through the *coincidentia oppositorum,* grasps the infinite beyond the world of objects.

In this darkness is born the light which now illuminates all finitude and is the source of our true awareness of being. It discloses truth in the finite itself. For not until the birth of this light is the finite recognized as such by virtue of its reference to the infinite, which is unlike any finite relation. In the finite we become conscious of the infinite, in relative being of absolute being, in rational knowledge of the supra-rational presuppositions which give meaning to finite knowledge.

Although between the infinite and the finite there obtains no relation that would enable us to think the infinite (which would then become finite) by relating it to the finite, the infinite can guide us. Freed from limitations, it sets the standards of the finite.

D. *Man's task. To strive toward becoming an ever closer image of God.*— Man is great by virtue of his task. By carrying it out he becomes himself. But whatever he achieves for himself is given him by God. His task is to become an increasingly closer copy of the original, though not to become the original itself. Nor can the copy of the original achieve perfection in the finite, in time. A man in process of becoming himself is exalted by his sublime awareness of being attracted to the original mind of God.

All our intellectual thinking is tied to enigmatic images and metaphors; but a perfect intellect would jump over the wall and contemplate the eternal truth itself. These two themes are to be found in all Cusanus' writings.

Cusanus calls perfect insight in contemplation *filiatio,* which is his translation of the Greek term *theōsis* (*De filiatione Dei*). Once again the twofold theme: True, eternal contemplation goes beyond every possible contemplation in this world; but it is present in the believer as the experience of divine filiation.

The Platonic idea of participation and St. John's concept of divine filiation seem to merge into one in Cusanus.

E. *Man seeks God and God wants to be known.*—Man is created in order that he may seek God and find peace in this quest alone. Yet God is not to be found in the world of the senses; discursive reason is too weak to know God; our abstractions fail to arrive at any similarity to God. But if the world of the senses and of discursive reason were of no use in the quest for God, man would have been set down in the world in vain (*De quaerendo Deum*).

What is the purpose of the world? Cusanus answers: God wants to be known, to be seen in His omnipotence. Therefore simultaneously with the world He created man, who comes to know the world and, through it, God.

The world is the order of all existents, of every object of cognition, from sensory knowledge to intellectual insight. The objects of the senses are disclosed by their colors, thanks to light, by their sounds, odors, etc. Man is a sort of cosmographer to whom messages are brought through five different gateways (the sense organs). From this image of the external world, which he creates, he rises above the various modes of knowing objects to the contemplation of the Creator of the world, the objective cosmographer (*Compendium,* 8). Thus we obtain a ladder of spiritual ascent from the senses and discursive reason to the intellect.

The unknown God attracts us to Himself. He can be known only when He shows Himself. But He wants us to seek Him. To those who seek Him, He gives the light without which they could not go on seeking. Man shuts himself off from the truth so long as he holds true only that which he can measure with discursive reason (*De quaerendo Deum*).

F. *Metaphors for the ascent through thought.*—Just as our body needs food, so our spirit needs spiritual nourishment. Our intellect is on the *"hunt* for wisdom," guided by an innate knowledge of what kind of nourishment it needs. By means of our thinking we strike out in every direction in our search for immortal food (*De ven. sap.,* 1).

Our erratic search for the way is illustrated by a comparison with a game Cusanus invented, "the ball game" (which is the title of one of his works, *De ludo globi*). It is played with a wooden ball with a spherical hollow off center. When the ball is bowled, it does not, since one side is heavier than the other, roll in a straight line, but takes a spiral path. The players toss the ball over a surface divided into ten concentric circles. At the center is the king—Christ. The winner is the player whose ball has touched the greatest number of circles and comes closest to the center.

Our mind has the nature of *fire.* God sent it into the world for the sole purpose of burning, of becoming a flame. The flame increases when the mind is kindled by wonder. The wonder we experience in contemplating God's works is the wind that increases our longing by turning it into love for the Creator and into contemplation of wisdom (*De quaerendo Deum*).

Man's consummation in the world is the joy we experience through our senses of sight, hearing, taste, touch, and smell, through feeling, life, and movement, and through the use of our discursive reason and our intellect. Its culmination is an infinite, ineffable joy, in which all joy, all delight come to rest (*De quaerendo Deum*).

G. *To become Christ.*—Magnificently as Cusanus points out the successive philosophical stages along the path to selfhood, the crucial part of the journey, the part on which everything depends, is not, in his view, philosophical. Man cannot help himself, he must rely on God. Consequently, the one thing that can help him is implicit trust in the promise of Christ.

Man "knocks at the door in fervent prayer, confident that he will not be abandoned if only he continues without cease to enter into Christ" (*De possest*).

Did we not believe in Christ as the Son of God, says Cusanus, we would never follow His teaching as the teaching of the One true God. All the great philosophers and sages were merely men, and "every man who is not God may be a liar." We must therefore believe—nothing can be more certain—that He is the Son of God. Therein lies our salvation (*To Albergati*, 37). "No believer in Christ has ever been disappointed" (*ibid.*, 54).

At the close of *De docta ignorantia* (III, 12) we read: "Nothing can resist the man who enters into Christ, and nothing will be difficult for him, neither the Scriptures nor this world, for he has been transformed into Christ by the spirit of Christ that dwells in him, which is the goal of intellectual yearning [*intellectualium desideriorum*]."

What is the meaning of "transformation into Christ"? What is the meaning of "the spirit of Christ dwells in me"? Such questions cannot be answered in other terms, but perhaps they can be elucidated indirectly.

We may call such expressions ciphers for the presence of the eternal within me, for the experience of "absolute consciousness," manifesting itself in empirical consciousness. But such paraphrases do not satisfy a believing Christian.

To us the "Christian within me" signifies roughly a way of understanding the eternal, not in the subjectivity of Existenz with the objectivity of ciphers, but on the basis of an objective revelation. The physical presence of the God-Man in time, the physical presence of the Church as the incarnation of spirituality, sole authority for proclaiming the one absolute universal truth—all this the nonbeliever would at least like to understand. No analogy from our own experience can serve, but for centuries down to our own day philosophical, or at least philosophically intelligible, accounts of such an experience have been repeatedly put forward.

The Stoics tell us: My reason is identical with the reason of the universe, my *logos* with the cosmic *logos*. Since Plato we have been told about the light "from above," the radiance of the Ideas and the Idea of Ideas. We are told how our "knowledge participates in the creation." We are told about being given to ourselves in love. We are told about the inner constitution of Reason as the bond connecting the modes of the Encompassing, about the Encompassing of all Encompassing as the presence of transcendence. The difference between what is philosophically expressed in such formulations and the thesis of belief in the God-Man which Cusanus puts forward with such manifest fervor is this: My certainty that Christ is in me, based on the belief that God revealed Himself in the man Jesus, is so absolute, so far-reaching, so exclusive, and lays claim to a certainty so radically different in origin, that all philosophical certainty seems to pale before it. But the consequences of this belief often include a restriction of vision, an inhuman intolerance. Even a man of Cusanus' stature did not wholly escape these consequences (as we shall see in discussing the ideas advanced in *De pace fidei* and elsewhere). And the Christian certainties have made possible a kind of dishonesty unparalleled in history and disastrous to the entire Christian world. The remoteness of transcendence in spite of the nearness of being-given-to-oneself excludes approximation to God and the possibility of becoming godlike. Something far more difficult is required: the striving to apprehend man's being in itself, to fulfill it, to advance in it without knowing exactly what it is.

H. *Comparison with Pico della Mirandola (1463–94).*—Cusanus' extraordinary self-confidence has little in common with the Renaissance conception of the *uomo singolare* perfectly content with himself in his own uniqueness, with his own greatness as exemplified in his finest achievements; it has just as little in common with the conception of the *uomo universale,* who desires to realize humanity in a superhuman way, to be and to know all things, while remaining untrammeled by the ecclesiastic-political-social order.

Pico's *Oratio de dignitate hominis* (1486) provides an instructive contrast to Cusanus' conception of man's task. The two are in agreement in respect of the creativity of the human spirit and man's God-created freedom. Pico, too, adhered to the ecclesiastical faith and was a friend of Savonarola. But Pico's image of man is as follows:

Man is a great marvel, the most admirable thing on the vast stage of the world. But though he is placed at the center of all creation, represented as the bond between the world and the angels, as spiritually akin to the supraterrestrial world, as the lord of all creatures, all this does not constitute man's true greatness, which Pico finds in man's origin:

The world had been created in its magnificence, from the supraterrestrial down to the material regions. All beings had been assigned their proper places within the hierarchy. The world was complete. Then the Divine Architect was moved by a desire to create a being capable of discovering the laws of the cosmos, capable of loving its beauty and admiring its grandeur. But to create such a being God had neither a worldly model nor particular treasures at His disposal. Above all, there was no place left on earth for him, who was to make the universe the object of his contemplation, to live in. For all the places were taken.

Therefore God made man in His image and likeness, ordained that he should possess the endowments that every individual calls his own, and said to him: We have given you, Adam, no definite form, no special inheritance. We have subjected all other creatures to specific laws. You alone are in no wise restricted, but free to take whatever gifts you choose according to your desire and judgment. I have placed you at the center of the world to enable you to look around and see whatever you wish. You will be your own artisan and sculptor and fashion yourself from the material that appeals to you. You are free to degenerate to the basest animality or to rise to the highest spheres of divinity. And after putting these words into the mouth of God, Pico cries out jubilantly: What good fortune! Man can be what he desires. The animals possess at birth all they will ever possess. The higher spirits are from the first all they will be for eternity. In man alone God planted the seed of every form of activity and the germs of every form of life. Who can fail to admire this capacity for change! It was for good reason that mankind was symbolized by the figure of Proteus in the mysteries.

The Creation had been completed. Only then did God decide to do something more than to create a world. Did He then proceed to create something which, once created, would be removed from His control, namely, freedom? Pico replies: It is a sign of His omnipotence that He was confronted with a dilemma in creating the last living being—a sign of His wisdom that He hesitated as to which gifts He should confer upon it—a sign of His love that He compelled Himself to endow that very being with original sin from the outset.

Pico holds that man was not created according to a model; subject to no standard, he is the inexhaustible possibility of freedom. He has unique dignity, for thanks to God's creative will, man is entirely on his own. Pico omits to tell us in what sense man is dependent on something other and hence limited in his freedom, how he experiences the source of his freedom in his very consciousness of freedom.

Though no less aware of the sublimity of man's task, Cusanus limits it by what he interprets as man's imitative character. He never yields to the temptation of asserting an absolute freedom, which would lead to boundless corruption. Cusanus' conception of freedom as freedom of choice, a choice to be oneself (*eligere*), is in Pico perverted into the freedom to create oneself.

Both see man as in and at the same time outside the world. In Pico, man is not originally a part of a world complete in itself, but a later addition, set down in a world that has no particular place for him. To Cusanus, man, with his freedom and the possibilities it opens up, remains at a distance from God as His image and likeness sheltered in the world by the Creator, who also encompasses his freedom; for all the possibilities of his freedom, man stands within the world. To Pico, he is opposed to the world as a whole. He can make it an object of his cognition, but he can also shatter it.

Pico's conception strikes us as the aesthetic game of a recklessly self-sufficient mind, but in actual fact his mind was bound to the rituals and dogmas of the Church and was sustained by the promise of immortality. Cusanus' conception of man bespeaks the earnestness of a thinker whose ventures are marked by humility. Pico seems to forget all about the Church when he is writing, just as in his adherence to the Church he must have forgotten what he had written. There is in Pico a recklessness that anticipates a number of later errors and superstitions. Cusanus is more temperate—his thinking is a painstaking development, he takes account of contradictions. He formulates speculative and existential ideas, the truth of which remains open and which appeal to us even now.

We may ask today whether there is not a third possibility, a safer position than either Cusanus' adherence to the Catholic Church or Pico's reckless assertion of freedom as an absolute. May we not find strength in awareness of the great destiny of freedom, in our progress toward the uncertain—a progress illumined by ambiguous ciphers—bound to time by our historicity (without which freedom remains empty) and encompassed by transcendence?

II. PEACE

Fundamental reality of the Church. Cusanus' thinking in the Concordantia

The task of humanity living in community is to preserve the peace. Peace is the subject of Cusanus' first book, and it was the objective of his political activity on behalf of the Church. If both Church and Empire were adequate to the divine archetypes, peace internal and external would be achieved through the unity of Church and Empire.

In Cusanus' day, the Church as an eternal reality was taken for granted by Western man. The deeply religious Cusanus was no different. The Pope might be held prisoner, priests and monks might be openly abused and held in contempt, but nobody rejected the Church. Men could neither live nor die without it. The widespread dissatisfaction was not with the Church as such, but with its condition at the time. The corruption of the Church, the need for reform, was the great political issue of the day.

Cusanus, who lived in God's unity whose image is the one world, shows us how this illumines all present reality, even now giving us an intimation of eternal peace. Peace through unity is the God-created reality. The only way to restore it in the world is to make the image a better likeness of the original. However muddled the relations of Church and Empire may be in reality, they owe their existence to this harmony which resides in the cosmos—in individual man and in the order of Church and Empire.

Although the individual becomes himself only in confrontation with God, he is not on his own, but a member of the entire community of mankind. While the individual is himself through participating in the infinite, his participation in the world makes him a member of a community in bond with God; every individual is united with every other within the world.

The harmony of this world, which is an image of the divine original, is all-embracing concord (*concordantia catholica*) and manifests itself as the agreement of all men (*consensus omnium*).

Nothing in the universe is to be loved save as an aspect of the unity and order of the universe. No man is to be loved save as an aspect of the unity and order of human nature. Every love has its truth in love of the One God who is absolute, infinite love and the source of all unity.

Peace unites because in it oppositions are stilled. Through peace all things are linked with the center, so that the whole is preserved from disintegration. Peace is the object of our longing, for without it nothing can subsist. Only in peace can truth endure. All those who have written subtly about truth have for this reason sought to present in a peaceful way the truth contained in divergent opinions. The philosopher who is caught up in opposites cannot see peace. Peace, the home of truth, cannot be attained by discursive thinking; it can only be intuited above and beyond all opposites (*Exc.*, V, 487; Scharpff, p. 532).

On the other hand: Although God is at peace with all men, not every man is at peace with God. For by virtue of his freedom, man can not only move closer to peace, but can also move away from it. He has only one recourse: "We are born as the children of wrath, but through faith in Christ we are reconciled with the author of peace." Hence Cusanus' certainty: "For the peace of Christ all things have been prepared from the beginning, so that there may be one world and in it the final goal of Christ."

1. *De concordantia catholica*

De concordantia catholica (1433) is Cusanus' first and longest book; *De docta ignorantia* (1440) is his first comprehensive philosophical work. Did some change take place between the writing of the one and the other? Not really. The fundamental idea of the *coincidentia oppositorum* methodically developed in *De docta ignorantia* probably occurred to him as a sudden illumination, but his deeper fundamental attitude, part of which is his thinking on unity, harmony, peace, as well as his method of symbolic interpretation of all things, had remained unchanged.

In methodically surmounting the operations of discursive reason by another kind of thinking, he attains new awareness, but not a new fundamental attitude. The new idea is anything but revolutionary. It merely provides a deeper foundation for his original view of harmony.

De concordantia catholica argues the cause of Church reform and was written for the Council of Basel. It is based on sources which Cusanus studied in monastery libraries. He took for his model the Councils of the early Church and the ideas of the Fathers. The juridical and political conceptions of the patristic and scholastic past are examined and co-ordinated. According to Cusanus, the power of the Councils had been allowed to lapse, to the detriment of the Church. The spirit of the enlightened ancients should be revived. Cusanus' projects for reform, which he justified historically and theoretically, are based on his insights into the origin, nature, and purpose of both Church and Empire. He invokes no irrevocable authority, but rediscovers in the thinking of the early Church Fathers his own answer to the problems of a later day.

In *De concordantia catholica* he draws a picture of the ideal Christian society, comprising both Church and Empire. Its unity derives from God, who as Christ is its head. The Church is His representative on earth, the Empire looks to Him as to a guide. The two institutions are of different origin.

A. *The supernatural origin of Church and State.*—Because of its supernatural origin, the existing community must be looked upon as a copy of the original. The copy points to the original, expresses it symbolically. Because the mind grasps this, it can continually improve the form of the copy.

In the copied reality of the world, unity lies in the concord (*concordantia*) of the many. It is unification with God through Christ in the Holy Spirit. The Church is grounded in the Trinity, the sole source of life. Through faith and love all men are united with God. No man is grounded solely upon himself.

The Church in its purity, as eternal order from the beginning of time until the Resurrection of the Dead, is *Christi ecclesia triumphans,* but in the world it is *ecclesia militans*. For as long as we live here below, there must be a steady increase of faith and love. Every many must strive to surpass the degree he has already achieved, knowing that there will be no completion in time.

Among many vividly concrete metaphysical interpretations of the foundation and early manifestations of the Church, we shall mention only a few. God, the angels, and the saints in Paradise are the Church triumphant in eternity. Within the Church in time, the sacraments correspond to God, the priests to the angels, the people to the saints. Sacraments, priesthood, and the body of the faithful are the principal elements of the Church militant.

God alone knows the Christians united with Him through love. The angels know those who are allied with God through faith. An act of faith is like the striking of a chord which reverberates throughout the heavenly kingdom. The angels perceive it the moment a believer touches the chord.

B. *The idea of unity. Pope and Council.*—The main theme of the Council of Basel was the relations between Papacy and Council. How can they work together? Which should have precedence in the event of disagreement? From what does each derive its legitimacy?

Fundamental and exceeding all else in importance is the idea of unity. To Cusanus, the unity and harmony of all things are present everywhere in the world. The unity of the Church is the unity of the faith. A difference of views is justifiable, as long as it is not maintained with obstinacy. To set one's own views above the welfare of the Church is to deny the possibility of unity.

Concord (*concordantia*) is a unification of differences. The less the differences, the less will be the antagonism between them and the stronger the concord. Here below there can be no perfect concord, although life would be impossible without some measure of concord. Only in eternity, where there are no oppositions, is perfect concord possible.

On the practical plane unity is the supreme consideration. It takes precedence over everything else. It tips the scales in every difference of opinion. Conversely, schism signifies absolute corruption. Which should prevail in policy-making decisions, the Pope or the Council? Do the Pope's orders have to be obeyed under all circumstances? What appeal is there from them? Does a Universal Council have the authority to enforce its decisions against the Pope, and can a Council prevent him from dissolving it? Does a majority decision in the Council represent the truth for all, even for those who voted against it? Can a consensus be obtained in this way? From whom does the authority of the Universal Council emanate? Can a Council be summoned by high-ranking ecclesiastics, by the entire priesthood, by the body of the faithful? Since not all members of the Church can attend, how should representatives be elected? Do all bishops automatically have the right to sit as members of the Council, as true representatives of the entire body of Christendom? To all such questions Cusanus gives no final answers. Studying his statements, we find him giving clear enough answers in one context, but contradicting them in another. On the whole, we have the impression that he sees the problems as they really are and formulates them clearly, but that his metaphysical interpretation obscures his statements. The splendor of the supernatural is expected to hold everything together, but as soon as practical issues arise, the splendor is dimmed, if not extinguished. The following arguments are cases in point. Unity, hence power, reside in the Church, but *de facto* supreme authority resides either in the Pope or in the Council or in both. The resolutions of the Council are absolutely valid, but only if the Council is really universal, approved by the entire body of Christendom (that is, as I see it, never). The Pope's privileges, which had been defined by earlier Councils, are inviolable—but only if the motives of the Pope who invokes them are pure, untroubled by extraneous considerations (which, I believe, can occur only in exceptional individuals and never completely). Council and Pope should work together because both are rooted in and unified by the Church—but the resolutions passed by the Council become binding only after the Pope has confirmed them.

The foregoing is not intended as an absolute condemnation of this gigantic effort to establish peace and unity in theory as in practice. But it does discredit this particular historical event as an expression of the absolute truth. To be honest we must acknowledge that the world cannot be perfectly organized. We are always on the way.

c. *State and Empire*.—Cusanus ascribes a separate origin to the secular power. Side by side with the Church, we have the autonomous Empire. *Sacerdotium* and *imperium* constitute a unity of different elements.

Just as the vicar of Christ takes Christ as his model, so the prince is to be guided by Christ. His power has both a divine and a human origin.

It follows from the unity of mankind that there should be a single emperor whose power surpasses that of all other princes. The emperor is the equal of the Pope. In matters of government the emperor takes precedence; in religious matters, the Pope. The latter's claim to temporal power had been based on the spurious Donation of Constantine. Imperial power, by its very nature, is independent of the Church; it is dependent only on God.

d. *Repraesentatio*.—In the discussion concerning the respective roles of the Pope, the Council, and the body of the faithful, one concept plays an essential part—"representation" (Kallen). In its practical application this concept was a source of endless confusion.

In the first place, all things, *qua* finite copies, represent the infinite original. In the second place, the forms of the Church and the Empire represent the permanent spirit of these communities. In the third place, elected members of the Council represent the limited number of those entitled to vote, who in turn represent the entire body of the faithful.

The confusion of symbolic representation with actual representation (in other words, of the expression of the spirit of a community with its specific institutions) leads to obscurity and untruthfulness. Particular institutions are justified by *ad hoc* arguments.

How do the will of the universal religious and political community, both supposedly "copies" of the divine will, and the *consensus omnium* supposedly flowing from the divine spirit, become manifest? In practice, this will is determined by advisory and executive bodies which are appointed or elected. The characteristic of truth is unity, but here it becomes unanimity.

Cusanus reflected to an equal extent on the unifying spirit of the truth, on the meaning of metaphysical *repraesentatio,* and on the technique of elections. He desired institutions whose actual power would be legitimate in a technical-juridical sense and sanctioned supernaturally. Such congruence of secular and spiritual power cannot be realized in practice, except at unusual, unpredictable, and short-lived moments when a whole community acts unanimously.

e. *The method of symbolic interpretation*.—Cusanus' method of symbolic interpretation employed for the purpose of justifying practical demands strikes us as very strange today. To us, it seems that interpretation of this type can be varied almost at will. This lies in the very nature of symbolic interpretation. It embraces opposites and shifts the emphasis as needed within one and the same over-all view. The dangers that result are two-fold. First: When such a method is employed to justify practical measures, it leads to contradictions which encourage real or seeming opportunism. Second: Through rationalization, the interpretations degenerate into schematic thinking and playing with words. In either case, the symbolic truth of the ciphers, the language that motivates the earnestness of action, is lost. Symbolic thinking remains true only so long as it remains in suspense, confines itself to creating a background, leaves room for the communal spirit to make itself felt and communicable. To use it for rational arguments on behalf of practical ends is to abuse it.

Because language can elucidate meanings, it can communicate truths for which there are no rational criteria. Truth is tested rather by the emotional effectiveness of the language, by its consequences in the conduct of life.

Cusanus has full mastery over symbolic thinking. It gives spiritual force to his ideas. Perhaps it is in his conception of the imitative, reflected, metaphorical being of all finite things that his symbolic thinking achieves its greatest clarity. Everything that is, everything that is thinkable, everything that is to be done, he envisages in terms of metaphysical "meaning." As we put it: he reads the ciphers. Yet, for all the magnificence of his images, the fact that in his arguments and justifications he, like so many others throughout history, mistakes this meaning for reality itself leads him time and again to practical-existential confusion.

The metaphysical images, the juridical forms and arguments, the real decisions are interrelated. Traditional faith, rational form, practical interest support and combat one another. Any one of the three may prevail for a time. On the plane of language they slip and slide into one another. In concrete situations, the real will can be obscured by metaphysical ideas and beguiled into surrendering to brute force. Conversely, practical interests can make use of metaphysical ideas in the actual struggle, deceiving the adversary without gaining the commitment of those who proffer them. The power of the practical interests is veiled. Multiple interpretations on the merely rational plane do not make for clarity. Because of their very depth, metaphysical ciphers, unless their methodological character is clearly recognized, can becloud vision and obscure the real powers at work.

Metaphysical interpretations cannot serve as arguments for a worldly goal save by deceiving. No specific course of action can be adequately based on them; their real function is to elucidate one's own faith. Universally valid justifications in the world cannot be based on historically documented contracts, unless the principle that contracts are binding is accepted. Nothing can be justified as a means to an end unless the end is recognized as such, in terms rationally defined, by all the parties concerned.

Characteristic of this bewildering confusion is the double meaning of *repraesentatio*—metaphysically, image of the one whole; juridically, representation by election or appointment. The proposition, *concilium repraesentat ecclesiam*, tends to imply the idea of juridical representation. The proposition *papa repraesentat ecclesiam* is more metaphysical, denoting the symbolic incarnation of the *corpus mysticum ecclesiae* in one person, who is primarily the representative of Christ on earth and only secondarily the representative of the historical Church. Conflict arose between the two propositions as a result of the opposition between the conciliar and the papal movements. At the time, the papal party was victorious, but the victory reflected only the actual balance of power. It had nothing to do with the validity of the arguments used by either party.

Cusanus' ideas have to be grasped within the framework of his encompassing interpretative thinking. To isolate any one of them is to do him an injustice. He did not foreshadow the absolutist state, the absolutist Tridentine Church of the modern era, or the parliamentary constitutional state. Cusanus advocated neither absolutism nor popular sovereignty. Rather, he had both in view as articulated within his over-all conception of the political order.

F. *Comparison with Dante.*—Cusanus' purpose is to encourage reform in the Church and the Empire; his philosophical thinking is intended to assist in this task. When we compare him with Dante, we see how very modest a role he assigned to philosophy as such.

Both conceive the unity of the world order in two forms: Church and Empire, Pope and Emperor; the two forms are related by virtue of a higher unity. The unity of mankind is the guiding idea of both Dante's *De monarchia* and Cusanus' *De concordantia catholica*.

The picture painted by Dante is clear, simple, and beautiful. Cusanus not infrequently seems to lose his way in his tremendous subject. Dante's exposition is concise and moves rapidly from point to point. Cusanus is forever running off into digressions and side issues.

Dante's picture has monumental beauty. There is a certain beauty in Cusanus' ideas, images, and metaphors, but the work as a whole is formless. The unity of Dante's work, though rationally constructed, is enchanting. The unity of Cusanus' work, though less pure in its logic and its images, is intellectually convincing. Dante's unity is charged with tension; it calls for heroes and saints. Cusanus' unity appears as a temperate harmony of balanced forces.

Philosophically speaking, the great difference between the two is this: Cusanus speaks as an ecclesiastic, Dante as a layman. Dante was in reality the great layman of whom Cusanus merely talked. In both, philosophy achieves autonomy. But Cusanus raises no claim to independence for his philosophy, while in Dante the autonomy is explicit and takes a highly questionable form.

In Dante, philosophy appears as a third power, superior to Emperor and Pope alike, but not yet embodied in human institutions. By virtue of their offices, the Emperor and the Pope head the orders of the world. Above them, but without official status, stands the individual man, any man or every man, in whom we glimpse the archetypal man. Philosophy is always a given philosopher, never an impersonal authority.

It would be a mistake to identify this third power with *studium* in accordance with the medieval classification *"sacerdotium, imperium, studium"* having their summit in Italy (Rome), Germany, and France (Paris), and thus to rank *studium* above *sacerdotium* and *imperium*. For this *studium* is a theological discipline, and thus remains within the province of the Church. Dante's philosophy, though permeated with *studium* as it is with his experience of Church and Empire, is autonomous and lays claim to an authority superior to both Church and Empire. The enormity of this claim prevented Dante from saying directly where he stood. He concealed his real position in allusions. Although he manages to convey what he really thought, he nowhere states explicitly that he lays claim to an authority superior to Church and Empire—a claim that would be extravagant for any human being. How, indeed, could he have designated himself as the man to whom he refers as the *veltro!* * (Olschki). He plainly describes himself as a poet, a teacher, not as a superhuman individual endowed with authority over other men. Nevertheless, in respect of the great cause of truth, justice, and freedom, which can be realized only by persons, he staked out such a claim for the great philosopher, whom he identified with himself, not explicitly, but in effect.

Plato said: the Good will never attain to reality until the philosophers have become rulers or the rulers philosophers. Dante aspires—though not explicitly—to rule the world without holding office, through the authority of his counsel, by virtue of his intellectual superiority, his earnestness, and his poetic power. Neither Plato nor Dante envisaged the solution which to Kant seemed the only practical one: a form of government which Kant called "republican" (because it realizes political freedom in the public interest—*res publica*—as the foundation on which everything else rests), which leaves suprapersonal authority to be achieved by thinking persons debating issues with one another. Such an authority embodies the public spirit; the rulers are influenced by it because it has educated them to be what they are, and the people regard it as their own authority though it has no official status. Because it does not lay claim to official powers, because it represents the spirit itself, because it is embodied in individual personalities rather than in collective bodies, it effectively influences education, manners, and customs, and provides guidance for rulers and professional men. What appears as superhuman in a single individual's irrational claims and leads

---

* Translator's Note: The symbolic Greyhound (Deliverer of Italy?) mentioned in *Inferno*, Canto I, line 100.

to violence and despotism, can be humanized only through full and open discussion of differences. This is merely to recognize that we are never in possession of the truth whole and entire.

Dante was under the delusion that his towering artistic and intellectual gifts placed him so far above his contemporaries that by his own strength he could achieve what is actually possible for finite men only through a process of communication and recognition of differences by responsible citizens, a process by which they make themselves capable of a public exercise of authority. Dante demanded too much, and on the whole his example proved to be disastrous. Nicholas of Cusa, on the other hand, demanded too little. Essentially he did not adopt the role of the autonomous philosopher, though he helped to pave the way for independent philosophy.

2. De pace fidei

The conciliar struggle provided the occasion for *De concordantia catholica* with its program of reforms; the conquest of Constantinople by the Turks (1453) provided the occasion for *De pace fidei*. In both cases the main idea is the will to peace and unity.

Cusanus starts from the mistaken assumption that the conflict with the Turks was a religious war which could be stopped if only there were agreement on religious matters. He did not see that Islam was a religion of warriors interested in dominating the world and only incidentally in converting it. Religious constraint, which Cusanus rightly regarded as hideous and inhuman but falsely ascribed to the Turks, had in fact been a specific feature of Christianity whenever the Church had had the necessary power. In his old age even Augustine, breaking with all his earlier thinking, wished to force men to believe.

De pace fidei is a utopia in the form of a conversation in Heaven around the throne of God. Whether a letter subsequently addressed by Pius II to the Sultan was inspired by Cusanus' work is as uncertain as whether the letter ever reached the Sultan. The speakers are God, the Logos, Peter, Paul, and representatives of seventeen nations—a Greek, an Italian, an Arab, a Hindu, a Chaldaean, a Jew, a Scythian, a Frenchman, a Persian, a Syrian, a Spaniard, a Turk, a German, a Tartar, an Armenian, a Bohemian, and an Englishman. The substance of the conversation is familiar to us from Cusanus' other writings. No attempt is made to describe the doctrines of the other great religions.

In the face of the terrible evil of war between religious faiths, an archangel begs God to emerge from His concealment. Then swords will be idle. All mankind will become aware that for all the variety of rituals, there is only one religion (*una religio in rituum varietate*).

God replies, however, that He has left man free and by this freedom created him capable of human society. Because earthly man was held in ignorance by the prince of darkness, God sent down the prophets and finally the Logos, Christ, through whom He had created the world. Their mission was to show mankind how to find for themselves the immortal food of truth.

Now the archangel, the same who had begged God to come out of His concealment, replies that the Logos is bound by God's decision: man has to find the truth by exercising choice upon which his freedom of will depends. But man's situation is this: Since nothing in the world of the senses is permanent, since views and conjectures, like languages and inter-pretations, change according to circumstances, human nature requires frequent re-examination of the essentials. Only thus are errors dissipated and the truth enabled to shine through enduringly.

How is this to be accomplished? Since there is only one truth and since every free will can apprehend it, it would be expedient to reduce all different religions to the one true faith. Strange! No sooner has Cusanus opened the door to the possibility of man's constantly testing himself, striving in freedom for the truth, than he shuts it again by invoking the one truth, which the free will *must* recognize as one and indivisible.

Cusanus does not condemn the existing diversity of religious faiths. According to his context, he notes several reasons for it. Diversity is required by the sheer richness of the manifestations of the One. Earlier, in *De coniecturis* (III, 15) we read: The unity of intellectual religion is received in different aspects of otherness (*in varia igitur alteritate unitas intellectualis illius religionis recipitur*). Let the nations retain their various ceremonies and exercises in piety. Competition between nations to surpass one another in the splendor of their worship may even contribute to the growth of reverence for religion. The diversity of rites should be tolerated in view of mankind's weakness, so long as they are not offensive to the god-head. The main point is the thesis to which all the speakers subscribe: Differences between religions are purely a matter of usage. Common to all is worship of the one true God. However, the common people, led astray by the prince of darkness, have not always understood the meaning of their own actions.

The work concludes with the statement that "A general agreement among religions in keeping with these reasonable considerations was decreed in Heaven." God orders the sages to lead their respective nations to join together in knowledge of the true God. They are to be invested with full powers and to meet in Jerusalem, the center of the world, to accept one faith in the name of all, and on this basis to conclude a perpetual peace.

3. Faith and communication

It is often thought that once an event has been understood "historically," it has thereby been justified. But man is forever confronted by a task that goes beyond his historical circumstances. Thus we shall take no account of so-called "historical necessity" in considering the meaning of Cusanus' will to peace.

A. *Speculative thinking, fanaticism, communication, loving struggle.*—Taking as his premise a metaphysically grounded unity, Cusanus sets out both to define and to bring about union in the world, that is, to achieve peace. He relies on the power of speculative thinking, which transcends discursive reason. His adversaries are all fanatics (whether Christian or non-Christian); they assume in others a hostility to God, which they regard as a challenge. Fanatics always try to compel their adversaries to embrace the true faith and, when this fails, to destroy them.

Cusanus agrees with the fanatics, however, that there is only one true religion. Like the fanatics, he overlooks the only way in which men can achieve peace and unity. The one truth cannot be the possession of any one individual, community, or Church, an absolute possessing objective validity for every thinking mind. Communication among men is the only medium in which different faiths and ways of life can meet; because these are incompatible, they cannot exist simultaneously in any one man, but they can look upon one another with sympathetic interest once it is assumed that all contain truth as a possibility. Where no faith raises a claim to exclusivity, men, though engaged in loving struggle, will be able to live in peace with one another. For all the disparity of their ways of life, they will try to understand each other and learn to love one another. Disparity among faiths and ways of life does not preclude peace, for peace requires only one resolution: never to resort to violence in the name of religion, never to subordinate religious belief to practical interests.

In the temporal world, my ultimate duty is to enter into communication with other men, never claiming to know definitively what I myself am or what the other is. In perceiving the transcendent meaning of the ciphers, we can never attain universal validity. Transcendence is accessible to us only through the reading of ciphers, but the meaning we derive is never without ambiguity. All we know is what others say and what we ourselves say, and in neither case can we be sure of understanding correctly. For the speaker can misunderstand himself in the very act of expression. He comes closer to himself through a process of understanding that never ceases to test itself, he deepens his understanding by asking questions—whether to defend himself against adversaries suspected of hostility to the truth or for motives arising out of concrete situations. Only in this way can we learn to know ourselves in the face of the transcendent which is hidden and becomes clearer only in the experience of the ciphers. We live with one another as companions in the journey of human fate.

In matters of practical life, agreement is achieved by compromise on the basis of rational considerations. For practical problems are not absolute, but finite; they can be taken one by one, and in solving them we may be guided by what is merely expedient. However, the will to peace as such has a metaphysical source: although it leaves room for reasonable settlements of practical problems, it has an absolute character. Only this metaphysically grounded will to peace separates honest readiness to compromise from dishonest opportunism.

This distinction between questions of faith and practical problems is presupposed when an agreement concerning external matters involves a spiritual struggle to establish communication between irreconcilable faiths. Even on points where the adversaries are furthest apart, they try to establish contact, recognizing that their will to peace offers a common ground despite the diversity of its manifestations. Such contact does not of itself bring about unity, but is oriented toward the One, which neither party possesses exclusively. In such contacts the solidarity of common action in the empirical world is less important than the possibility that even radically different faiths have a common source. When this possibility is kept in mind, the deeper unity between man and man can be respected despite practical differences of opinion. Then the contending parties act "chivalrously."

The question is: Must the plurality of faiths, ways of life, attitudes to life, and metaphysical modes of existential awareness lead necessarily to contention on the empirical plane? At just what point are spiritual attitudes perverted into practical claims? What kind of faith is needed to link all men and to keep practical problems clearly separated from questions of faith? What faith—or what element present in every variety of faith—must be common to all men if mankind is to be united in peace?

This element is faith in freedom, faith rooted in freedom. This is the only faith that gives rise to demands for freedom at the social and political levels. I shall not deal here with the idea of how political freedom reflects man's will to secure the conditions of human fulfillment. Within the framework of political freedom, the freedom which itself creates this framework leads to loving struggle between rival faiths. On the empirical plane, rivalry may stoop to methods dictated by discursive reason or the passions, it may induce hatred and culminate in violence. Only faith in freedom can persuade men to distinguish practical problems from questions of faith. Such faith is not grounded in politics, but is itself the ground of politics, that is to say, of all politics deserving of the name—a politics aimed unconditionally at freedom, unity, and peace in empirical existence. Only when these ultimate objectives have been achieved will man be able to realize his potentialities and experience the full grandeur of his destiny.

B. *The individual and the historical.*—Cusanus' conception of individuals, each unique and irreplaceable, enjoying his own life as it is and wishing to be no other, rests on the following assumption. Since, by the nature of the divine creation, each individual is content with himself, while admiring those who are more accomplished or more outstanding, unity and peace prevail without ill-will. But he adds directly: "In so far as this is possible." For although peace is the power that makes possible the life of all men, it is disturbed by the disparities prevailing in this world of mere images (*De doc. ignor.*, III, 1).

Although Cusanus recognizes the diversity of substantial individual existence, he rejects the idea of a plurality of substantial faiths. There can be only one faith, the one true faith. But many religions and conflicting revelations divide mankind. Dismayed by this fact, Cusanus distinguishes religious rites—infinitely various—from faith itself, which can only be one. He strives vainly to make all men realize that they are actually living in one and the same faith; at the same time he acknowledges their right on the empirical plane to unfold the richness of the one faith in a variety of rites and customs.

No clear line is drawn, however, between the permissible diversity of religious customs and the true faith which is supposed to be the same for all. This lack of clarity is not accidental. Human faith discloses an original substantial diversity such that unification is impossible at the deepest level. What limits Cusanus' perspective is his certainty that the Christian faith is absolutely true, a certainty that excludes the other truth and seeks to impose on all men its own unacknowledged limitations.

Cusanus does not distinguish between the diversity of individuals and the plurality of the historical forms of selfhood. He gives magnificent expression to the all-important philosophical idea of unity, but he weakens it by positing a particular historicity as universal, thereby going counter to his own will to peace.

c. *The metaphysical awareness of being and action.*—Because Cusanus considers the problems he deals with in their metaphysical ground, he gains an exceptionally wide horizon in which he considers particular instances. Since this horizon transcends the concrete, temporal issues, he has room for contradictory practical decisions and is able to cope with new situations.

This is why the impact of a particular situation never determines his deliberations (not even when, in behalf of Pope Eugenius IV, he tried to dissuade the Germans from their attitude of neutrality). The historically unconditional stand of the great statesman was utterly alien to him. So long as peace has not been achieved, a statesman, as a man in the world, must confront other men in the struggle for survival, championing his own community as one power against other powers. Precisely because he is caught up in such struggles, he can take an unconditional stand only on historically limited truths.

The divine truth is eternal. Attempts to ascertain it in terms of transcendence lift us out of the world (at the peril of our lives) and we are in effect cut off from the world even when we look back upon it from on high.

For then we see the world as a marvelously transparent metaphor or allegory. When we follow this path, we do not attain the truth we are capable of attaining, for truth exists only as we create it by our actions in the world. Because the finite is never more than an inadequate image of the original, man must improve the world by championing the cause of finite truth in real situations. But this is an endless task which cannot be laid out in advance in any program or determined by any rules. It can only be carried out in history.

D. *The spirit of a whole.*—Nicholas of Cusa has a highly developed sense of "the spirit" of a whole—that is to say, of the Encompassing—which holds a community together and sustains it through all dissensions, the common, life-giving element which is as natural to the community as the air it breathes. But to Cusanus himself this spirit is so self-evident that we cannot go along with him without certain reservations.

Sheltered in such a spirit and relying on it unconsciously, we can feel its presence, or—this possibility could not have occurred to Cusanus—we can remain unsheltered, perpetual refugees in the world, when the world becomes a dispersed congeries of rationality, technology, and violence, lost in self-destruction.

If, however, we conjure up such a spirit in order to share in it more lucidly and more fully, and on this basis address men as our companions in fate, we shall conceive of it as a kind of substance that contains and sustains everything. Cusanus' philosophy may be regarded as just such a conjuring up of the spirit incarnated in the world, on the strength of which he means to live along with all others.

But when we try to understand this "spirit" or even to survey the variety of "spirits" that have lived in the course of the centuries, we apprehend none of them as a whole. Each comes to us in an image, and this image is not unitary. The understanding apprehension of a "spirit" is achieved, rather, through an unlimited plurality of ideal types, constructions of meaningful relationships which more or less reflect the historical reality of a spirit. The more consistent our constructions, the more instructive they are, but also the falser they are if we mistake them for reality itself. The endless historical reality of a spirit is always more or less than such ideal types disclose. They enable us to see the spirit of a whole as the result of countless factors produced and handed down in the medium of education, language, forms of social life, patterns of conduct, ideas. These produce the "spirit" of a historical epoch, and within it great men produce the supratemporal in works and actions that break through the spirit of an age or a community.

E. *The modes of "tolerance." Vilification of Saracens and Jews.*—To Cusanus "tolerance" signifies willingness to put up with foreign customs and even to approve of them, provided the inner faith is the one truth of Christian revelation. Actually, this is not tolerance at all, for it presupposes that the adversary shares the same "self-evident" faith. Cusanus' tolerance is neither an indifference toward the other (as in the shallow variety of rationalism) nor freedom to see the originally alien in the depths of the other's faith, to respect it as such, and to be moved by it (as in genuine tolerance). Rather, it is an unconscious intolerance; Cusanus' own Christian faith remains for him the only true faith, absolutely valid for all men everywhere. Cusanus either rediscovers his own faith in the outwardly alien manifestations of the other's faith or sees this other faith as the work of the Devil.

Because Cusanus believes that no religion can lead to peace unless grounded in faith in the God-Man—who is the Word, the Light, and the Life (John)—he can make statements which in fact exclude peace. He speaks of the "superstitious aberration (*absona credulitas*) of the Saracens, who deny the godhead of Christ. Without reason they persecute the Cross, they are blinded (*obcaecati*). The Jews are afflicted with the same diabolical blindness (*eadem diabolica caecitate*), for they, too, deny the godhead of Christ" (*De doc. ignor.*, III, 8). Can such a scorn be so inherent in the Christian faith that even in a man like Cusanus, whose will to peace was a basic motive of all his thought, it must raise its ugly head? When I read such passages in Cusanus, I am amazed, shaken with indignation, and I think of the Gospel according to St. John in which the author has Christ (who is not the historical Jesus) say to the Jews: Ye are of your father the devil (John 8, 44).

Part Five: Political Action and the Conduct of Life

Did Cusanus' theories spring from his experience of life, and if so, did they in turn influence it? At what points was there agreement, and at what points not?

We are not asking whether he lived in accordance with his beliefs. His reflections were not such as to provide practical prescriptions for man's conduct (nor does any real philosophy). What we are asking, rather, is in what way his philosophical thinking affected his fundamental attitudes toward life. Were his pious speculations matched by equal piety in his practical activities?

Did a specific practice of life attain self-understanding in this philosophy? Did his philosophy help him to achieve self-certainty in respect of his political activity, for example? To what extent did his life motivate and reflect his philosophy? Did his philosophical composure remain unshaken throughout the vicissitudes of life?

Reality shattered nearly all his deeper convictions and practical aspirations. Did his vision of Being turn out to be an illusion for not having withstood the test of practice? Was he unable to immerse himself in his historical tasks because he clung so fervently to the promise of eternal bliss held out by Christian revelation?

In the last analysis, such questions cannot be answered. All we can attempt here is to look at the factual data in relation to which such questions arise.

1. The Council of Basel

Sent to the Council of Basel by Count von Manderscheid to press the Count's claims to the bishopric of Trier, Cusanus became a leader at the Council after presenting his great work, De concordantia catholica (1433). At that time he was a supporter, along with the best among those present, of the conciliar party, which advocated reform and opposed the Pope. The Council seemed to be united in its views and was at first victorious over the Pope.

But the situation was modified by the prospect of another Council, summoned by the Pope to discuss a union between the Latin and the Greek Church, and by dissensions arising within the Council of Basel, which Eugenius IV shrewdly exploited. In the course of a crucial session on May 7, 1437, the split within the Council burst into the open. Cusanus now voted with the papal minority. The supporter of the Council had become a supporter of the Pope. His defection was interpreted by many as a betrayal, and his political attitude has remained a subject of discussion to this day.

Cusanus left Basel with the minority on May 20, 1437. As minority spokesman he accompanied the papal envoys on a journey to Constantinople to lay the groundwork for the Council which was to promote unity between the Latin and Greek branches of Christianity.

Meanwhile the conciliar idea lived on. The German princes took a neutral attitude. In the prime of life, Cusanus devoted himself to the cause of Eugenius IV, expending inexhaustible energy, his superior intellect, and uncommon eloquence in an effort to win over the princes to the Pope. This he did on repeated occasions: in 1438, at the Imperial Diet in Nuremberg; in 1439 at the Diet of Electors in Mainz; in 1440 and 1442 at the Imperial Diet in Frankfurt; in 1443 again in Nuremberg, and in 1447 at the Diet of Princes in Aschaffenburg. Piccolomini, his humanist friend, later Pope Pius II, at this time still a partisan of the Council, called him Hercules Eugenianorum.

In a letter to Cesarini (Posch, p. 169) Cusanus says that on one occasion he spoke in a "a strong virile voice" from seven to eleven very effectively, as he hoped, and that he feared danger to his person. The upshot of all this activity was the concordat of 1447–48, a victory for Cusanus. The Germans declared their obedience to the Pope. The Council of Basel had disbanded in 1443.

Why had Cusanus defected from the conciliar party? The determining factor was the threat of a new schism. In reality the Pope alone could preserve the unity of the Church. The Council had failed. The *consensus omnium* had given way to endless quarreling and sanctimonious factionalism. The Holy Spirit no longer seemed to be guiding the proceedings. The authority of the Council to represent the entire Church had declined. It no longer had any real power, although it continued to promulgate decrees. At the time when Piccolomini was still undecided and wrote "There was no Christian there who did not weep, the Holy Spirit could not have been among us," and "God sees where the truth lies, I do not," Cusanus had already made up his mind.

The unity of the Church was the all-important consideration. Unity could not survive unless backed up by power. As a mere article of faith, a mere opinion, it was meaningless. If there was power anywhere now, it was not with the Council but with the Pope, however objectionable his personal character may have been. To work for unity does not mean to believe in it and do nothing. It has to be fought for in the real world, with the world's own methods, that is, politically. Cusanus did just that. His actions were widely interpreted as a betrayal of his ideal conception of the Church, but in shifting his position on this particular question he remained faithful to his primary objective of unity. As he saw it, this now required a new orientation on the plane of reality.

There is no doubt that he made a political volte-face. Did he at the same time change his opinions and formulations? There is no doubt on this point either. Many of his statements seem to reflect some fundamental change in his interpretation of the respective roles of Pope and Council. Closer scrutiny, however, shows that statements about the role of the Pope in his first pro-Council work foreshadow his later thinking—for even then he had expressed himself in favor of the Pope. Nor did he subsequently abandon altogether his views as to the ideal role of the Council. But an unchanging belief in the absolute importance of Church unity guided his interpretations of the realities of the day, which are reflected in statements that vary to the point of being contradictory. Though his justifications are of great philosophical interest, they are anything but easy to grasp.

A. *His arguments*: (1) *Is the Pope above the Council or is the Council above the Pope?*—The question presupposes unanimity regarding Church organization. In the discussions of that time no one contested the principle of the One Church, unique and infallible, not to mention the theological status of God or Christ or the Gospels, or the dogma of the Church as the mystic body of Christ.

Both Pope and Council possess their high and inviolable significance. Both are in their temporal reality represented by persons whose "spirit" must have qualities that meet the requirements of the institution.

The Pope must not fail to carry out his duties as Vicar of Christ, as interpreted by the decisions of his predecessors and the early Church councils whose decrees are binding upon him. The councils, under the guidance of the Holy Spirit, must express unanimously the inner dispositions of their members, and their decrees, moreover, must be universal, must represent the entire Church.

But what is to be done when one of the two chief authorities—or the men who embody authority—fails to act in accordance with the principles stated above? Can the Council depose the Pope? Can the Pope dissolve the Council? Who is to decide which of them is right? There exists no authority superior to both, no supreme court of judgment, to which appeal can be made in the case of conflict between Pope and Council.

The idea of the One Church, in which Pope and Council are interrelated parts of a single whole, loses its force when a state of corruption prevails in the body of the Church. In the event of conflict a judge is needed to settle it. But his verdict can be enforced only if Pope or Council is clearly recognized as superior, and by all concerned, or at least by a majority. But this is a merely juridical and political solution; it is not a matter of faith. What actually takes place in the event of such conflict becomes a question of power and political adroitness; which party will gain the support of princes and governments? The weaker "the spirit," the more decisive becomes the role of brute force. And this is what happened at that time.

(2) *The contradictory formulations.*—From the outset Cusanus looked upon Pope *and* Council as the highest authority within the One Church. He regarded them as equally indispensable. But faced with actual situations, he arrived at contradictory formulations.

At first he wrote that the Church is more certainly and infallibly represented by the Council than by the Pope alone (*De conc. cath.,* II, 18; Basel edition, p. 687). As the presiding member, Cusanus says, the Pope is part of the Council, and since the whole is superior to its parts, the authority of the Council is superior to that of the Pope. He salutes the Council of Basel with these words: "Oh, that in spite of everything God may have gathered His elect in this holy Council and revealed His glorious Coming in these troubled times" (Jaeger, I, 22).

Later, however, he asserts the superior authority of the Pope, though by no means recognizing his absolute autocracy. The Pope is limited by the rulings of his predecessors, by the canons of the Church, by his status as the head of the ecclesiastical hierarchy (Posch, 165 ff., report on the letter to Rodrigo Sanchez, May 20, 1442). Such limitations, however, merely describe what is valid in principle; they could not legally be imposed by any other authority, not even by a council. This is why in the same letter Cusanus declares that the Pope is completely free. He depends on no one, no one can pass judgment on him. Because the Council of Basel had done just that, he called its action dreadful sacrilege, vain presumptuousness, rebellion against the Apostle (*horridum nefas, vanissima ambitio, apostolica rebellio*).

The most significant statements are quoted by Posch from the records of the imperial diets. Cusanus now grants the Pope constitutional rights he had formerly denied him, and develops this new idea in great detail. The Pope, for example, has the right to grant prebends (that is, he is not bound to respect the choice of the local chapters). And a council representing all of Christendom save the Pope would not be a council.

But this is the crucial point: The question of how the Church is to proceed against a bad Pope should not even be discussed; to do so would be disrespectful and unedifying. At a diet in Frankfurt he said: "The Council can do nothing about a fallible Pope" (Posch, 170). He does not deny that the Pope, like any other man, may be fallible (*deviabilis*), but "We are to asume that he is less fallible than other men" (Kallen, 81).

The Pope holds his powers directly from Christ, whereas the powers of the Council derive from the Pope. The Council without the Pope is like a tree without leaves. It would be absurd to maintain that the power of individual leaders in the Church can equal that of the Supreme Pontiff. He rules absolutely. To argue that he both rules and obeys would be absurd. Within the Church each separate authority is valid only when it is subordinated to the single supreme authority.

(3) *An example: the argument involving the role of Peter.*—No man who does not worship at the throne of Peter is a believer; such a man stands outside the unity of the Church (*De conc. cath.,* I, 14; Basel edition, p. 685). There is only one *cathedra* of St. Peter. All of St. Peter's successors to the throne have the same rights as he. Just as Peter was prince among the Apostles, so the Bishop of Rome is prince among the bishops (*De conc. cath.,* I, 15).

Yet, in another passage of the same work, these emphatic statements on the position of the Pope are seemingly retracted by a number of finely drawn symbolic distinctions concerning the role of St. Peter. Their effect is to limit the extent of papal power. The rock of the Church is Christ. Just as Christ is the truth and the rock (*petra*) is a figure or symbol (*figura sive significatio*) of Christ, so the Church is the rock of Christ and Peter is a figure or symbol of the Church. Or again: Just as Christ is the truth and the rock His figure and symbol, so the rock of the Church is the truth and Peter is a figure and symbol of the truth. This shows clearly that the Church is above Peter, just as Christ is above the Church (*De conc. cath.*, II, 18; Basel edition, 739).

(4) *Argument based on changing historical conditions within the Church.*—What was true of Church government when the Church was being founded is no longer true of the Church in its present form. Since then there has developed a specific hierarchical order allowing for degrees of power. Furthermore: what was true for such an emergency as a schism within the Church is no longer true for a period of unity, when the Pope enjoys universal recognition but is threatened with a new schism. Thus, many of the decrees promulgated by the Council of Constance were emergency measures and as such appropriate only for the duration of the schism. For at that time, beyond any doubt, there was no legitimate Pope able to dissolve the Council. Now that there is such a Pope, the Basel Fathers insult the Council of Constance when they invoke the earlier body as a precedent (Posch, 170).

(5) *Free elections and the majority.*—A universal council can be convened only through elections. All lawful authority is based on free election (*De conc. cath.*, II, 19; Basel edition, p. 687).

The Fathers assembled in council require a majority of votes to pass a resolution. But Cusanus makes contradictory statements concerning the powers of the majority. At first: According to St. Augustine, a majority of the Council can overrule the Pope, because it is a more reliable and less fallible *repraesentatio* (representation, manifestation, presence) of the Church (*De conc. cath.*, II, 18; Basel edition, p. 687). But later Cusanus condemns the majority principle (holding that the minority at the Council, to which he himself belonged, represented the truth). Where the unity of the Church is at stake, he says, mathematics has no bearing. Only the practical consequences of a course of action decided upon by the ballot can determine whether it furthers the cause of unity. For example: from the standpoint of the Council for uniting the Latin and Greek Churches, planned in opposition to the Council of Basel, the Council of Basel was a mere incident without universal significance.

B. *The meaning of such arguments.* Today they are called "ideological." What do they mean in themselves? What lies behind them?

(1) *Rationalization and dialectics.*—Cusanus thinks in ciphers, drawing inferences from them as to practical decisions. But this kind of thinking is bound up with a "spirit" which is not itself definable. When the spirit is absent, the multifarious practical interests and aims, as well as sophisms of discursive reason, make all arguments futile. In the end everyone does what he wanted to do in the first place, putting forward arguments as a smoke screen. When this point is reached, all the parties to the dispute work inadvertently toward their own destruction.

Interpretations derived from thinking in ciphers are by nature dialectical in the sense that opposites are combined to form a unity, so that one opposite tilts over into the other and opinions change while the underlying will to unity remains unchanged. The shift of opinions becomes sophistical when it serves the will to power, which is not itself dialectical. It can avoid sophistry only if it remains within the bounds of some substantial spiritual whole.

It does not seem likely that Cusanus was aware of the dialectical relativity of the various positions he maintained theoretically. That he had a dim intimation along these lines may be attested by his use of expressions like "the basis of this consideration" (*fundamentum huius considerationis,* Basel edition, p. 687).

Only with meaningful, not sophistical dialectics, rooted in a sense of the whole, could Cusanus have served both the conciliar and the papal party without dishonesty. Actually his idea of unity—which, being metaphysical, is adequately grounded only in the *coincidentia oppositorum*—remains unchanged. Unity has to be realized unconditionally, though just how depends on the situation. Thus there is nothing to show that Cusanus was unfaithful to his fundamental goal when he shifted allegiance. His faith remained the same; he merely altered his means of attaining it in finite reality.

(2) *Source and logic.*—The source of faith and of a will grounded in it cannot be rationally justified. The doctrine is not the faith itself, but only one manifestation of it.

The force of logic is compelling only to the extent that it avails itself of definable concepts. The presuppositions of faith can be expressed in ciphers, but they are not rationally definable. Communication in indefinable concepts—which despite their rational aspect are in themselves without rational content—is existentially convincing only when a shared faith gives meaning to the concepts and guides the thinking. And since agreement in faith can never be rationally certain on the plane of the utterable, it discloses itself only in the struggle of ideas. In philosophical thinking logic gives way to sophistry whenever it ceases to be guided by the content of faith, and the discussion bogs down in the contingency of sham concepts.

The openness of self-understanding can be founded on rational propositions only when these are in close union with the content of the faith. Without such union the result is first emptiness and then sophistry, because the words, exposed to endless ambiguities, lose their original meanings.

(3) *Arguments of faith.*—There are extreme cases where faith is experienced with purity, also cases where faith deceives.

In the former, faith speaks directly as such, as "the spirit." It is conscious of man's task in the world as the imperative of a higher authority.

Formulated as a doctrine, faith is no longer the same. The doctrine may invoke a revealed God, historical necessity, natural necessity, some metaphysical necessity governing all happenings, or something else.

Any such doctrine, in which faith seeks to understand itself, is the product of our own thinking and indemonstrable because its ultimate higher authority can never be demonstrated. Historically, there have always been several such doctrines, mutually exclusive on the rational plane even though attempts have been made to combine them all in a single great systematic structure. Likewise, there are several historical faiths, and there is no Archimedean point outside them from which one man can survey them. With few exceptions, each faith not only lays claim to unconditional truth but also looks upon its doctrine as absolutely valid for all. Vainly it struggles to assert itself against other doctrines by means of arguments. It owes its existence to a human claim to power.

The claim to power also leads to blatant religious deceit—the other extreme case, opposed to pure religious experience. Discussions ostensibly of religious matters may in fact be motivated by selfish interests; religious feelings are exploited for material purposes.

In real life, pure religious experience is as rare as the pure claim to power; the motives are usually mixed. Who can claim to penetrate another person's mind, who can be sure he knows his adversary's true motives? In ideological quarrels we often complain about the endless argumentation, the possibility of proving or contradicting anything at all. When men who have lost their faith speak in the language of faith on a rational plane, we may say with the poet,

> You speak of reasons, ah, be still,
> With reasons I can all your reasons kill.

The existential force of metaphysical thinking apprehends events and actions in another dimension, as though eternity were present in them. Such thinking is truthful. But when speculative thinking in ciphers harnesses the propositions it arrives at to worldly ends, the result is bewilderment and confusion, a permanent deception in speech and argument.

(4) *Cusanus touches upon the problems of truth and freedom but does not grasp them.*—Because Cusanus believed the truth he possessed through revelation and speculative thinking to be the voice of God in the world, he was unaware of this great problem: Since only the individual can gain insight into truth, freedom, and peace—not an isolated individual, but only one who shares his thinking with others—how can the best individuals concerned with community welfare gain the support of the many? How can the co-operation of the best and the many produce not merely external decisions, but rather express the inner moral and political reality of the community? In discussing the conciliar controversy, he touches upon the questions of institutional freedom and of the way in which the co-operation of all the faithful is to be attained, but these problems are never brought to full awareness.

(5) *Cusanus did not disguise the shift in his allegiance, but obscured the fundamental human situation.* After Cusanus' defection, his adversaries in the Council criticized him for his inconsistency, and rightly so.

Did Cusanus try to conceal the fact that he had turned his back on his earlier position? Did he refuse to admit that his opinions had undergone a radical change? Did he dodge the issue? I believe that his manner of thinking prevented him from attaining clarity on this score. This was why, on the one hand, he felt that he had not contradicted himself with respect to the inner disposition of his faith, and why, on the other hand, he did not take seriously the contradictions that are so clearly evident when his statements are considered from a rational point of view.

Logically unclear statements as to the relations between Pope and Council occur both before and after his shift of allegiance. In the course of his hesitations, he occasionally encompasses the two opposites, but then he also speaks as an extreme advocate of each position.

He never grasped clearly the dialectical character of his approach to practical problems. The reason for this (we shall discuss it in greater detail later) seems to be that his metaphysics postulates a harmony realizable in the world. He thus loses sight of the fundamental situation of our existence in the world.

2. Brixen

In 1450 Cusanus became Bishop of Brixen. He was appointed by the Pope against the wishes of the local Chapter. His administration proved disastrous to the province of South Tyrol. He was opposed by the clergy who had been bullied into accepting him, by the monastic institutions (especially one convent under an energetic abbess) which he tried to reform, and by the Archduke Sigismund of Austria from whom Cusanus tried to regain certain prerogatives of which the Church had been deprived. His miserly financial policy was unpopular. He gained the support of a number of peasants and of some enemies of the Habsburgs, such as the Swiss—who made use of him to the same extent as he tried to make use of them. In the struggle he applied the harshest measures, including excommunication. He enforced a ban on foreign trade, so that the province lost the income it had derived from commerce between Venice and the north. With the loss of prosperity political and moral standards declined. Violence and contempt for the Church increased (Jaeger, I, 4). Cusanus himself was absent for long periods; at first his duties as papal legate kept him traveling in Germany, and his last years were spent in Rome.

When he died, the new Pope and the Emperor quickly settled the conflict. The claims Cusanus had fought so stubbornly to have recognized were abandoned. A partisan of Cusanus, who realized what a great blow this was to the prestige of the Church, wrote: "Ah, if only they had never begun this dispute that has come to so shocking an end" (Jaeger, II, 432).

During the years in Austria, Cusanus was often exposed to personal danger. In 1457 he went to Innsbruck to negotiate with the Archduke

(Koch, 63 ff.; Meuthen, 15) and on his way back he saw some armed men. On the basis of rumors he publicly accused the Archduke of plotting to ambush and kill him. Koch, who studied all the relevant documents, wonders whether the Cardinal was not more frightened than the situation called for, and suspects that he exploited it for all it was worth. Koch believes that the incident was deliberately staged to intimidate the unpopular foreigner and severe reformer. Cusanus tells us, however, that he escaped only with God's help. The castle of Buchenstein on the southern boundary of the diocese seemed to provide him with some measure of safety. He resided there for a year, and in September 1458 moved to Rome.

From there he carried on his struggle against the Archduke. He returned to his diocese in 1460, taking every precaution to protect his life. The journey was anything but a success. When the Archduke laid siege to the castle of Bruneck, Cusanus capitulated. He signed an agreement giving in on all points at issue, and when the Curia protested, he defended the Archduke. But once back on Italian territory, he declared that he had been made to sign the agreement under duress. The episode marked the lowest point in his career; both materially and spiritually it was a defeat. For he was well aware of how badly he had behaved. In a letter to the Bishop of Eichstätt, dated June 11, 1460, he writes: "I had hoped to end my days with a glorious death in the cause of justice, but I was not worthy of that honor" (Jaeger, II, 62). A short time later he said (*De ludo globi*): A Christian is a man who puts the honor of Christ above his own life. The test is how he stands up to persecution. "Christ lives in him, he himself does not live." A Christian despises this world and this life. "It is a simple matter for one who has the true faith. . . . But it is impossible for a non-believer." Are we to conclude that Cusanus broke down when put to the test because he did not truly believe, but only believed in faith—that he failed at the crucial moment?

Yet in the same letter he goes on to say: "I did not wish I had not suffered what happened to me, I was glad of my suffering. . . . Moreover, I became convinced that a bishop's duty is not to increase the *temporalia* [financial resources, etc.] of his church, but only to preserve them. . . . Alms for the poor, not the wealth of the bishops, are what ought to be increased. Therefore, I rejoice in my misfortune, because it has enriched my knowledge. . . . At the time I did not see my error, but I see it now, for I was punished for it. . . . This is what I thought, to comfort myself and to recover my peace of mind, and we can congratulate each other that God has been willing to show us our imperfections by sending us such little trials" (Jaeger, II, 62).

There are also glimpses of Cusanus' thoughts about himself in his letters addressed a few years earlier to his friend the Abbot of Tegernsee: "If only I might hope for some results, I would not be deterred by the work, for after all there is no peace anywhere in this world; but to spend oneself for nothing at all is absurd. . . . I bear the difficulties with patience, sooner or later I shall surmount them with God's help" (1458). A year later: "It is impossible for me to concentrate and get on with it [the composition of the work]. If I am not given more freedom, I shall be lost . . ." (1455).

Do not such reflections sound like those of a man who is uncertain of his goal and, instead of striving to become transparent to himself, falls back on traditional ideas?

3. The reform movement

The best among Cusanus' contemporaries demanded thoroughgoing reform of the Church (extending from the papacy down to the parish level), and reform of the Empire as well. Cusanus himself reflected on these matters all his life. The intention was to bring back to living reality the eternal elements of faith within the Church organization. The reform movement, however, proved a complete failure.

In 1451–52 Cusanus was sent to Germany with the mission of spurring on reform. The churches and monasteries received him with honors, but when the question of reform came up, they resisted or made token gestures that lasted only as long as his visit. Later, in Brixen, his attempts at reform met with violent resistance from both the monasteries and the clergy. Commissioned to reform the Church in Rome itself, he failed completely because the Pope and the cardinals had no intention of allowing their own authority to be interfered with. Lastly, at Orvieto—apparently no place was too large or too small for Cusanus to be sent to reform it!—the burghers were at first overjoyed at the presence of the great man, but soon they resisted him stubbornly. Why did all these attempts at reform end in failure?

No reform conceived merely as an external change of institutions can succeed. Reform presupposes a change of heart by the participants, a serious resolve to make a fresh start. Cusanus himself never experienced any such change of heart. He remained within the world of faith he inherited. His personal life was modest and irreproachable. All this is respectable, but there was no passionate devotion to a cause. A few isolated individuals among the clergy and the monastic orders were alone willing to accept reforms. That so many attempts at reform were fruitless or violently resisted shows that the reformers were not really in earnest, were not prepared to make sacrifices. Cusanus was not motivated by his philosophical ideas concerning man's task (which he expressed so magnificently in his meditations), nor did he go back to the Bible. He merely invoked doctrinal considerations and the ascetic principles sanctioned by the Church. He sincerely advocated reform, but he did not realize that reform is meaningless unless the men who carry it out have undergone an authentic change of heart.

Cusanus' failure on both the material and the spiritual plane teaches us to see more clearly how difficult the task of the truth is, what tremendous obstacles must be surmounted by those engaged in it. Quite possibly no one has ever surmounted them. Socrates and Jesus came closest. But we also learn that all evil springs from lack of sufficient truthfulness.

4. The crusade against the Turks

The conquest of Constantinople by the Turks shook the West to its foundations and was felt to be a turning point in history. The humanist Enea Silvio de' Piccolomini (later Pius II) lamented the fate of the land of Homer, overrun by barbarians. Cusanus wrote *De pace fidei* in the hope of restoring peace through union of the faithful of all religions.

When Piccolomini became Pope, his main goal was to launch a crusade against the Turks. Cusanus saw that the project was unfeasible and repeatedly warned the Pope against vain hopes. He advised, for example, against convoking a congress of princes at Mantua, predicting that not even the Emperor would attend. And indeed, the congress proved a humiliating failure for the Pope.

A crusade could have been successful only had there been political peace in the West and if the Church had been reformed and unified. An internally united West conscious of its common danger would have been strong enough to carry out such a crusade. Cusanus saw clearly how unrealistic the project was because he knew that Europe was divided. Faithful to his principles, he nonetheless served the Pope obediently in his hopeless cause. He accompanied him to Mantua and conducted himself thereafter as though he shared the Pope's views about the crusade.

The humanist Pope dreamed his irresponsible dream. As he lay dying in Ancona on the Adriatic coast, a few Venetian ships he had long been awaiting suddenly appeared in the harbor. With tragic irony he reflected: Formerly I had crusaders but no fleet, now I have a fleet but no crusaders. It had been Cusanus' responsibility to look after the penniless adventurers who rallied to the Pope's banner, to keep them out of trouble and prevent them from pillaging the countryside. A few days before Pius II, Cusanus himself died, quietly and undramatically, in Todi, while on his way to join the Pope.

5. Ecclesiastical benefices

Cusanus lived on revenues from benefices—as was perfectly normal for a Church dignitary. As early as 1427 (when he was twenty-six years old) he obtained a dispensation granting him the right to hold several mutually exclusive benefices. During the 1430s he was given more benefices (Münster-

maifeld, St. Martin in Worms). When he took over a richly endowed archdeaconry in Liège, the local clergy found fault with him for being unable to
administer the office himself.

An exchange of letters with Jacob von Sirck, Archbishop of Trier (1453),
deals with a benefice which Cusanus had verbally promised to turn over to
the Archbishop. He wished nevertheless to keep it for himself, and his
attitude in the matter is ambiguous. To Sirck: "I will be giving up the
archdeaconry one of these years." On the same day, to a friend in Rome:
"I have no intention of rushing my resignation." Although he had promised
to pass on the benefice to Sirck, he wrote to Rome that he would submit
his resignation to the Pope—which meant that another candidate would be
appointed. When Sirck learned of this, he was indignant. And actually
Cusanus held on to all his benefices until he died. He gives several reasons
why he could not surrender them. The most important was the home for
the aged he founded at Cues: "What God hath given should go to the
poor" (Koch).

Despite his influential position in the Curia (which rested solely on his
friendship with Pius II), Cusanus never amassed a personal fortune. But
in acquiring his comparatively modest benefices, he showed himself at
times to be a scheming realist, inconstant, and occasionally untrustworthy.
The consequences of his Christian philosophizing did not reach into these
domains.

6. His conduct of life—summary

A. *Historical situation.*—The historical situation confronted Cusanus with
a plurality of powers. This was the age of the sovereign individual, indifferent to good and evil, a type that was gaining ground within the Church
as elsewhere. In the end the Renaissance Popes, who carried this kind of
individualism to extremes, discredited the Church completely, though they
helped to produce an unprecedented flowering in the arts. Ruthless representatives of territorial and national particularism reduced the office
of Emperor to a purely decorative function. The Emperor enjoyed a
measure of authority only in the country he ruled by hereditary right;
otherwise he was scarcely more than a figurehead. Nevertheless those who
were eligible aspired to the title, for it retained a certain traditional prestige
and various prerogatives that could be exploited. Within the Church there
were conflicts, both major and minor—occasioned by the conciliar movement, the Hussites, and contending ecclesiastical and secular claims. In
Rome there were rivalries between the cardinals, and intrigues of French,
Italian, and Spanish factions. The Papal State was involved in conflicts
with many city states and tyrants, and problems of world-wide importance
were interwoven with local Italian interests. Particular interests might join
in common cause or press their claims separately, depending on the situation

of the moment; everyone tried to make use of everyone else. Diplomatic intrigues were rampant, everything was in a state of flux. Cusanus lived in the thick of all this complicated activity, which historians find so picturesque.

B. *Adaptability and inconsistency.*—In order to take an active part in this world, Cusanus could not avoid making certain adjustments and involving himself in certain inconsistencies. He could not get ahead with the great task he had set himself—the achievement of peace and unity—unless he first tackled the lesser concrete tasks that Rome set him. As a result, he virtually lost sight of his primary task. As adviser and agent plenipotentiary to the Pope, he played the part assigned him, and like everyone else took a hand in events which brought about no significant change.

Good will, such as Cusanus possessed, was not enough to produce results. Only a force as elemental as the ruthless destructive forces of that epoch could have opposed those forces effectively. Cusanus was not such a man. What he lacked above all was a passionate faith based upon a real change of heart.

Examples of Cusanus' inconsistencies: He condemned the project of a crusade against the Turks, yet participated in the preparations for it. He looked upon the Emperor's rights as inviolable—on the ground that the Emperor represented the unity of the Empire and was the protector of the Church—yet appealed to the real power of the King of France against him.

How did Cusanus become involved in such a situation? Active by nature, especially at the beginning of his career, he wished to be where public events were being decided, a penchant that remained with him to the end of his life. The impression made by his intellectual superiority, his talents as a preacher and negotiator, made him a valuable servant of the Church. And he himself not only identified the ideal unity of the Church with the unity of mankind, but also championed the power of a Church which was not in fact universal but merely laid claim to universality. He also sought power for himself. Although Cusanus took life more seriously than the humanists, Thomas More was far superior to him in his conduct of life.—Cusanus lacked the consuming seriousness of faith. He lacked the courage of his convictions, the courage of the truly responsible statesman. He was a man of half-measures, too easily satisfied. No doubt it was quite an accomplishment for a boy from a village on the Moselle to become a cardinal and the vicar general in Rome. But, except for persuading the neutral Germans to support Pope Eugenius, he failed in all his undertakings, and brilliant representative of the Church that he was, he attained none of his objectives.

C. *Violence.*—Cusanus' moral and political failure can be accounted for by his attitude toward violence.

We discern in him a will to power that sought to subordinate everything to his Church, to his faith, to his vision of the world order. He was not motivated by a will to communication, such as strives for the peaceful co-existence of fundamentally different faiths. Rather, his faith was that of a doctrinaire Churchman. In pronouncing the words "We Christians," he was so sure of his cause and of himself that he was incapable of active tolerance. He had no sympathetic understanding of other religions, no readiness to recognize that they are fully entitled to their different rituals and customs, whose importance he minimized. He failed to see that other faiths may be just as wholehearted, true, meaningful, and comprehensive as his own. For all his concessions, he naïvely assumed and asserted the absolute truth of Christianity in the specific form of his own Church. To achieve peace he did not resort to communication but, in the last analysis, to violence.

To carry out his reforms he needed the support of the princes, a secular power at the disposal of the Church. He appealed to them in vain; they refused to help him. Again, it was naïve of him to take for granted that the secular princes would serve his (and the Church's) will to power. Clearly, he did not rely solely on the freedom of faith and the word, on the power of philosophical arguments.

In actual fact Cusanus took the path of compulsion. But he had no power. We shudder to think what his life and character would have been had he possessed power and made use of it!

As a philosopher Cusanus was more understanding, more profound, and more communicative than he could ever be in his practical activities. In his best works he often moves us deeply by his magnificent open-mindedness and the vast range of his vision. The obtuseness of his political practice is something else again. Was he lacking in the honesty that is inseparable from the unremitting will to understand oneself? Was he incapable of seeing how incompatible his philosophy was with his ecclesiastical practice?

D. *Is his philosophy discernible in his conduct of life?*

(1) *De docta ignorantia* marked an important step forward in his philosophy, but despite certain new formulations his fundamental political attitudes never changed. The fact that he eventually applied the concepts of *complicatio* and *explicatio* to Pope and Church, or to Peter, Pope, and Church, amounts only to a slight enrichment of his symbolic language. For example: the Pope is "implicitly" what the Church is "explicitly," or: Peter is "implicitly" what the entire Church with the Pope as its head is "explicitly." This means: the Pope is not Peter, but together with all the bishops and the rest of the clergy he is part of the *explicatio* corresponding to the *complicatio Petri*.

The *coincidentia oppositorum* makes it easier to advocate contradictory theses (successively or even simultaneously) about the one and the whole regardless of the actual alternatives involved in practical, temporal decisions: Pope vs. Council, Empire vs. nations, etc.

(2) The original model of the eternal order as we see it in *De concordantia catholica* goes back to the patristic epoch and the Middle Ages. Cusanus was not in search of something new, but trying to restore the old. What had become virtually powerless in reality, remained for Cusanus the guiding idea. But after having used it for a time to justify practical decisions, Cusanus made no further mention of it. The more deeply he became entangled in practical politics, the less he resorted to justification.

Eventually he stopped trying to justify his actions by his philosophy as he had done so impressively in connection with the conciliar question. To attempt anything of the kind today would merely produce an empty construction. Cusanus' own inability to do so throws a significant light on his politics, which was always a pursuit of short-range objectives and which dissatisfied him because it had gradually lost all philosophical meaning.

(3) Down to the last year of his life, as some of the finest and most mature of his minor works show, he meditated with undiminished energy. But there was no point of contact between his philosophical meditation and his politics. He conceived of philosophy as the one and only possible happiness in the world. It was an accompaniment to his practical activities but did not influence them. The hours and days he was able to devote to philosophical reflection were especially precious, the retreat of a monk unwilling to give up his whole life and withdraw from the world. In the world he found disorder and disappointment but was compelled to play the game in order to survive. In philosophy he found justification and the often repeated satisfaction of piety. This was the refuge of a man lost in the world.

Part Six: His Place in History

1. Between the Middle Ages and the modern era

Cusanus lived in a complex, disintegrating, intellectually flourishing world. The schism within the Church seemed to have been averted by the Council of Constance, but it remained a threat. A general awareness of the disorder into which the Church had fallen gave rise to demands for internal reform whose need no one contested. The impotence of the Empire, the arbitrary power of the German princes, of the city tyrants in Italy, and of the King of France had undermined all secular authority. Each of these potentates was determined to assert himself in his own way and to rely on himself alone.

Since the rediscovery of Cusanus (in the nineteenth century) he has been looked upon as a transitional figure between the Middle Ages and the modern era—sometimes as the last great medieval thinker and sometimes

as the founder of the modern era. To Cusanus himself the notion of the
Middle Ages was entirely unknown. He was not conscious of living in a
transitional age, at the dawn of the modern era. It was only the genera-
tion after him that became aware of its novelty and referred to the Middle
Ages as a thing of the past.

We may see in Cusanus a last culminating point of the Christian ecclesiastical faith, which was still Catholic and constitutive of the unity of the
West, illumined with the clarity of philosophical understanding for one
last time, before "modernism" made its appearance on the stage of history.
He never doubted that he was at home in eternity; in the teeth of all evidence
he asserted the essential unity of life in its plurality, and was confident that
the existing organic whole would survive. He perceived the language of
God everywhere in the world, incorporated within one all-encompassing
Church. The vision with which he sought to temper and surmount the
chaos of his age was one of the noblest concord, uniting a universal authority
which understands and educates all men with sublime freedom under God's
guidance.

No less impressive, however, is the other, opposite aspect of Cusanus.
Measured by the spiritual coherence and infinite richness of Thomas
Aquinas, Cusanus' thinking marks a decline. He lived with a consciousness
of the whole, but no longer made use of it to create an all-embracing system.
We have seen that, although he did not take the path of modern science,
he contributed to the intellectual climate which heralded the advent of
modern science (and philosophy), especially by his conception of the mind
as creative activity. He sensed that mathematics could be an important tool
of investigation, that the world is infinite, that individual beings are the
true reality—all insights that foreshadowed the science to come. His speculative ideas are harbingers of subsequent modern philosophizing (Bruno,
Leibniz, Hamann, Schelling).

To Cusanus, the two aspects of his intellectual world (as we think of
it today)—the medieval and the modern—were not incompatible. Whatever
tendencies to "modern" aggressiveness and destructiveness might be
detected in his thinking are still entirely overshadowed by his faith, which
is safely wrapped in official Christian doctrine. True, his passion for finding
the truth at the source by independent inquiry and his discovery of the
"layman" point to a later anti-authoritarian, revolutionary element. But
none of his ideas has explosive force.

The view that Cusanus represents a transitional figure between the
Middle Ages and the modern era does not strike me as very fruitful. It is
in fact misleading if the spiritual essence of this great metaphysician is taken
to reflect the inner conflict of his epoch. Such a view would imply that
Cusanus, as the last medieval thinker, was engulfed in contradictory currents
which he neither understood nor tried to surmount, and that as the first
modern thinker he was buried under the ruins of the medieval tradition.

Both these pictures are false and obscure Cusanus' originality. It is not true that the duality of his nature resulted from the transitional character of his epoch.

The truth is that his thinking displays features that can be met with in any period: strength of metaphysical insight, weakness in practical adaptation, willingness to put up with a climate of equivocation, the germs of an intellectual approach to the structure of the future—a structure which is always superseded by the time it becomes a reality. But before we come to grips with these matters, a brief digression.

2. On historical interpretation

Historical views of the course of things as a whole are often plausible but never compelling. The idea of a historical necessity, ascertainable by men, is a fallacy that deprives historical thinking of its meaning: "trends" are never inevitable. The unexpected, the "leap," "the miracle" of the fresh start are essential characteristics of knowable history, within which particular chains of causal necessity and meaningful relationships which are always susceptible of different interpretations play a part.

The idea of absolute historical necessity (the content of which can never be known) is contradicted by man's authentic possibilities. By virtue of his faith and his reason he can fight against the allegedly inevitable, against ideas intended to make him follow a path determined in advance. Those who are caught up in such ideas try to persuade him that he has no alternative. Some enthusiastically applaud history; others resign themselves to its absurd "necessity"; both views are paralyzing. Authentic men are those who take risks in their thinking or their actions, those who, far from being "shown up," are on the contrary transfigured by failure, who, perhaps by their very failure, exert a real influence on the future of mankind.

When philosophers are explained in terms of their epoch or national origin, this is done under the tacit assumption (which, today, under the influence of Hegel and his follower Marx, we are in danger of mistaking for self-evident "fact") that history is a substantial process and that the various philosophies, ideas, poems, and works of art are its by-products or epiphenomena. Unwittingly influenced by this conception of history even when we contest it, and making use of its facile methods, we employ such inaccurate expressions as "Greek thought," "Christian thought," "modern thought." Such expressions have a relative meaning when applied to certain phenomena, but in reality they are no more revealing than physiognomy is revealing of character. At best they remind us of men's complexity, which increases with their stature.

In connection with Cusanus it is particularly important to keep in mind these dangers of historical interpretation. It is much easier to avoid the shoals of pure historicism in dealing with the greatest—Plato, Spinoza, Kant—than in approaching philosophers who fall short of classical clarity and simplicity in their language, thinking, or conduct of life. But even these, if they are in any sense philosophically significant, cannot be treated as mere by-products of history. To take a purely historical view of Cusanus would be to relegate him once again to oblivion, to lose sight of what he really was and thought. Our task is to let him speak for himself.

Like all important philosophers, Cusanus is neither old nor new, neither medieval nor modern. Living in time, he is timeless in spirit, one of those who, clad in the raiment of their day and nation, meet as equals over the millennia to discuss the destiny of man.

So long as we remain aware of their limited significance, we can formulate historically meaningful comparisons without deluding ourselves. They serve merely as ideal types, intellectual constructions that never do full justice to reality. Such constructions combine particular insights with over-all metaphorical views. With their help we, inspired by our own tendencies, our own complaints and accusations, and our own hopes, ask questions of history. Let us attempt to formulate a few such questions.

3. Cusanus' life and thought in relation to subsequent history

A. *The decision at the Council of Basel.*—For all practical purposes, Cusanus' choice was between corruption through conciliar rule and corruption through papal rule. Either way he was bound to fail, whether he opted for the idea of unity or for that of internal reform.

Had he decided to go along with the conciliar movement, however, his failure would have reflected personal impotence in a corrupt world. He might have become a monk, devoted himself entirely to philosophy and meditation, composed works revealing the corruption of the conciliar, papal, and governmental powers, and thereby run the risk of being branded a heretic and incurring martyrdom. Then, with his intellectual clarity he would have disclosed the seemingly inevitable evil and proclaimed the truth of the original Biblical faith with all its historical consequences. He would have become a beacon to all thoughtful men and have helped to awaken moral and religious impulses.

But because he decided in favor of the papacy his failure was associated with a prominent position in a corrupt world. He became powerful amid the confusion and blundering of the epoch, but was powerless to realize the truth and the good. A man of vast knowledge, but not a thinker striving for concrete clarity at any cost, he became unwittingly "coresponsible" for what actually happened.

He was not in the least aware of this either-or. Our formulation implies no accusation. But it characterizes Cusanus in his historical situation.

B. *Cusanus was not a precursor of Protestantism, of the Counter-Reformation, or of the Enlightenment.*—After Cusanus came Protestantism, the Counter-Reformation, democratic (republican) and absolutist developments, the Enlightenment and the anti-Enlightenment.

Cusanus was not a precursor of Protestantism.—His efforts to reform the ecclesiastical establishment are not to be confused with the Reformation which was eventually to shatter forever the unity of the Western Church. The condition for the preservation of which he worked remained a condition of untruth, of continual momentary expedients. He had no understanding of the gathering storm of fanatical Protestant faith in alliance with regional interests. The precursors of Protestantism were hostile to Cusanus: the monks and priests who opposed the rule of celibacy, the laymen who condemned the wealth of the Church and the interference of Rome, and the princes who chafed at sharing their power with the Church. Allied with these forces was Luther's courageous faith, unknown and alien to Cusanus, which at its best was marked by a seriousness and depth that Cusanus never achieved.

He had no premonition of what was coming. The shadow of the religious wars had not yet descended on the world. There was still a liberality of spirit; for all the chaos, the prevailing atmosphere was still one of serene piety and inspiring faith. The spirit of the Catholic Church was still, to some extent, truly universal.

The Reformation came as a storm because the reforms so long clamored for and fitfully attempted for more than a century had all failed. But the Reformation itself led into new blind alleys; it curtailed and finally did away with the freedom that had prevailed in the medieval world. The unleashed forces spent themselves in religious wars between the various sects, and Catholicism ceased to be anything more than a sect. A new and modern freedom, which had been merely latent in the Middle Ages, came into being in the wars of religion, but it was a different and much more dangerous political and philosophical freedom than anything the Middle Ages had known.

Nietzsche believed that the Catholic Church had been well on the way to achieving a magnificent new "paganism," a true freedom of the spirit, and that the Germans disastrously prevented this with their religious fanaticism. But the fact is that the new freedom of science and philosophy developed most notably (though not exclusively) in the Protestant countries.

Cusanus was far from being a champion of humanistic paganism, let alone the precursor of a Reformation that destroyed Church unity and released a profound Biblical impulse with the force of a volcano. Compared with Nietzsche's vision or the Protestant revolution as it actually occurred, Cusanus' thinking strikes us as intellectually noble, but pale and feeble in its practical effects. For all the brilliance of his intellect, his activity helped, paradoxically enough, to make the Church more contemptible, with the consequence that entire nations were led by faith to turn their backs on a Church they no longer trusted.

Cusanus was not a precursor of the Counter-Reformation.—The gloomily magnificent, dogmatically ferocious, sensually enchanting, strictly papal and absolutist Church created after the Council of Trent was not Cusanus' Church. His Church had not yet lost its spiritual breadth.

He was a champion of Church unity (and hence, in the situation as he saw it, of papal supremacy), but not by any means of an absolutist papal Church, a new organization with a fundamentally new attitude, such as emerged in reaction to Protestantism. Taking as his standard the eternal original model, he wanted the Church to be reformed profoundly—in all its members, the Pope and the princes of the Church, the secular clergy and the orders. But this was not to be achieved through a rigidly disciplined power structure, holding every member in subjection and leaving no room for the development of a plurality of autonomous individuals.

Today we know that the subsequent course of history has been marked by a parting of the ways between the conciliar, "parliamentary" reality and the papal "absolutist," totalitarian reality. Cusanus had no clear idea of either, and wanted neither. He wanted unity in plurality and plurality in unity, unconditionally guided only by the idea of unity. It never occurred to him that such a unity can develop only in free human communication, through institutions of a federative type, through agreement and co-operation. He was bound to forfeit true unity in the real world, because he took for granted that it could be achieved by compulsion.

Thereby he helped to prepare the way not back to medieval Catholicism, but to modern, fanatical Counter-Reformation Catholicism animated by a new spirit of a mere spiritual and political violence, a mere denomination among denominations, its claim to catholicity unjustified and pointless after the definitive schism. This Catholicism was by nature alien to Cusanus.

Cusanus was not a precursor of the Enlightenment.—He was interested not in a rational interpretation of symbols, which, as in the shallow rationalism of the Enlightenment, makes them superfluous, but in speculative thinking, in which the symbols illumine ever greater depths but retain their enigmatic and metaphorical character. Cusanus' world is not the enlightened world of "dis-enchanted" realities, but a sensual and intellectual world, illumined by the radiance of the supernatural. He did not think that things are "never more than" what we know about them, that there is nothing "behind them," but was led by his nonknowing knowledge to unfathomable depths.

His political philosophy is not a program; he elucidates the political domain, guided by his vision of the divine model. His operative idea is not that of rectilinear progress toward an ever better future, but the idea of a steady, ever renewed ascent to the ideal. What he has in mind is not the *modus operandi* of such an ascension, but the idea of the whole to which we come ever closer by virtue of our spiritual essence.

Shallow rationalism loses sight of the intellect by raising discursive reason to the level of an absolute and by exalting sensory experience. It believes in progress, rejects speculative philosophy along with theology, and allows the roots of personality to become stunted. Cusanus was the very opposite of all this.

But neither was Cusanus a precursor of the other, constructive kind of Enlightenment, represented by Kant and Lessing, which avoids superficial rationalism and embodies an infinitely continuing will to enlightenment.

The true Enlightenment implies communication between originally different sources, and no one who follows this path can lay claim to possession of the truth, even if he chooses to pursue an unconditional course in his relations with men. Such a possibility of unrestricted extension of one's mode of thinking falls outside Cusanus' conscious perspectives.

When Cusanus envisages the union and peaceful coexistence of all religions, he assumes that they are all essentially Christian. When the false Enlightenment envisaged the unity of all religions, it had in mind a universal religion, a kind of distillation of the element common to all religions, under the assumption that the contents of the religions can be formulated rationally, perhaps at religious congresses.

Transcending both is the philosophical approach, which aims, not at securing the uniformity of all historical religions, but at discovering their deeper roots, under the assumption that they stem from different sources and that communication between them is the thing to be achieved. Then— and this goes counter both to Cusanus and to superficial rationalism—the goal is not unity of the explicit contents (in the form of a credo accepted by all), but boundless communication in respect of the deeper contents. The presuppositions of such communication may be sought in a common fundamental knowledge, which is not itself formulated once and for all time. The only alternative to this search is the breaking off of communication and a consequent recourse to brute force.

Cusanus stands apart from Protestantism, the Counter-Reformation, and the Enlightenment. He cannot justly be regarded as a forerunner of any of these movements. Although Cusanus championed the papal cause, he did not really adhere to any cause, for he saw everything from the lofty height of his awareness of God and the world. He advocated no radical solutions, though the practical problems of the day cried out for them. His political activity never went deeper than the superficial skirmishing which continued until the situation was altered by definitive schism within the Church and by the rise of sovereign national states.

Cusanus was not aware that the immediate future belonged to the powers against which he fought. Because he was not farsighted enough to envisage the possibility of such a future, he fought blindly. He lacked the mighty energy of faith because he relied entirely on the Church. He unwittingly helped to give the Church a form he himself rejected.

c. *The "crisis" since Cusanus:* (1) *From Cusanus to our own day.*—Cusanus can seem modern because he thought at a time of progressive moral and political decline (a time like our own), and because the purpose of his thinking was to check this decline. His insights lacked the power to penetrate the deceptions of his time. His thinking could not become real in the hearts and minds of his contemporaries. He followed paths that did not lead to the centuries succeeding his own.

Protestantism took hold of the people with a violence long unknown in religious matters. The Catholic world exploded in a series of schisms. The Empire, meanwhile, gave way to an aggregate of regional absolutisms. A new, seemingly stabilized European world emerged from the chaos. Just as the medieval order attained a seeming perfection in the twelfth and thirteenth centuries, so in the seventeenth century a European order attained its apogee, after which it too was destroyed. Once again, in the nineteenth century, the semblance of a liberal order came into being despite the Revolution, and its collapse in turn has produced the contemporary situation, a state of affairs which, in theory at least, can no longer produce a European but only a world order. In each historical instance, seeming perfection and stability concealed the seeds of self-destruction, brought about by its own shortcomings.

The age of Cusanus may appear as the first major spiritual crisis of Europe's upper classes, foreshadowing the crisis of modernity as such. It was a first upsurging of the flood that has repeatedly risen and threatened to overwhelm us, though each time in a different way. Since Cusanus much the same situation has occurred several times. Light-mindedness and half-measures have led to anarchy, the reaction to which was violence justified in terms of fanaticism. By recourse to violence the state (with the help of the Church or some similar institutionalization of doctrine, Marxism being the latest) managed for a time to enforce an absolute order. In the end, the revolution of the Enlightenment, which was rooted in reason, engendered political revolution and its reign of terror justified by a degenerated discursive reason.

Later, liberalism gave rise to a more sophisticated totalitarian rule. Our picture of the course of things is that of a whirlpool which changes shape from time to time, but engenders no lasting order.

Until now the ineradicable forces of darkness have been repeatedly victorious in the world. They have triumphed over reason, humanity, and freedom, over all such "weakness," which they despise.

(2) *The crisis generated by the sciences.*—Cusanus has no place in the history of modern science, nor did he correctly understand its spirit; at the same time, his philosophy is relevant to the scientific world which has developed since his epoch.

The attitude toward life characteristic of the modern world was shaped by a science and a philosophy independent of revealed faith. This world has generated evils against which it has carried on titanic struggles. The human spirit became confused when it lost its existential roots, science became meaningless when it lost sight of its goal, philosophy ceased to be serious when it conceived of itself as a science and behaved accordingly. Freedom turned to anarchy and irresponsibility, liberal-mindedness into doctrinaire liberalism, the intellect into mere discursive reason. This vast fragmentation has led to radical reversals that ostensibly re-established an order; as formerly it led to absolutism, so in our time it has led to total domination.

Freedom has been replaced by command and obedience. Like the monarch's will under absolutism, so the Leader's under totalitarianism is recognized as the supreme law, whether or not it happens to be expressed in laws. The people have been freed from freedom. All, those who command as well as those who obey, are turned into slaves. The road to such a condition is paved with illiberal thinking and violent conduct in the little things of everyday life. Neither those who command nor those who obey are amenable to reason. They break off human communication, ceasing to recognize it as a goal, or seek only a semblance of it, hedged round with every sort of mental reservation.

It is a matter of the most crucial importance that we achieve clarity as to what science can accomplish: namely, progress in the cognition of objects, indefinitely, and what it cannot do: namely, give purpose to our life. This the contemporary forms of superficial rationalism—positivism and Marxism—fail to grasp. Superstitious reliance on science has led to the confusion embodied in conventional slogans and turns of speech in all walks of life, especially in politics.

Anyone who is willing to think can free himself from such conceptions. All he needs to do is remove the scales of falsely self-evident truths from his mind's eye. It cannot be accomplished in the manner of a Baron von Münchhausen pulling himself out of the swamp by his own pigtail, but in communication with other thinking people, who can achieve in common and in freedom what an individual cannot achieve for himself alone. This is not a utopian idea. The alternative is to despair of humanity.

In our world today, an understanding of the nature of science is essential. Cusanus said that a science indiscriminately concerned with everything is "a whore." The provocative phrasing points to the existential problem of all rationality, including that of modern science. Let us cast a glance at the world of modern science, even though it carries us beyond the scope of Cusanus' thinking.

Is "disenchantment of the world" the necessary consequence of science? By no means, for the disenchantment extends only as far as science extends. By experiencing its limits, pure science serves only to enhance our consciousness of the mysterious depths of all things that are in the world.

Total disenchantment is brought about not by science, but by scientific superstition posing as science: when we absolutize our changing epistemological assumptions, mistaking them for the truth as such and our changing scientific theories for knowledge of Being; when we declare that science is an end in itself, or when science asserts that it leads us to true faith, true art, true poetry, true happiness, true Being.

Authentic science, which is aware of its limits and does not transgress them, does not leave the world disenchanted. It clears the way for new ciphers and does not destroy the old ones when it shows that they fail to provide us with tangible, real knowledge; it does not destroy the miracle which lies beyond everything we call "meaning."

To pure science, things are no more than what we know of them—finite, fragmentary phenomena. We can never know things as an all-encompassing whole embracing all phenomena. To the questions—What is this whole? What is the meaning of the world? or What do the things we know signify?—science gives no answer. The answers are given in ciphers. These are understood at the level of human Existenz, the "meaning" of which transcends all meaning.

Transcendence is not encountered by science, but can be apprehended in the meaning of the ciphers. The ciphers do not exist in themselves, but for Existenz, just as the objects of science have no universally valid existence in themselves, but only as phenomena for consciousness as such.

In Cusanus there is no trace of the modern "disenchantment" of the world. Following him in his speculations, we enter a world where all things are symbolic, where their "significance" is perceived with naïve wonderment.

In recent decades, the movement toward recovery of metaphysical freedom has been furthered by what has been called "the crisis in the sciences." It is a crisis of the nonscientific element in the sciences, of scientific superstition still unsurmounted. It is a cleansing process, which has purified and broadened the sciences. The "crisis" has in no way affected science itself, but only a pseudo-science based on fallacious axioms, which advanced "scientific" conceptions of the world—when there can be no such things as a scientific conception of the world. Scientific minds that had gone astray have sought a way out of this error. As a result, new scientific discoveries and a purer science have become possible, and a purer philosophy as well.

To be sure, "the crisis in the sciences" signifies that the process of disenchantment with the world has become complete within the scientific framework itself. But complete disenchantment, including the rejection of all unproven metaphysical assumptions, such as the absolute validity of causality, is necessary to clear the way, so that a further domain—long obscured by scientific superstition—can at last be experienced and elucidated: the domain where all things and the existence of science itself become ciphers. At this point, however, universal validity ceases, though it does not necessarily follow that we must surrender to ever-changing subjective fantasies. Here begins a struggle of powers, which no man can ever survey as a whole.

It is in this domain that Cusanus is situated with his magnificent cipher world. But because he himself was unaware of this, he did not achieve complete philosophical freedom.

4. Lack of influence

For all the brilliance of his career, Cusanus remained a secondary figure in the history of his times. Highly respected for his superior mind, he had no real power even as a prince of the Church, because he was not sufficiently wealthy. Toward the end of his life he exerted a certain influence as favored adviser to Pope Pius II, an old friend.

Nor, apart from a few monks, did his philosophical ideas exert any influence. As we have seen, Cusanus was not a precursor of such Western developments as the Reformation, the Counter-Reformation, absolute monarchy, the Enlightenment, and modern science. Nor is he cited by those who at an early date chose the path of human reason and freedom (certain humanists, Italian humanist heretics, the great philosophers beginning with Spinoza). Only one of the great figures remembered him at all (we need not count Faber Stapulensis and Bovillus). The famous eulogy by Giordano Bruno (in his speech at Wittenberg) stands alone across the ages: "Where is there to be found a man comparable to that native of Cusa, who was the less accessible the greater he was? If his priestly robe had not now and then veiled his genius, I would go so far as to say that he was not the equal of, but far greater a figure than, Pythagoras." Through Bruno's writings, Cusanus' ideas became known to others who had no direct knowledge of him—Leibniz, Hamann, Schelling. Probably the first to rediscover him was Schlegel, though nobody paid attention at the time. Why was Cusanus forgotten for so long?

It would be rash to say that metaphysical speculation as such cannot influence the multitude. Speculative thought does exert a powerful influence when it is originally embodied in a way of life (as in the case of the Buddhists), or when it constitutes a real cultural world (as in the case of the Roman Stoics), or when it is expressed in a religious way of life (as in the case of Christianity). It is through such practice that speculative thought gains in influence.

On the other hand, when speculative thought serves only to procure aesthetic gratification, when it is pursued as a mere hobby or avocation, it exerts no influence. So pursued, speculation may lead to profound insights, but as it does not affect everyday life, it falls into oblivion. Although it is a kind of liberation, it is not a real liberation because it does not put its own consequences to the test. There is a momentary feeling of liberation, but the impetus is soon absorbed by some religious belief or by some nihilistic mode of life concealed by social convention.

Cusanus does not fall within either of these two categories. As a metaphysician he was a creative thinker meditating in solitude and finding no echo. Metaphysics has efficacy only in the independent selfhood of the thinker himself. Cusanus' independence had limits of which he was not aware:

First: Cusanus did not battle for true faith; indeed, he was scarcely aware of any challenge to it. The Catholic Christian Church was for him eternally one and the same, the physical object of faith, which leaves no room for even the slightest doubt. *Second:* Out of some innate, inherited disposition, stimulated perhaps by the turmoil of his age, he set out to recognize in the real world the pattern of eternal order which is always present, and to restore it by his call for unity, peace, and faith.

Cusanus is the only important philosopher of his century who did not belong to any school or found a school. He is a solitary figure, standing completely alone—rather like Duns Scotus Erigena in the ninth century. Like Erigena a metaphysician, Cusanus was attracted to him, though Erigena's views were then considered heretical.

Are we closer today to Cusanus than were the intervening centuries? Did he, long before the upheavals of recent generations, aspire to unity and order based on an encompassing metaphysically grounded knowledge (though in a sense that is no longer possible today)? Do we keep going back to him from our own chaos because we are asking the same questions as he, only more urgently and with greater awareness of our danger?

Similar questions are suggested by every philosopher. We hope to find in each some help in exploring our own possibilities. We should like to appropriate the truth of their insights without falling into their historically conditioned errors.

Part Seven: Critical Estimate

INTRODUCTION

The Meaning of Criticism

To apply finite logical standards to Cusanus' metaphysical thinking would be to miss its import entirely. It is not an "object" but a meditative movement of thought in which objects serve only as guideposts. We must place ourselves within the movement if we are to criticize it adequately.

To grasp Cusanus' thinking we must not draw up a set of alternatives, trying to clarify his "point of view" by envisaging an opposite point of view. Everything has to be referred to the infinite mind of which our own mind is an image. A critical estimate of Cusanus is possible only if we too examine this infinite mind under his guidance.

The essential questions are: What is the existential meaning of his conceptual ciphers? What is their truth? What new perspectives does he open up to our experience? What perspectives does he shut off? Such a critique cannot be carried out by logical methods alone.

Philosophy is not a "point of view" but a "mode of thinking." Studying it, we can understand it by making it our own, or we can miss its point entirely, deceiving ourselves with secondary rational interpretations. We can choose to go along with the philosopher or refuse to do so. We can, looking at it eye to eye, as it were, participate in the struggle between antagonistic powers which is the essence of every philosophy. But we must never put it in the straitjacket of a "point of view" and then, on that basis, decide for or against it.

Like every great philosopher, Cusanus can be approached in terms of his ideas, his life and background, and his place in the philosophical tradition. But we should like to go further. We should like to gain an inkling of what he himself really was underneath all this, to meet him face to face, as it were, with reverence but not without questioning and criticism.

In attempting a critical characterization, we are fully aware that we can never recapture the whole of Cusanus. To criticize we must have the courage to expose our own limitations. What we are attempting will be corrected, supplemented, or rejected for deeper insights by other students of this philosopher, provided that, aided by their own philosophizing, they base their judgments on documents and texts.

1. *The significance of Cusanus' contradictions*

A. Cusanus' speculations do not give rise to a systematically ordered conceptual system. Divergent trains of thought run side by side, presenting contradictions which are sometimes methodologically meaningful and sometimes not. Often ideas are set forth in no particular order, and their content is obscured by digressions. Cusanus used such contradictions as a method of saying what he could not convey in other fashion. His statements often sound as if some crucial truth has just been discovered, and as if this is a step forward in knowledge rather than yet another variation in a meditation forever unresolved. We do not encounter the pure play of a mind surveying and methodically mastering its categorial inventions. Let us discuss the significance of the many contradictions to be met with in Cusanus' practice and thought.

B. Cusanus speaks of God and yet he knows that to do so is impossible. This contradiction is unavoidable and implies no lack of clarity. Cusanus knew that speculative truth can be elucidated only in the form of contradiction.

False contradictions arise only when ideas that are paradoxical from the standpoint of discursive reason, though meaningful from that of the intellect, are perverted into rational concepts or imaginary physical realities.

Criticism fails in its purpose when it transforms speculative ideas into rational statements or theorems. Speculative insight is lost when it is frozen into a lesson that can be learned.

C. Cusanus did not believe that the negations of "negative theology" mark a terminal point of thinking, beyond which we are left in a vacuum. On reaching the point where he was confronted with a choice between mysticism (in the sense of an experience from which the world and the self are absent, perhaps infinitely meaningful but completely incommunicable) and the world as a reality without transcendence, Cusanus rejects both alternatives, and embarks upon the way of speculation, which is the medium of lucid human Existenz in the world.

D. The questions arise:

How is it possible to prove or disprove any statement or idea if we cannot refute it by discovering that it contradicts itself?

If we admit contradictions in our thinking, if they become a characteristic of the truth, how can such a thinking be convincing, how can it have the ring of authentic truth?

Can we distinguish between a meaningful speculative contradiction and an empty, rationally destructive contradiction?

Is not the door to intellectual anarchy opened by the admission of any contradictions whatsoever?

The answer is: We can only try and see what happens. There is no criterion outside speculative experience itself, unless it be the criterion of how such experience affects the man who has it.

E. One fundamental contradiction in Cusanus is this: God is separated from mankind by an unbridgeable gulf: the infinite and the finite are incommensurable, and God is unknowable. But at the same time God is present in the world He created. He can be known by human beings, and all things reflect His essence, for God is in all things. God is completely separated from the world, yet God is in the world—the contradiction is stated too unmistakably to be overlooked. Our human limitations being what they are, we cannot avoid falling into this contradiction, but we can be aware that we are doing so. When we reach this point, the contradictory terms cancel each other out, and the intellect is free to go on in pursuit of speculative insights which transcend this form of objectivity.

It is a different matter when we are confronted with contradictions in practical situations that require a choice. The conciliar movement and the papal claim are not in contradiction as Cusanus subordinates them to the idea of unity. But in a concrete situation involving a real Council and a real Pope, their meaning is perverted into antagonistic arguments, which meet and clash.

On the practical plane, choice between alternatives is inevitable. It is imposed by the reality of the temporal situation. Now there is a line of reasoning that might be taken here, which is not implicit in the vision of unity. The unity of the Church makes it imperative to support the Pope in the real situation of a council that is spiritually a failure. The exactly opposite choice might be made if a universal council, demonstrating by its unanimity that it is inspired by the Holy Spirit, were able to assert itself against an inadequate Pope without causing a schism. But Cusanus does not reason in this way. Without being conscious of doing so, he breaks up his philosophical vision of the Church into two mutually exclusive rational theories. He employs one as an argument in support of his own choice and drops the other, which is now taken by his adversaries. Thus Cusanus contradicts himself by regarding the papal theory as the only true one. In the actual polemical struggle he fell a victim to the concrete situation. In this case, Cusanus cannot be defended against the accusation of objective rational inconsistency, although his mode of thinking and the fundamental attitude expressed in *De concordantia catholica* need not have led to such a contradiction.

Cusanus might be justified on the ground that alternatives between which a choice must be made in real situations cannot be maintained simultaneously in theory without weakening the contestant's position. But such a weakening is possible only if the philosophical theory itself is abandoned. Philosophy need not sacrifice its total vision for the sake of alternative arguments, nor is the philosopher's resolve weakened by a concrete situation. But in practice he must choose even if his choice is not adequately grounded in universal principles; he must take a calculated risk, conscious of his historical responsibility. Because he was not clearly aware of this, Cusanus was led into needless contradictions.

F. In the meandering course of his speculations Cusanus uses incompatible expressions. It is impossible to expound his works at an internally consistent system.

He himself says that the ungraspable One can be usefully designated by many terms. To know what he means it is more important to keep his aim in mind than to make a comparative study of the terms he employs.

To understand Cusanus one must be willing to meditate with him, to bear with him when he repeats the same idea in different words. We must experience the ever-present speculative attitude as well as the prevailing mood of pious perspicacity, of ascent through thought.

G. We should distinguish (1) contradictions forcefully expressed, which lead to further speculative thinking and have been sought and found with this purpose in mind (their effect is liberating); (2) contradictions which seem to result from shifts in linguistic usage (they are not real contradictions and their clarification merely requires a certain effort); and (3) false contradictions, which demand correction, have nothing to do with the speculative method, and occur on the rational plane purely as a result of negligence (they lead to error and obstruct the course of the meditations). One defect in Cusanus' philosophizing is that he does not distinguish between contradiction and such related concepts as difference, polarity, and opposition. Nor does he put his thinking to test categorially and systematically (we have to go to Hegel to gain clarity on this point). He sometimes identifies opposition (*oppositio*) with contradiction (*contradictio*).

The philosophical limits disclosed in Cusanus' life, ciphers and speculation

At moments, certain of Cusanus' ideas seem to burst the bounds of his philosophy. But these ideas remain inoperative, because he holds to the view that the universe is essentially harmonious. Contemplation of the harmony of all things in the ground of being is the supreme goal of all his speculative endeavors.

A. *His interpretations of his own epoch.*—The type of criticism which holds that he failed to recognize the emergent forces of the future, that he waged a losing battle for the past, the view that he was an "extraordinary man who lacked nothing but an understanding of his own epoch" (Jaeger, II, 425), has significance only for those who believe in a necessary course of history and suppose that they can tell what it is by the results. I am interested here in something else, namely, Cusanus' explicit evaluation of his own epoch.

We find it in a New Year's sermon of 1440 (Scharpff, *Reformator,* p. 292) and in a work of 1452, *Coniectura de ultimis diebus* (Akademieausgabe, 1959). Cusanus' reflections follow a traditional pattern. The course of history (he writes in 1440) reproduces the course of Jesus' life: the former is to the latter as an image is to the original. One year in Christ's life corresponds to fifty years in the history of the Church (for the following reason: time runs in septenaries—in periods of seven days, seven years, and seven times seven or forty-nine years; the fiftieth year is the Sabbath that completes the laborious cycle). Jesus was twelve years old when He appeared in the Temple: these twelve years correspond to the first six hundred years of our era, down to the epoch of Gregory the Great. For the next seventeen years Jesus seems to have done nothing—these correspond to the 850 years following the epoch of Gregory the Great. Now begins the period of His Epiphany which extends down to the Crucifixion and the Resurrection. "Therefore I make it known to you," says Cusanus in his New Year's sermon (1440), "that what is now beginning for us is the last fifth of the twenty-ninth year of Jesus' life, the time when He appeared in public and was baptized in the Jordan." This means: the time of the betrayal and the Passion is approaching.

In 1452 Cusanus once again foretells what is to come (in 1450, the twenty-ninth Sabbath had been celebrated in Rome as a jubilee year by representatives of the whole Western world): The body of Christ, i.e., the Church, is to be purified so that the spirit of God may enter it visibly, as it were, just as it descended upon Christ in the form of a dove. Some saintly souls will withdraw and practice a more severe asceticism, until, after vanquishing the Tempter, they will come back into the world to spread the word of eternal life. They will suffer persecution, but the number of the faithful will increase rapidly, until the thirtieth Jubilee has been attained.

Then the satanic spirit of the Antichrist will touch off a persecution against the body of Christ, the Church. This will be a time of sore affliction. The Passion of Christ will be repeated. The Church will seem to have become extinct. The holy apostles will desert it and flee. There will be no successor to St. Peter upon the throne.

But this will not be the end. Holy men will gather their strength and repent, because they will see the Church rising anew, in greater brilliance than ever before. Peter will shed bitter tears at having fled, and so will the other apostles, the bishops, and the priests. Gloriously resurrected, the Church will calmly envisage eternal peace. But the consummation will not come at once. First the Church, the bride of Christ, must become worthy of her bridegroom, cast off her blemishes. Then Christ will come to judge the living and the dead, and to destroy the world by fire. He will take the bride to Him in all His Glory, so that she may rule with Him for all eternity. This "Resurrection" will coincide with the thirty-fourth Jubilee—corresponding to the Resurrection of Christ—that is, it will come after 1700 and before 1734.

This is how Cusanus interprets the present and foretells the future. Characteristically, he calls such interpretation "conjecture." For, he says, we should refrain from "curious investigation of the future," if only because almost all who have so far tried to predict the course of future events have been mistaken, even the Fathers of the Church, whose holiness of life and profound learning we lack entirely. And yet such thinking is not reprehensible. Although the decrees of God remain hidden even to the wisest men, "He, in His great kindness, permits us, worms that we are, to make conjectures about things He alone knows." Only God sees all things from outside time. Only He can determine the moments of time. In such traditional schemata of history Cusanus sees catastrophe ahead; but it is followed by apotheosis.

So general a characterization of the epoch may seem to us mere trifling, but his inner attitude toward contemporary events was serious. In a letter to Jacob von Sirck, dated October 1453, he had the following to say of the Turkish peril after the conquest of Constantinople: "I fear greatly that this violence may defeat us, for I see no possible uniting in resistance. I believe that we must address ourselves to God alone, though He will not hear us sinners." What does he mean? His insight into the situation does not result in an urgent appeal for action. He speaks in general terms of sinners, not of the need to understand very specific contemporary sins, which must be surmounted if men are to unite against a deadly peril. The only action he recommends is prayer—though he himself judges it to be ineffectual under the circumstance. A keen appreciatioon of impending disaster simmers down into passivity.

B. *Cusanus' attitude toward death.*—He speaks about death in three ways.

First: "Nothing is entirely destructible, but every individual thing can pass into another mode of being. A given mode of being comes to an end, and yet, as Vergil said, no real death occurs: For death seems to be nothing but the dissolution of a compound into its elements" (*De doc. ignor.*, II, 12). This implies a certain conception of nature: the thinker looks serenely upon himself as partaking of the changes undergone by an indestructible substance, the nature of which he does not investigate.

Second: When a man feels that the burden of his body has become an obstacle on the path to eternal wisdom, he desires to be separated from it and does not fear death, for he wishes, as an immortal soul, to feast on God's eternal wisdom. Fired by such love that they renounce themselves and all else, those worthy of this wisdom prefer it even to their own life (*De ven. sap.*, 15).

Third: Cusanus comments on the voluntary character of the suffering and death of Christ in his letter to Albergati. This text is incomparably more profound than the two just quoted. We do not really know, he says, what death is. No one, save only Jesus Christ, ever possessed or will possess the knowledge of death and suffering. Because He had this knowledge, He was "exceeding sorrowful, even unto death" (Mat. 26, 38) and prayed in agony at Gethsemane. And His sweat was like unto drops of blood. The death of Christ encompassed the suffering of all who die here below. Indeed, none of us knows what death is. Therefore only the death of Christ is the perfect death. Christ died for all and gives life to all.

Therefore Cusanus says to the young monk: "Learn to imitate Christ, when He prayed on the Mount of Olives. Do not imagine that you are praying unless you struggle unto death and rise from your prayer at least mentally drenched in your blood and scalded by hot tears. Then you will be comforted as Christ was and be filled with joy, victorious over the death of the body and the sufferings you have taken on yourself."

But what if the experience is not merely mental, but actual? We must not forget how Cusanus conducted himself when his life was threatened. Did Cusanus even remotely imitate Christ? Did he not, rather, evade the concrete situation by taking refuge in a metaphysical magnificence unjustified by his own existential experience?

What does it mean "to be victorious over death"? We have found the following three ideas in the texts just referred to: The first is impersonal, a vision of nature, a cipher of the eternity of Being; it expresses an attitude, unmarred by transient self-interest, of serenity in the face of death. The second idea contrasts soul and body. The body denotes everything that is natural and inescapable, everything that limits us and holds us in subjection. The soul is conceived of as incorporeal and immortal, as yearning for the joy of God's presence, of perfect philosophical knowledge conceived as a desirable permanent state. This is an artificial notion without real substance: the conception of eternity as endless time and of the incorporeal soul as existing in time is no more than a self-deluding form of our will to survive. This is not a victory over death. The third idea is that the more painful death may be, the more likely it is to usher in a most blessed union with God, that an agonizing death can confer victory over death. This third idea raises the following questions:

(1) Is the experience of "reliving" something in one's mind comparable to actually experiencing it? When I imagine that I can imitate Christ as He was on the Mount of Olives and die like Him, I am on an entirely different plane of reality, I am envisaging a mere possibility and running no real risk. (2) Is not true imitation of Christ an essentially boundless readiness to die in mortal anguish, a readiness that proves genuine only when actually put to the test? To become Jesus' mirror, freed through Him to one's own freedom to speak and to be the truth: that is, really to repeat His sacrifice? (3) Can we speak of an imitation of Christ in connection with every case of agonizing torment, even suffered involuntarily? Can imitation of Christ give us the strength to rebel no more but to assent, and even when deserted by God to counter our despair by addressing to Him the question, My God, my God, why hast Thou forsaken me?—those unfathomable words from the Psalms, which were Christ's last questioning words on the Cross?

Cusanus does not ask such questions. Accordingly, we find no answer to them in his writings. For it cannot be called an answer when, after his profound interpretation of Jesus' prayer on the Mount of Olives (though he does not really convince us that he takes it seriously), he says to young Albergati: Victory over death lies in the obedience of the monk who lives away from the world, who has died to the world. "Great is the privilege of the monk who always has Christ present in his father superior so that he may die to himself and live forever in Christ."

His attitude toward death and immortality remains unclear. This is not surprising: crucial insights can be achieved in philosophy only if the philosopher applies them in practice. Otherwise scientific ideas, sublime emotional flights, extravagant dreams are all self-deceptions. They are not errors, but reflections of existential failure, of blindness to reality.

In Cusanus theological and philosophical discussions, occasional flashes of truth, are overshadowed by traditional arguments. For example (from the letter to Albergati): Only God has the immortality to which we aspire. Only He can give it to us.—A man who suffers for justice and truth suffers for God. If he chooses to die rather than to offend against justice, God will not let him lose his life, but give him immortality. Therefore if a man accepts death, which has no end, for God's sake, God will confer upon him immortal, everlasting life, and it will be a life that knows it is living.

Cusanus has neither theoretical nor practical knowledge of the courage a man must have to risk his life without renouncing his will to live, but rising above it, mastering it, to die calmly like Socrates, without expectations, in the serenity of nonknowledge.

c. *Freedom and evil.*

1. *Freedom of choice.*—Cusanus asserts the freedom of choice: "The faculty of free will in no way depends on the body, as does the faculty of desire." Our freedom of choice remains entire even when the body is weakened. "It is never impaired as are the desires and senses of old men."

Freedom is here meant in its full sense. "The ability to choose implies the faculty of being, the faculty of living, and the faculty of understanding" (*posse eligere in se complicat posse esse, posse vivere et posse intelligere*).

Capability as such (which we have discussed above) is powerfully and indestructibly present in the capability of the mind. As we know from experience, it possesses a being separate from the body (*De apice theoriae*).

What a man really is, is not determined by natural necessity nor by what is called predestination, fate, ill fortune. "For every man has the freedom to choose, namely, to will or not to will. He should choose the good and shun evil. For he has within him the king and judge over these things. Because the animals do not know all this, this power is a human attribute" (*De ludo globi*).

2. *Evil has no real existence.*—What is evil? Cusanus gives the old answer: Evil exists, but has no reality of its own. "Being is good and noble and precious. Hence everything that is has some value. Nothing can be without having some value" (*De ludo globi*).

There is only one principle, God, Capability as such. What is actual is actual because if reflects Capability as such. "What does not reflect it has no essential original being." "Futility, defectiveness, error, vice, sickness, death, corruption, and other such things lack all the quality of being" (*De apice theoriae*). In this view, which identifies misfortune, suffering, defect, and error with evil, evil is flattened and shorn of all reality.

Ideas that assert the nonbeing of evil greatly reduce its significance, unless, in the face of the reality of evil, they scan its abysses and ciphers and reach out beyond all ciphers.

3. *The origin of evil: freedom.*—Though evil does not originate in being, it is present. How is this possible? Cusanus answers: God willed that man, who without free will could not have been a noble creature, should be capable of error and sin. God did not create man a vulgar slave subject to the yoke of necessity, but free and ready to carry out the divine tasks in freedom of choice, out of love. This implies that those who serve of their own free choice can also choose not to obey (*Exc.*, VI, 527).

Evil is rejection of God in favor of something that is preferred to God. "How demented is he who seeks Thee," Cusanus says addressing himself to God, "and while seeking Thee, withdraws from Thee. . . . Every sinner, then, strays from Thee and departs afar off" (*The Vision of God*, chapter V, *op. cit.*).

4. *The origin of evil: chance.*—Does evil arise solely through misuse of freedom? Cusanus sees another source which evil has in common with all bad things, all disasters, all imperfections. None of these things comes from God. For things derive from God their essence, their unity, their perfection—but not their finiteness. And the origin of finiteness is chance (*contingentia*). In *De ludo globi,* Cusanus tells us how this comes about. God creates all things, including things subject to otherness and change and passing-away, yet he does not create otherness and changeability and passing-away, as such. It is by chance that things perish, change, become imperfect. God does not produce defectiveness, but only opportunity (*opportunitas*) or possibility. Defectiveness is only one consequence of possibility, and is added only by chance. "Evil and potential sin and death and becoming-other are not God's creations."

This is illustrated by the following image: "When we throw several peas down over a plane surface, no single pea moves in exactly the same way as any other . . . this otherness, this difference does not originate with the man who has thrown them down together, but comes about by chance [*ex contingentia*]. For it is not possible that they should move in the same way or stand still on the same spot."

Must we conclude, then, that chance is a condition of freedom? Cusanus may appear to think so. In his metaphysical analysis of finitude and its consequences, "the freedom to do evil" is relegated to the domain of chance. But in his psychology, he recognizes that man has the freedom to choose.

We have here two points of view. On the one hand, an objective analysis of finitude which reduces all imperfections to a common denominator (and one of these imperfections is the possibility of freely choosing evil); on the other, a more subjective analysis of freedom, which is attributed exclusively to man. When the two points of view are combined, the meaning of freedom is lost. We ask: Is freedom possible only thanks to the imperfection of the finite world, with chance marking the point at which evil can enter? This would be the kind of freedom that is supposed to characterize the motions of intra-atomic particles and that is today foolishly asserted to be the condition of the possibility of human freedom.

Or does Cusanus here touch upon an idea of which he is not conscious, does he for a moment attain an extreme point without seeing it? This idea, which is alien to Cusanus, can be formulated as follows: Is not finitude inseparable from order just as infinitude is inseparable from chaos? Are both inseparable from the truth of the being in which we find ourselves? The concrete answers of our Existenz and the speculative answers of our metaphysical thinking are true only if both—finitude and order on the one hand, and infinitude and chaos on the other—are not lost sight of. Existential seriousness does not deal with chaos by denying its reality.

The order of finite things must be wrested from chaos, there is continual struggle between the two; similarly, there is a continual struggle between the light of existential reason and the darkness of passion which is all- and self-destructive. The struggle may take place with no communication between the two, each side aiming only at destruction of the other; it may take the form of a frank exchange of views, without practical results; or finally, the form of a life and death struggle, tempered only by awareness of a common purpose transcending the inevitable conflict. We shall not go into all this here, but merely note the limitations of Cusanus' thinking: When he fails to distinguish between imperfections and evil, reducing everything to the level of the negative, he misses the true significance of both freedom and evil. The insoluble conflict between the two, which, as far as we can see, reaches down to the very ground of things, gives way to an illusion of a harmonious whole.

D. *The view that the universe is fundamentally harmonious.*

1. Cusanus' attitude toward life was not affected by his profound ideas on freedom. Of the problem of evil he was scarcely aware. In his eyes the world was beautiful, self-contained, and fundamentally harmonious; consequently, any sort of radicalism was alien to him.

Nor does Cusanus belong to the tradition exemplified by works such as *De miseria conditionis humanae* (by Pope Innocent III). Pascal said, "The I is always hateful." Cusanus said, "We cannot hate ourselves" (*The Vision of God*, p. 74, *op. cit.*).

2. The view that reality is fundamentally harmonious implies that the

goal of eternal peace has already been achieved. In this view, knowledge is inseparable from faith and love. The single articulated totality of Cusanus' harmony casts its light over every one of its elements, even rationality, even sensuous beauty, even the vital impulses. What may appear to us as transitory on the plane of the finite, remains for him an image of the original and, seen with the eyes of faith and love, reflects its light. Nothing is isolated in the hierarchical structure of the truth. Robbed of the hardness and violence of the particular, all things can be recognized as a reflection of the eternal truth. Such recognition is effected through an enthusiastic, selfless, objectless love of the truth—an emotion related to mystical experience. It is opposed to any feeling of power in possession of the truth (such as peremptory satisfaction in logical correctness) and to the sort of dogmatism that is impervious to argument, leads to ruthlessness in action, and is destructive of the truth of the whole. Here violence begins and peace becomes impossible.

Visions of universal harmony can function as ciphers. Their beauty appeals to us at certain moments, but soon we come to question their truth. At all times two ciphers of the world have been current. One is expressed in the philosophical view that the world and all things in it are governed by a fundamental harmony; the other, in the view that the world originated in deviltry and that its existence is a kind of fraud. Both must be rejected. They are to be taken only as symbolic expressions or ciphers of passing experiences; apart from this, they have no validity.

The image of a harmonious universe is a cipher; as such, it may appeal to us because of its reassuring quality, but we must not be seduced by it. Because it gains the upper hand consistently in Cusanus, it sets limits to his philosophy.

Harmonious to whom? Even to men driven to despair by suffering and death, tortured, abandoned by all? Or only to a God who takes pleasure in the hideous sport, for whom the dissonances are resolved in a whole unknown to us, yet into which we are helplessly flung? To men given to the practice of false humility and existential self-deception?

3. As we have said, Cusanus takes the truth of official Christian doctrine for granted. His faith is anything but a belief in Christ softened by intellectual liberalism. It seems absolutely unreflective, childlike, imperturbable, and this proves a barrier to the speculative movement of his reflections, though Cusanus never seems aware of it (save perhaps occasionally in sermons addressed to listeners whose faith is in danger). He does not transcend the endless movement of reflection. Nor does he have any sense of the fermenting forces which were undermining the Christian faith and every faith—forces such as asserted themselves with fanatical savagery a century later, in Protestantism and in the Counter-Reformation. To these earnest believers Cusanus' faith in universal harmony must surely have seemed superficial.

4. This is how Cusanus interprets the imperfection of earthly existence: in the realm of the finite, every thought and deed, life and existence alike, are merely "conjectural," nowhere complete or completable, never more than approximations. To Cusanus, however, this does not throw everything open to doubt. On the contrary, the conception of all things as conjectural becomes itself a source of reassurance. For according to this conception, things are not corrupt but merely inadequate, there is not wickedness but weakness, not destructive evil but only limitation.

Cusanus' belief in universal harmony has something to do with the fact that he has virtually no feeling for human greatness, let alone the ability to perceive greatness even in one's mortal enemy. He did not, like the humanists, admire heroes, poets, and thinkers for their sheer greatness alone.

Thus, he sees in oppositions and contradictions only the possibility of surmounting them, not symptoms of some fundamental conflict. He does not see how mankind and the world are torn by conflicts, or how contending forces can rage within a man who remains unaware of this and believes himself to be at peace.

In Cusanus' eyes, revealed faith is not opposed to philosophy, any more than the authority of the Church to genuinely free thought. On the contrary, he believes that in both cases the former implies the latter, and that the two form one harmonious whole. Thus Cusanus was anything but a battlefield for the conflicting tendencies of his age. He stands in the vortex of the creative whirlpool itself, rather the advocate of a questionable subjective harmony than a classical thinker.

The belief in universal harmony gives false reassurance in practical affairs. It authorizes shams and half-measures. It provides an illusory security, which leads to complacency in respect to avoidable evils. In the midst of great activity, it gives rise to spiritual paralysis, great energy is coupled with helplessness, impatience, or capriciousness. Such are the psychological consequences of this basic untruth, a belief in universal harmony which rules out all inconvenient experience.

Once we perceive the limitation of the cipher of harmony, we ask: What is the real core of Cusanus' over-all attitude? Or has it no core? Are we merely dealing with different attitudes in juxtaposition? Should we conclude that he never attains full clarity about the concrete situation, that he never makes a resolute existential choice? That he arrived neither in his thinking nor in his life at a clear-cut either-or? That he never took on the full, awe-inspiring burden of responsibility?

Against the background of his belief in universal harmony, how are we to account for his peculiar helplessness in practical action, for the uncertainty that overwhelmed him at crucial moments despite the firmness of his claims? He fought for the power of the one Church rather than for the authenticity of Existenz, and yet the potential grandeur of Existenz is expressed in his philosophical thinking.

3. Cusanus the man

A. *Impotence of reason?*—Open-mindedness satisfies nobody in so far as everyone represents a party and seeks support for it. The completely open mind is at best a sky beneath which everyone in the world must occupy the place he does occupy. All that reason can do for a man is to help save him from falling entirely under the dominance of his place and party, from losing his selfhood. The open mind does not supply us with un-ambiguous, tangible principles. In so far as it aspires not only to understand everything but also to penetrate to the great heart of things, it accomplishes nothing. The strangely grandiose conception of a wholly rational man goes hand in hand with failure in matters of practice.

Or is all this untrue? Are we not, in accusing reason of weakness, blaming rather our own weakness, our inability really to rise to the level of reason? The weaknesses of the rational mind are inherent in the reality of this mind itself. They show that it is not rational enough, not mind enough. Once it believes it has attained the truth, it settles into self-complacent certainty instead of testing and renewing itself in the light of the resistances and incompatibilities it encounters in practical life. When it insists on the absolute validity of a specific point of view, it is anti-rational, it loses its grip on reality.

To what extent all this applies to Cusanus is shown by his limitations. Although his pure speculation—a mode of thinking that is by nature timeless—makes him at times free and open, it does not keep him suffi-ciently free and open in the flux of life. He soars to marvelous heights but cannot remain for long in the realm where all is metaphor and enigmatic image and even this metaphoric world is a metaphor for the state of detachment he has achieved.

His speculation becomes impure, tainted with foreign elements. It lapses into defense of the established Church and its dogmas, and because he fails to realize the historical character of his own faith, he cuts himself off from free communication with other human faiths.

While talking about peace in the name of the Biblical faith, the established churches split mankind into warring camps—a contradiction in terms if ever there was one. As a man of the Church, Cusanus was bound to acquiesce in such a practice. The self-certainty of his philosophizing does not remain at the proud level of independent human Existenz, which implies that the consequences of its immersion in historical reality are unpredictable. Instead, he arrives at an (objectively presumptuous) cer-tainty, based on a revealed faith defined as absolutely valid, and guaranteed by the reality of the only true Church. Since we reject such a faith, we must conclude that Cusanus shares responsibility for historical crimes and errors which he did not perceive, did not combat, and did not surmount.

As we follow Cusanus, sharing in his weaknesses, testing ourselves in our own, we discover that he was not a hero who faced extreme danger unflinchingly, not a man with the courage to look death in the face. He was not a martyr who would sacrifice his life for his faith and his Church. He was not a sage who, rising above himself, preserved his sovereignty and bowed only to the ambiguous language of transcendence. He lacked the aura of holiness possessed by certain other men in his time. He lacked the innocence, the mysterious charm, the poignant quality of a life sustained by pure spirituality.

Because Cusanus was not a hero, not a martyr, not a sage, not a saint, the failure of his reason to run the risk of total lucidity constitutes a weakness. His reason failed to assert its rights against the brutality and superstition of his time—nor does it help us to cope with such forces as they appear today.

Yet, for all his weaknesses, he is never base. There is genuine exaltation in his finest flights, in his knowledge of his true home, in the enthusiasm with which he pursues his philosophical path. We see how, for brief moments, he attains to great clarity and openness, but we also see how, in his life, he remained satisfied with the traditional dogmas. We see him animated by good intentions in his efforts to reform the Church. He is confident of success, and his failure does not shake his confidence but merely puts him in a bad temper.

On the whole, Cusanus is not one of those philosophers whose greatness is so pure that merely to think of them is gratifying.

B. *The modes of Cusanus' failure.*—Only in occasional moments did Cusanus' life match his ideas. When he became involved in political action, he did not achieve the grand style of the statesman. To an ever greater extent in the course of his life, his acts were incompatible with his ideas. Nor were his acts those of a man wholeheartedly concerned with realizing his goals—furthering political and moral salvation through education, institutions, laws.

He is neither an oak that stands unshaken (like Spinoza or Kant) nor yet a thinker so shaken to the depths of his soul (like Kierkegaard or Nietzsche) as to be compelled to utter truths never heard before. He was not—through the representative greatness of his humanity—a beacon to later generations.

Considering the profundity of his speculations, we cannot help being surprised by the kinds of failure he incurred. The following questions arise: Did his philosophical pursuits become for him a sort of refuge from the cares of everyday life, an edifying distraction for his leisure moments, comparable as such to the occasional retreat of a man of the world to a monastery? Do his ideas express no more than the heightened emotions that may touch us when we read poetry or listen to music, are they merely a purification and broadening of emotional experience? Can metaphysics remain detached from life (merely inspiring magnificent meditative flights), without the consuming and fulfilling seriousness that we experience in Plotinus or Spinoza? Does Cusanus, as has happened so often in modern philosophy, find some purely aesthetic pleasure in subtle speculation? Does such thinking generate a guiding force or does it evaporate in its failure to commit itself? Although when studying his works we participate in his speculative vision, are we not at the same time dismayed because this vision is not pure, because it is cluttered up with elements that have no connection with it, but come from a different source?

I hesitate to answer such questions by a simple affirmation. I feel, to be sure, that Cusanus is far from the purity of Plotinus or Spinoza or Kant. But what is true in his speculation is convincingly so. His limitations seem due not to any great tragic guilt, not to the violence of some powerful passion, but to commonplace shortcomings, such as forgetfulness, distraction, lack of consistency, conformism.

c. *Characterization of Cusanus the man.*—(1) Leaving home at an early age, Cusanus was prompt to take his fate in his own hands. While still very young, he was energetic in the pursuit of benefices. He played a leading intellectual role at the Council of Basel. He fought stubbornly in Brixen. As a propagandist and later as papal nuncio in Germany, he was indefatigable. He showed himself capable of making crucial decisions: when he left home, when he dropped jurisprudence for theology, and when he went over to the papal party at the Council of Basel.

Once he had decided on a course of action, however—as in Basel and later in Brixen—he was often inconsistent in his statements, uncertain in his reasoning, unclear in his over-all attitude. He did not consciously try to obscure issues, but he obscured them nonetheless. He countenanced the formation of an organized opposition to his views but did not always show a noble sincerity in his dealings with it. Like any diplomat, he occasionally made use of his great intelligence to dodge issues. Wherever he went, his intellectual superiority made a great impression, and to it he owed his personal success.

(2) Where his intellectual powers were best displayed was in his grasp and assimilation of all the movements of his age. He participated in the humanist movement, in the awakening of scientific curiosity, and in the political life of his day. At the same time, he was never caught up wholly in any of these developments. His true vocation seemed to be elsewhere. He expressed this "elsewhere" in an original speculative manner. His was a meditative as well as an active nature. Time and again he succeeded in tearing himself away from mere practical action, in finding time to think quietly and to set down his ideas in writing.

(3) Several times toward the end of his life, when he was serving as

adviser to his friend Pius II and engaging in the struggle against the Archduke, he expressed distaste for what he was doing. He wrote to the Bishop of Padua (quoted from Meuthen, 108): "If I manage to make peace [with the Archduke] I would prefer to live in the [Venetian] *dominium,* perhaps on the revenues of the [Brixen] church which is so close to his heart. There there is peace, and a climate suitable for me. I am tired of the goings on in the Curia."

Still more revealing is a scene at the Curia, which was noted by Pius II himself (quoted from Paolo Botta, *Nicolò Cusano,* Milan, 1942, pp. 103–06).

The Pope was trying to appoint a new cardinal. His choice was motivated by political opportunism and the cardinals opposed it violently. The Pope said to Cusanus: "We beg you not to take the side of those who think this way. You who esteem us, help us now!" Cusanus gave the Pope an angry look and complained of the Pope's ill-will toward him. Then: "You wish me to approve of everything you do; I cannot and will not be a flatterer; I hate sycophants." And he gave full vent to his bitterness. "If you are capable of listening to me, I want you to know that I dislike everything that goes on in this Curia; no one does his duty as he should; neither you nor the cardinals care anything about the Church. All are a prey to ambition or greed. When I try to speak about reforms in the consistory, I am jeered at. I am superfluous here. Give me your permission to leave. I cannot bear this kind of life. Let me withdraw, and since public life is intolerable to me, let me live by myself." And he burst into tears.

"You may censure everything that is done in the Curia," the Pope replied. "Nor do we ourselves find everything worthy of praise. Nevertheless, it is not your business to criticize. St. Peter's frail craft has been entrusted to us and not to you. Your task is to give honest advice. But nothing obliges us to take your advice. . . . The survival of the Church is at stake. I look upon you as a cardinal, not as the Pope. Up until now we have supposed you to be reasonable, but today you are unlike yourself. You ask me for permission to leave. It is not granted. . . . We try to act as a father, but we shall not yield to unreasonable demands. You say you wish to find peace and solitude outside the Curia. But where will you find peace? If you wish to find peace, it is not the Curia but your own restless mind you must escape. Wherever you may go, you will find no peace unless you temper your impetuousness and tame your spirit. Go home now, and you may come to see us again tomorrow if you so decide."

Cusanus wept. Silently, his features expressing shame and grief, holding back his tears with great effort, he made his way through the assembled dignitaries and went to his modest residence in the Church of S. Pietro in Vincoli. A little later he went back to see Pius II. "He displayed a more moderate attitude and gave up much of his foolish obstinacy, thus showing that the Pope's criticism had not been in vain." Cusanus had given in.

4. *Cusanus' greatness lies in his metaphysics*

Cusanus is not fully characterized when we list the issues of his day in which he was involved: humanism, secular scientific curiosity, mystical piety, conciliar and papal politics, the idea of universal reform, the rise of individualism. Our purpose has been to expound his metaphysics, to know and understand it, and only incidentally to raise questions that have a positive or negative bearing on it. Philosophy cannot be separated from the philosopher, but Cusanus' greatness lies wholly in his metaphysics.

The "authentic metaphysicians" arrive at a fundamental questioning which takes nothing for granted. In permanent ciphers of thought, they find answers on which everything seems to hinge. The peaks were Parmenides and Heraclitus, Plotinus, Spinoza, and some Asian thinkers. In their all-encompassing thinking the "seminal thinkers," as we call Plato, Augustine, and Kant, are also metaphysicians, and not lesser ones. But precisely because they were so encompassing, we do not include them in this series. They go deeper than metaphysics, which to them was a mere instrument. Cusanus is one of the "original metaphysicians," and no more. In the chain of the great metaphysicians he is an irreplaceable link. He projected in cipher a great and original vision of Being, which is of enduring value even without the Christian trappings.

Cusanus exerts a powerful attraction through his grasp of these fundamental truths:

First: Man's self-awareness in the face of transcendence. As the image and likeness of the Creator, man can be certain of his own creative powers, can be a second God. Yet as an image of the original, in his otherness, he is humble, because he is separated from the original as though by an unbridgeable gulf. He is never self-sufficient.

Cusanus' image of man is clearer to us than his image of God. But it is clear only because it reflects the radiance of the godhead.

Perhaps no earlier thinker so compellingly placed at the core of things an image of man's greatness and limitations in respect of his creative intellectual powers.

Second: The will to unity. Cusanus was anything but the *uomo universale* of the Renaissance, interested in everything, forever trying to produce something new. And yet he was always seeking new ways to unity. Without unity in multiplicity, thought and action would be dispersed. The meaning of the One is: the *truth,* in which nothing is forgotten; *thought,* because it points the way to the truth, sees it unseeing in its ground, touches it without touching it; *piety,* because truth has its ground only in the Encompassing One; *peace,* because all things must come together.

Third: The rapture of knowledge. With the freedom of the created mind (Cusanus knows himself as such) he takes wing in the sphere of the finite and soars into the sphere of the infinite. Speculative meditation makes him aware of his origin and goal. In it he experiences the meaning of cognition and of all science. All essential cognition by the intellect is achieved in images, metaphors, and symbols. It never attains the precision that characterizes divine cognition, but stays within "the conjectural."

Fourth: Man's task. In his finite existence as image and likeness of God, man has an obligation to move as close to the original as he can, though the process has no end, to discover in the unity of the ultimate ground the order of peace in which all things are joined.

In Cusanus' speculation we feel awareness of freedom certain of itself. This does not entitle us to look upon him as belonging to our own world, as though he intended and were able to guide it. Our world tries to found its existence upon political freedom, attains to the unrestrained freedom of the sciences and to the venture of unrestrained power to produce through knowledge, and plunges into the maelstrom of the inexhaustible possibilities of the mind. Our freedom has become license because it has no roots. It is already far gone toward its own destruction.

We are faced with the question of our destiny: Is it possible to save freedom on the basis of the freedom of the individual's Existenz? We still need help, which can only come from the ground of things. This help cannot be known. Hence we cannot rely upon it or compel it or obtain it by prayer. We trust in it when we trust ourselves. We hope to obtain this help to the extent that we truthfully and lovingly do what we can do in order to be free and deserve our freedom.

Freedom can be elucidated by metaphysical speculation which encompasses it. It can also be paralyzed by irresponsible retreat into the bliss of pure intellectual exercise. Freedom lives in the great millennial metaphysics of Europe and Asia, to which Cusanus bore witness. He is one of its representatives. Metaphysics alone does not bring freedom. But in keeping alive our consciousness of freedom, it performs its essential traditional function.

BIBLIOGRAPHY

EDITOR'S NOTE:

The Bibliography is based on that given in the German original. English translations are given wherever possible. Selected English and American works have been added; these are marked by an asterisk.

Anselm

SOURCES:

Opera omnia (vols. 1–2). Vols. 158–9 in *Patrologiae cursus completus (Series Latina)*, ed. by Jacques Paul Migne. Paris, 1863–4.

Opera omnia S. Anselmi Cantuariensis archiepiscopi, ed. by Franciscus Salesius Schmitt. 5 vols. Edinburgh and London, Thomas Nelson & Sons, 1940–51.

*Eadmer: *Life of St. Anselm, Archbishop of Canterbury*, ed. with introduction, notes, and a translation, by R. W. Southern. London and New York, Thomas Nelson, 1962.

Basic Writings, trans. by Sidney Norton Deane. 2d ed. La Salle, Ill., Open Court Publishing Co., 1962.

SECONDARY WORKS:

Barth, Karl: *Fides quarens intellectum: Anselms Beweis der Existenz Gottes im Zusammenhang seines theologischen Programms*. Munich, Kaiser Verlag, 1931.

*Clayton, Joseph: *Saint Anselm: A Critical Biography*. Milwaukee, Bruce Publishing Co., 1933.

Daniels, Augustinus: *Quellenbeiträge und Untersuchungen zur Geschichte der Gottesbeweise im dreizehnten Jahrhundert, mit besonderer Berücksichtigung des Arguments im Proslogion des hl. Anselm*. Münster, 1909.

*Gilson, Étienne: *History of Christian Philosophy in the Middle Ages*. New York, Random House, 1955.

Hasse, Friedrich Rudolph: *Anselm of Canterbury*, trans. by W. Turner. London, 1850.

Koyré, Alexandre: *L'Idée de Dieu dans la philosophie de Saint Anselme*. Paris, 1923.

Steinen, Wolfram von den: *Vom heiligen Geist des Mittelalters: Anselm von Canterbury; Bernard von Clairvaux*. Breslau, Ferd. Hirt, 1926.

Nicholas of Cusa

SOURCES:

Nicolai Cusae cardinalis opera. 3 vols. (Reproduction of 1514 ed., Parisiis in Aedibus Ascensianis.) Frankfurt am Main, Minerva, 1962.

Nicolai de Cusa Opera Omnia, ed. by Ernst Hoffmann and Raymond Klibansky. 14 vols. Leipzig, F. Meiner, 1932–64.

Texte seiner philosophischen Schriften, ed. by Alfred Petzelt. Vol. I. Stuttgart, Kohlhammer, 1949.

*The Vision of God, trans. by Emma Gurney Salter. New York, F. Ungar Publishing Co., 1960 (first published, 1928).

*Of Learned Ignorance, trans. by Germain Heron. London, Routledge & Kegan Paul, 1954.

*Unity and Reform: Selected Writings, ed. by John Patrick Dolan. Notre Dame, Indiana, University of Notre Dame Press, 1962.

*Oeuvres Choisies de Nicolas de Cues, French trans. by Maurice de Gandillac. Aubier, Éditions Montaigne, 1942.

Schriften des Nikolaus von Cues in deutscher Uebersetzung, ed. by Ernst Hoffmann. Leipzig, F. Meiner, 1936.

Predigten 1430-1441, German trans. by J. Sikora & E. Bohnenstädt. (Vol. 2 of *Schriften.* . . .) Heidelberg, 1952.

Ueber den Ursprung, German trans. by Maria Feigl. (Vol. 1 of *Schriften.* . . .) Heidelberg, 1949.

Die Kalenderverbesserung, German trans. by Viktor Stegemann. (Vol. 3 of *Schriften.* . . .) Heidelberg, 1955.

Scharpff, Franz Anton, tr.: *Wichtigste Schriften.* Freiburg, 1862.

Billinger, Martin: *Das Philosophische in den Excitationen des Nicolaus von Cues.* Heidelberg, C. Winter, 1938.

Bredow, Gerda von: *Cusanus-Texte, IV. Briefwechsel des Nikolaus von Kues. 3d Sammlung. Das Vermächtnis des Nikolaus von Kues. Der Brief an Nikolaus Albergati nebst der Predigt in Mont Oliveto (1463).* (Sitzungsberichte der Heidelberger Akademie der Wissenschaften. Philosophisch-historische Klasse, Jahrgang 1955.) Heidelberg, C. Winter, 1955.

Kallen, Gerhard: *Cusanus-Texte, II. Traktate, 1. De auctoritate presidendi in consilio generali* (Latin and German). (Sitzungsberichte der Heidelberger Akademie der Wissenschaften. Philosophisch-historische Klasse, Jahrgang 1935/36.) Heidelberg, C. Winter, 1935.

Marsilius of Padua: *Defensor Pacis: Der Verteidiger des Friedens* (Latin with German trans., trans. by Walter Kunzmann), ed. by Horst Kusch. Berlin, Rütten & Loening, 1958.

**Previté-Orton, C. W., ed.: *The Defensor Pacis of Marsilius of Padua.* Cambridge, Cambridge University Press, 1928.

**Enea Silvia Piccolomini: *Commentarii rerum memorabilium: The Commentaries of Pius II,* trans. by Florence Alden Gragg, with historical introduction and notes by Leona C. Gabel. *Smith College Studies in History,* XXII (Nos. 1–2, October, 1936–January, 1937); XXV (Nos. 1–4, October, 1939–June, 1940); XXX (1947); XXXV (1951); XLIII (1957). Northampton, Mass., Smith College Department of History, 1936–57.

**Gabel, Leona C., ed.: *Memoirs of a Renaissance Pope: The Commentaries of Pius II: An Abridgment of the Translation by Florence A. Gragg.* New York, Putnam, 1959.

*Enea Silvio Piccolomini, Papst Pius II: Ausgewählte Texte aus seinen Schriften, ed. and trans. by Bertha Widmer. (Latin and German.) Basel, Benno Schwabe, 1960.

SECONDARY WORKS:

**Bett, Henry: *Nicholas of Cusa.* London, Methuen, 1932.

Bredow, Gerda von: *Das Sein der Freiheit.* Düsseldorf, L. Schwann, 1960.

Cassirer, Ernst: *Individuum und Kosmos in der Philosophie der Renaissance; Liber de mente* (Nicolaus Cusanus) trans. into German as *Über den Geist* by Heinrich Cassirer. Leipzig and Berlin, Teubner, 1927; 2d ed., Darmstadt, Wissenschaftliche Buchgesellschaft, 1963.

Creutz, Rudolf: *Medizinisch-physikalisches Denken bei Nikolaus von Cues*. (Sitzungsberichte der Heidelberger Akademie der Wissenschaften. Philosophisch-historische Klasse, Jahrgang 1938/39.) Heidelberg, C. Winter, 1939.

Falckenberg, Richard: *Grundzüge der Philosophie des Nikolaus Cusanus mit besonderer Berücksichtigung der Lehre vom Erkennen*. Breslau, W. Koebner, 1880.

Fromherz, Uta: *Johannes von Segovia als Geschichtsschreiber des Konzils von Basel*. (Basler Beiträge zur Geschichtswissenschaft, Vol. 81.) Basel and Stuttgart, Helbing & Lichtenhahn, 1960.

Gandillac, Maurice Patronnier de: *La Philosophie de Nicholas de Cues*. Aubier, Éditions Montaigne, 1941.

Glossner, Michael: *Nikolaus von Cusa und Marius Nizolius als Vorläufer der neueren Philosophie*. Münster, 1891.

Haubst, Rudolf: "Johannes von Segovia im Gespräch mit Nicolaus von Kues, und Jean Germain über die göttliche Dreieinigkeit und ihre Verkündigung vor den Mohammedanern," in *Münchener Theologische Zeitschrift, II* (2d year, No. 2, 1951), 115–29.

———: Das Bild des Einen und Dreieinen Gottes in der Welt nach Nikolaus von Kues. Trier, Paulinus-Verlag, 1952.

Hoffmann, Ernst: *Nikolaus von Cues und seine Zeit; Nikolaus von Cues und die deutsche Philosophie*. (Two lectures.) Heidelberg, F. H. Kerle, 1947.

———: *Cusanus-Studien, I. Das Universum des Nikolaus von Cues*. (Sitzungsberichte der Heidelberger Akademie der Wissenschaften. Philosophisch-historische Klasse, Jahrgang 1929/30.) Heidelberg, C. Winter, 1930.

Jäger, Albert: *Der Streit des Cardinals Nicolaus von Cusa mit dem Herzoge Sigmund von Österreich als Grafen von Tirol*. 2 vols. in 1. Innsbruck, 1861.

Kallen, Gerhard: *Nikolaus von Cues als politischer Erzieher*. (Wissenschaft und Zeitgeist, Vol. V.) Leipzig, F. Meiner, 1937.

———: "Die politische Theorie im philosophischen System des Nikolaus von Cues," *Historische Zeitschrift* (Munich), CLXV (1942), 246–77.

———: *Die handschriftliche Überlieferung der Concordantia catholica des Nicolaus von Kues*. (Sitzungsberichte der Heidelberger Akademie. Philosophisch-historische Klasse, Jahrgang 1963.) Heidelberg, C. Winter, 1963.

Kleinen, Hans, and Robert Danzer: *Cusanus-Bibliographie 1920-1961: Mitteilungen und Forschungsbeiträge der Cusanus-Gesellschaft*, Vol. I, published by R. Haubst. Mainz, Grünewald, 1961.

Klibansky, Raymond: *Ein Proklos-Fund und seine Bedeutung*. (Sitzungsberichte der Heidelberger Akademie der Wissenschaften. Philosophisch-historische Klasse, Jahrgang 1928/29.) Heidelberg, C. Winter, 1929.

Koch, Josef: "Nikolaus von Cues 1401-1464," in *Die grossen Deutschen*, I, 275–87. Berlin, Propyläen-Verlag, 1935.

———: "Nikolaus von Cues als Mensch nach dem Briefwechsel und persönlichen Aufzeichnungen," in *Humanismus, Mystik und Kunst in der Welt des Mittelalters*, pp. 56 ff. Leyden, Brill, 1953.

———: *Nikolaus von Cues und seine Umwelt. Untersuchungen zu Cusanus-Texte, IV. Briefe, 1st Sammlung*. (Sitzungsberichte der Heidelberger Akademie der Wissenschaften. Philosophisch-historische Klasse, Jahrgang 1942/43; Jahrgang 1944–48.) Heidelberg, C. Winter, 1948.

Kymeus, Johannes: *Des Babsts Hercules wider die Deudschen, Wittenberg, 1538, als*

Beitrag zum Nachleben des Nikolaus von Cues im 16. Jahrhundert, ed. by Otto-
kar Menzel. (Sitzungsberichte Heidelberger Akademie. Philosophisch-historische
Klasse, Jahrgang 1940/41.) Heidelberg, C. Winter, 1941.

Meuthen, Erich: *Die letzten Jahre des Nikolaus von Cues.* Cologne, Westdeutscher
Verlag, 1958.

——: "Die universalpolitischen Ideen des Nikolaus von Kues in seiner Erfahrung der
politischen Wirksamkeit," in *Quellen und Forschungen aus italienischen Archiven
und Bibliotheken* (Deutsches Historisches Institut, Rome), XXXVII, 192–221.
Tübingen, Max Niemeyer Verlag, 1957.

Olschki, Leonardo: *Dante "Poeta Veltro."* Florence, Olschki, 1953.

Posch, Andreas: *Die "Concordantia catholica" des Nikolaus von Cusa.* (Görres-
Gesellschaft zur Pflege der Wissenschaft im kath. Deutschland, Veröffentlichun-
gen der Sektion für Rechts- und Staatswissenschaft, Vol. LIV.) Paderborn,
Schöningh, 1930.

Rotta, Paolo: *Nicolò Cusano.* Milan, Bocca, 1942.

Scharpff, Franz Anton: *Der Cardinal und Bischof Nicolaus von Cusa.* Part I: *Das
kirchliche Wirken: Ein Beitrag zur Geschichte der Reformation innerhalb der
katholischen Kirche im fünfzehnten Jahrhundert.* Mainz, Kupferberg, 1843.

——: *Der Cardinal und Bischof Nicolaus von Cusa als Reformator in Kirche, Reich
und Philosophie des fünfzehnten Jahrhunderts.* Tübingen, Laupp'sche Buchhand-
lung, 1871.

*Sigmund, Paul E.: *Nicholas of Cusa and Medieval Political Thought.* Cambridge, Mass.,
Harvard University Press, 1964.

Stimming, Manfred: "Marsilius von Padua und Nikolaus von Cues: Zwei politische
Denker des späteren Mittelalters," in *Kultur- und Universalgeschichte: Walter
Goetz zu seinem 60. Geburtstage dargebracht von Fachgenossen, Freunden und
Schülern,* pp. 108–26. Leipzig and Berlin, Teubner, 1927.

Übinger, Johannes: *Die Gotteslehre des Nikolaus Cusanus.* Münster and Paderborn,
Schöningh, 1888.

Vansteenberghe, Edmond: *Le cardinal Nicolas de Cues (1401-1464): L'action—la
pensée.* Paris, Champion, 1920.

Vogts, Hans: "Hospital St. Nicolaus zu Cues," in *Deutsche Kunstführer an Rhein und
Mosel,* Vol. IV. Cologne, Augsburg, and Vienna, Filser, 1927.

Zimmermann, Robert: "Cardinal Nicolaus Cusanus als Vorläufer Leibnitzens," in
Studien und Kritiken zur Philosophie und Aesthetik, I, 61-83. 2 vols. in 1. Vienna,
W. Braumüller, 1870.

INDEX OF NAMES